The Gift of Empathy

The Gift of Empathy

How generosity of spirit can transform your life

IMI LO

First published by John Murray One in 2025
An imprint of John Murray Press

SRD

A CIP catalogue record for this title is available from the British Library

Trade Paperback ISBN 978 1 399 81059 3
ebook ISBN 978 1 399 81061 6

Typeset by KnowledgeWorks Global Ltd.

Printed and bound in India by Manipal Technologies Limited, Manipal

John Murray Press policy is to use papers that are natural, renewable and recyclable products and made from wood grown in sustainable forests. The logging and manufacturing processes are expected to conform to the environmental regulations of the country of origin.

John Murray Press
Carmelite House
50 Victoria Embankment
London EC4Y 0DZ

www.johnmurraypress.co.uk

John Murray Press, part of Hodder & Stoughton Limited
An Hachette UK company

Contents

Introduction
Empathy – bridging the gap in a complex world

'Begin the morning by saying to thyself, I shall meet with the busy-body, the ungrateful, arrogant, deceitful, envious, unsocial. All these things happen to them by reason of their ignorance of what is good and evil.'

Marcus Aurelius

Empathy is a powerful tool. When combined with a deep understanding of why people sometimes act in puzzling or hurtful ways, empathy becomes a compass that navigates you through the complexities of human interactions. This compass not only helps you extend compassion in the most challenging situations but also ensures you maintain your boundaries.

My primary goal in writing this book is to make it genuinely useful in your everyday life. Rather than merely presenting scholarly debates and research, we will focus on relatable life scenarios – such as dealing with an emotionally unavailable partner or a demanding manager – and offer practical strategies for handling them effectively.

One pivotal section in this book addresses the trauma of having unempathetic parents and offers guidance on how to heal from it. This section is essential because without first addressing and healing your own wounds, any attempt to empathize with others risks becoming a mere intellectual exercise or a means to bypass and bury your own pain.

In this book, we delve deeper than generic advice. We will explore complex psychological factors that influence how we think, feel, and act, such as defence mechanisms, attachment patterns, and group dynamics. We will review the differences between constructive and destructive empathy, and how having 'too much' or 'too little' empathy can both have negative consequences.

Ultimately, we do not want to shy away from life's challenges or pretend that things are always smooth and easy. Instead, by confronting empathic challenges with clarity and precision, we can expand our hearts and fulfil our potential to be kind and compassionate beings in this world.

By the end of this book, I hope you will be able to:

- **Differentiate between constructive and destructive empathy**: Recognize when mental projection, intrusive actions, and co-dependency are mistaken for genuine empathy.
- **Identify your triggers and heal from past wounds**: Understand and address the impact of having less-than-perfect parents, allowing you to be less emotionally reactive and find greater peace in your life.
- **Develop 'self-empathy'**: Cultivate this critical skill to remain empathic while preventing compassion burnout, and use empathy to make meaningful contributions to the world.

This journey is neither easy nor superficial, it demands patience, courage, and a willingness to let go of preconceived ideas and biases. But I believe it will be immensely rewarding.

Warmly,
Imi

PART I

On being empathic

I
The paradox of empathy for the highly sensitive person

It is often said that highly sensitive people possess heightened empathy due to their innate emotional sensitivity. However, could their intense emotional experience have unintended consequences? Can having a lot of empathy paradoxically lead to emotional shutdown?

This book is not only for people who feel limited in their empathic potential, it is also for the naturally highly sensitive and empathic person, whose empathy went into overdrive and led them to eventually burn out. They absorb the emotions of others to the point of exhaustion, feeling the pain and stress of the world as their own. This book aims to help them understand their empathic gift and manage its intensity, so they can experience empathy without being overwhelmed by it.

In fact, many people who initially appear aloof and unfeeling may be empathically gifted, emotionally intense, and highly sensitive souls who have learned to hide their true nature. This detachment is not a conscious choice but rather a coping mechanism they have developed to protect themselves from the consequences of hyper-empathy.

If you have ever questioned whether you 'feel too much' or have faced criticism or rejection for being 'too sensitive', 'too dramatic', or for 'making things too complicated', the message in this chapter could strike a chord with you.

Who might be hyper-empathic?

The terms 'highly sensitive person' and 'empath' have gained greater recognition in mainstream awareness in recent years. 'Highly sensitive person' (HSP) is a term coined by Dr Elaine Aron. It describes people who are born with a heightened sensitivity to their surroundings and their own emotions. They notice subtleties, have intense emotional reactions, and are highly empathetic. This heightened sensitivity can be a strength as it brings them deep connections and creativity, but it may make them vulnerable to physical and psychological stress. Empaths, on the other hand, are known to possess a unique ability to understand and share others' emotions. They are deeply attuned to people's feelings, sometimes to the extent of feeling these emotions as their own. This makes them great at offering support but also prone to emotional exhaustion.

Growing awareness and curiosity surrounding these concepts have sparked research into the factors that contribute to heightened empathy in some individuals compared to others. Recent research suggests that a person's emotional sensitivity and empathy level are in part innately determined. Some people are naturally more empathic than others (Aron, 2013; Martin, 1996; Mehrabian et al., 1988). This may be because they are born with a more finely tuned nervous system, are more susceptible to emotional contagions, or have more active mirror neurons, making them naturally more empathic than others.

Environmental factors also play a significant role. For example, contrary to older research that links childhood abuse to the lack of empathy, more recent findings support the hypothesis that growing up in an unstable or chaotic environment can make someone exceptionally attuned to others' emotions (Greenberg et al., 2018). This is because they have to learn to interpret emotional cues as a means of survival. Being hyper-attuned helps them to anticipate potential conflicts or dangers at home so they can protect themselves. Even as a child, these individuals also have to train their empathic skills to navigate tense situations, resolve conflicts, and counsel family members. Sometimes, they have to take on a caregiving or nurturing role within their family – a process known as 'parentification'. Many highly empathic people have shouldered an excessive burden of responsibilities from a young age and were deprived of the carefree childhood they deserved. By the time they reach adulthood, they may already feel emotionally exhausted, with little capacity for self-love and self-compassion.

The loneliness of being hyper-empathic

If you were emotionally sensitive and highly empathic from the get-go, you will find that you tend to care and feel a lot more than others. Empathy is not something you occasionally practise but a way of being.

As a young person, you might have erroneously assumed that most people were like you. You might have been naive and hopeful about relationships and friendships. Your optimism and eagerness often drove you to seek deep and meaningful connections. However, you might have dived in too quickly, assumed too much good nature in others, but neglected or found excuses for their shadow side. Unfortunately, your openness left you vulnerable to the pain of misunderstanding and rejection. Your inherently empathetic and open-hearted nature could be misunderstood, where others label you as 'weird' or 'too much'. As a result, your childhood may have been marked by confusion and aloneness.

Being deeply empathic, or what some might call 'hyper-empathic', is a double-edged sword. Your heightened sensitivity allows you to experience the world's beauty on a profound level, seeing and feeling nuances that others often miss. This deep well of empathy creates a natural sense of connection with all living things, opening the door to spiritual insights and a richer understanding of life's interconnectedness. Your presence alone can be a source of comfort and solace for others, drawn to the warmth and understanding you naturally embody.

However, it can be exhausting when your empathy is dialled up to the max all the time. You find yourself acutely aware of the slightest mood change in those around you, picking up on every nuance in social situations. You may struggle to differentiate between your feelings and those of others, and you cannot help but carry the weight of their sorrow on your shoulders. You may also put others' needs above your own to the point of self-neglect.

As you look around, you may realize that only very few people see and feel the world the way you do. Most people seem to glide through life, barely registering the highs or the lows. They can shrug their shoulders and 'let go' of things, or turn a blind eye to injustice, while you struggle to. You may also feel that while people tend to emotionally lean on you and seek your counsel, you have no one you can open up to or depend on.

Building up a wall

As humans, we are wired with a protective mechanism geared to protect us. If your experience of 'being yourself', of speaking your mind without editing, and spontaneously expressing how you feel has repeatedly caused you to be hurt and chastized, you would inevitably shut down. You might have faced trauma, endured abuse, been harshly rejected, or found yourself encircled by toxic influences that preyed upon your sensitivity. Life's disappointments and losses may have left you feeling adrift, disconnected, and despondent.

Then, you may go through a time in your life where you consciously or unconsciously 'dial down' your sensitivity and empathy. As a result, you experience life with much less intensity. Everything seems more lukewarm, with less vivid colour. Whatever your circumstances, you might now grapple with a persistent sense of detachment and emotional numbness. You may find it challenging to establish meaningful connections with others, and despite being surrounded by people, you feel alone on the inside. As much as you want to preserve your innocence, passion, and hope in humanity, your wounds will no longer let you.

You may miss the old days when you were an open-hearted child who was exuberant, excitable, and loved freely, or when you were a young person who was imbued with hope, ambition, and drive, but somehow you can no longer re-open your heart. Your numbness and dissociation have taken over without you realizing it.

However, your empathic nature is not gone just because you try to deny it. After all, underneath the social persona you have adopted to conform to societal expectations and protect yourself, your true, empathic self is still there.

Fear of your deepest empathic potential

You might have hidden your true self because you were afraid of unlocking your most profound gifts and potential. A part of you feels that fully embracing your highly empathetic nature might lead you to be hurt again, or expose you to more criticism and rejection.

It could also be that embracing your true self would lead you on a different path from the one your family or traditions have set for you, possibly causing you to outgrow those around you.

For instance, you might be in a relationship with someone who is emotionally avoidant, and in their attempt to suppress their feelings, they deny yours. You may fear that reclaiming your true empathic self means ending this relationship.

Or, you may belong to a culture where expressing emotions is discouraged, so being your bold and expressive self means you deviate from the cultural and family narrative, which then leads you to be labelled as the rebel or black sheep.

Perhaps your expressive, exuberant, and creative self does not align with traditional gender roles (e.g. men should not cry, women should not express anger, even if it is justified).

You may have evolved spiritually beyond your religious upbringing and developed a more inclusive and interconnected worldview, but feel stuck in the conservative religious community you grew up in.

Inside, you now have a deep sense of knowing that you are wired differently, that you have extraordinary empathic gifts. If you listen to your calling, your highly sensitive nature may lead you down a path where you can impact the world in a meaningful way – perhaps in human rights, animal protection, ecological awareness, or anything you feel deeply connected with. But you fear your idealistic vision would be laughed at by those around you.

For instance, you may be surrounded by friends and acquaintances who prioritize material wealth and capitalistic values. Even when your heart is drawn to social and environmental activism, you may tone down your voice of advocacy to avoid standing out or stirring up disagreement.

You may dream of being closer to nature or dedicating yourself to community service and empathetic initiatives. But you hesitate to take on leadership roles for fear of becoming too different from your peers, who prioritize conventional notions of personal success over altruism.

In other words, you face the perennial human struggle between authenticity and belongingness – you know that if you fully live out your empathetic self, certain relationships will no longer align with your beliefs and goals.

Even what you are holding on to is merely false belongingness with people who do not see the real you; for someone who has struggled with loneliness all of their life, the idea of outgrowing family and friends can be daunting. However, holding back your empathetic nature is not a solution either, as it can create an enduring sense of disquiet, a lingering feeling that something in your life isn't quite as it should be. Inevitably, existential anxiety and guilt can take root when you suppress your true self.

The wake-up call

Fortunately, though often disturbing, life has a remarkable way of awakening us from denial and nudging us towards our authentic selves. These wake-up calls come in various forms. They may show up as burnout and exhaustion, forcing you to re-evaluate your priorities. Or they may come in the form of increasing tensions with those around you or relationship breakdowns, even a divorce. When tensions escalate, conflicts emerge, and patience wears off, it becomes apparent that something in your life is amiss. Health challenges and the loss of loved ones can also jolt you into awareness of your mortality, urging you to assess whether you have lived your life in alignment with your deepest desires. When the fragility of life becomes unmistakably evident, it compels you to seek meaning and purpose. Witnessing environmental crises, societal injustices, or global challenges can also rekindle your dormant desire to make a positive impact.

And then there are also those moments where your buried self makes its presence saliently known even when you try to 'forget about' it. These are the moments when strong emotions beneath the surface burst forth. Such moments might occur during a meaningful interaction with a group of kindred spirits or when you stumble upon a piece of art or music that resonates with the very core of your being. It might be a sunset that evokes memories. In those compelling moments, you are reminded of how much you miss feeling alive. It's a sensation that arrives in waves, washing over you with a deep longing for what once was or anxiety for what is yet to come. When a wake-up call comes, you instinctively recognize that your gifts for forming profound connections, showing compassion, and understanding others are there but not utilized, and you're not doing what you are made to do.

Reclaiming your empathic gifts

You may still be sitting on the fence, wondering whether it is worth it to reclaim your empathic nature. And of course, you would feel that way. Change can be daunting, and facing buried emotions and past wounds evokes fear of the unknown.

Perhaps we can find some guidance through the wisdom of existential philosophy. To an existentialist, living authentically means embracing your unique essence – like your signature, what makes you different, instead of conforming to external expectations. Jean-Paul Sartre, a prominent existential philosopher, believed that individuals are 'condemned' to be free. This implies that with freedom comes the profound responsibility to define ourselves and make choices that align with our authentic selves.

When you are empathically gifted, your empathic self is not just a facet of your personality, it is the very core of who you are. When you turn away from this intrinsic aspect of yourself, it is like denying your true identity. Whereas when you wholeheartedly embrace your empathic self, you liberate yourself from the constraints of societal norms that often promote emotional detachment and suppression. This glorious journey takes you beyond the superficial layers of existence and plunges into the depths of your soul, so even if it sounds daunting, it is one of the most meaningful quests of human life.

Simone de Beauvoir, another influential existential philosopher, stressed the significance of defining one's existence rather than allowing others to reduce you to an object or role. As you fully embrace your empathic self, you transcend the limitations imposed by societal norms. You move towards a more honest connection with your true nature – even if it involves a higher level of empathy and tenderness than society tends to accept as 'normal'. This is a significant endeavour because by boldly embracing your birthright to be unapologetically yourself – sensitive, intense, and expressive – you also extend the liberating permission for others to embrace their uniqueness. Thus, it is for sure not a selfish act but a noble one.

Reclaiming your empathic self is not just a journey of acceptance but also one of discovery. You will unearth layers of your personality you have long forgotten and discover new ones. As you peel away the layers of emotional suppression, you will uncover a treasure chest within you all along. It is likely filled with wisdom and creativity you have hidden all these years. When you release the shackles of emotional suppression and cease the constant overthinking of your actions and words, you might be astounded by the surge of creative energy within you.

It is undeniable that this journey can involve some pain. But this pain is not a sign of weakness, it is simply a growing pain and a testament to your courage and unyielding spirit. It is the raw, honest struggle of breaking free from the chains that have bound you to a life not your own – shaped by bullies, your parents' projections, the rules of schools, the mandates of institutions, and the influence of authority figures. This is a path where you will find your unique voice, dreams, passions, and, ultimately, a life that belongs to you and no one else.

While your abundant empathy may have resulted in wounds in the past, this does not have to be the case now or in the future. One of the goals of this book is to empower you with the skills needed to harness your empathy in a balanced and discerning way, allowing you to establish healthy boundaries while remaining authentically empathic.

Ultimately, reclaiming empathy is not just about feeling more, it is about living more. Your love for humanity and ability to delve deep within make you undeniably human.

Despite the complexity and weight of being you, I hope you would not trade your capacity for deep empathy for anything else. The fact that you are reading this now may mean you are already on a path of reclaiming who you are – deeply sensitive, empathic, and with a lot to offer the world.

PART 2

Empathy

What it is and what it isn't

2
Mirroring and mentalizing

Empathy, derived from the German term *Einfühlung*, which translates to 'feeling into', refers to the ability to understand and share the emotions of others. It allows us to connect with other people, feel their pain, and understand their points of view. It is often pointed out that empathy differs from sympathy, which involves feeling sorry for another's misfortune.

Numerous theories and debates surrounding empathy have emerged over the past few decades. In this chapter, we will briefly discuss a few concepts that are relevant to the aims of this book.

Empathy is a multifaceted construct. To break it down, it has two major components – a cognitive and an affective component. Cognitive empathy includes identifying and intellectually understanding others' feelings, thoughts, and behaviours. In contrast, affective empathy or emotional empathy is the capacity to 'resonate' with other people's emotions in an embodied way. The cognitive dimension of empathy involves complex cognitive functions like perspective-taking, whereas affective empathy means directly experiencing other people's internal states (Martingano and Konrath, 2022; Shamay-Tsoory et al., 2009; Shamay-Tsoory, 2011; Zaki and Ochsner, 2012), which, as we will see, is closely linked to something in our brain known as mirror neurons.

To understand the difference between cognitive and affective empathy, let us look at the two main ways empathy works: mirroring and mentalizing (Keysers and Gazzola, 2007; Waytz and Mitchell, 2011). These processes can happen separately or at the same time.

- **Mirroring**: Mirror neurons, discovered in the 1990s in the premotor cortex of primates, play a crucial role in the mirroring process. These special neurons in our brains allow us to perceive and experience the emotions of others directly and immediately. To put it simply, mirror neurons establish a fast link in our brains that feel the physical states of another person as if they were our own.

  For instance, studies indicate that when we observe others expressing disgust, the insula, a specific region in our brain, becomes active as if we were personally experiencing that same feeling. The level of activation in the insula even correlates with the intensity of disgust expressed by the faces we are observing (Wicker et al., 2003). Similarly, when we witness someone being touched, a corresponding area in our brain called the secondary somatosensory cortex will respond as if we were being touched. Social psychologists have also discovered that we often instinctively flinch or recoil when we witness someone being hit on their leg or arm, almost as an automatic reflex. In other words, the process of mirroring brings us beyond mere observation and into the realm of 'feeling with' others.

  What is unique about mirroring is that it is so automatic and natural that most of the time we are not even aware of it. The immediacy of the process allows us to connect with others even without words, and it transcends intellectual and cultural barriers. In our day-to-day lives, mirroring plays a crucial role in empathy, social bonding, and emotional regulation, and it allows us to feel instinctively connected to those around us without exercising a lot of conscious effort.
- **Mentalizing**: In addition to mirroring, another pathway to empathy is through mentalization.

> Mentalization is the skill of interpreting both our behaviour and the behaviour of others in terms of mental states, such as desires, intentions, beliefs, and emotions (Allen et al., 2008). It involves the ability to take perspectives and use our imagination to understand and make sense of what we observe in others that might otherwise be perplexing or unfamiliar (Hein and Singer, 2008).

Mirroring and mentalization are different. Mirroring allows us to grasp the emotions of others by experiencing their mental states vicariously. Through mirroring, we establish a connection with another person's mental state by synchronizing our bodily sensations with theirs (Keysers and Gazzola, 2007). On the other hand, mentalization involves inferring and deducing someone else's mental state through cognitive thinking processes. It requires us to use our mind's capacity to understand and interpret the thoughts, feelings, and intentions of others, rather than directly experiencing them in our bodies. Both mirroring and mentalization contribute to empathy, but they operate through different mechanisms.

The speed at which we can empathize differs between mirroring and mentalization. Mirroring is a rapid and immediate mechanism that allows us to connect with what another person is feeling in real-time. It occurs almost instantaneously and often operates on an unconscious level, surpassing the speed at which our conscious mind can fully grasp and process the situation (Corradini and Antonietti, 2013). In contrast, mentalization takes more time and may require conscious cognitive effort. It is a skill that can be cultivated and honed through practice and reflection.

Let's consider an example: a disagreement with your partner. Mirroring comes into play when you observe hurt on your partner's face or see tears streaming down their cheeks and you instantly experience a sense of sadness alongside them. It also occurs when you notice their body tensing up and you start to feel the tension in your own body. Mirroring allows you to immediately and intuitively resonate with their emotional state.

On the other hand, mentalization becomes relevant when you later reflect on the situation and attempt to understand why your partner was so upset. You engage in a cognitive process of thinking about possible reasons behind their emotional reaction. Was it a challenging day at work for them? Did something you said or did trigger their response? Mentalization involves the conscious effort of considering and interpreting the underlying thoughts, motivations, and circumstances that contribute to someone's emotional experience.

Here is another example. Imagine you are watching a movie and a sad scene comes up. Mirroring comes into play as you automatically and involuntarily experience the same sadness that the characters on the screen are portraying. Their body language, facial expressions, and emotional cues might trigger a response in you, causing tears to well up or a lump to form in your throat. Mirroring operates effortlessly, driven by the activation of mirror neurons in your brain.

In contrast, mentalizing in this scenario involves a cognitive process of trying to understand and analyze the characters' emotions and motivations. You may find yourself reflecting on why they are feeling sad, what events or circumstances led up to this particular moment in the story, and whether there is a deeper meaning behind their sadness. You may also consider how the director intends to convey these emotions and whether there are any personal connections or relatable experiences that resonate with you. This process of mental projection, analysis, and interpretation is slower, more conscious, and requires deliberate effort compared to mirroring. However, it can deepen your understanding of the characters, and their emotions, and even provide insights into your own psychology and emotional responses to the narrative.

Empathizing, fast and slow

Making the comparison to Daniel Kahneman's ideas in *Thinking, Fast and Slow* (2011) can help clarify the distinction between cognitive empathy (mentalizing) and affective empathy (mirroring).

Kahneman's concept of System 1 and System 2 thinking provides a framework for understanding different modes of cognitive processing. System 1 thinking corresponds to our intuitive, rapid, and effortless cognitive processes. It operates automatically, enabling us to make quick judgements and decisions based on heuristics and immediate emotional responses. This aligns with mirroring empathy, as it involves an automatic and instinctive emotional reaction to the emotions of others. Mirroring, like System 1, occurs swiftly and without conscious effort.

Meanwhile, System 2 thinking is characterized by slower, deliberate, and conscious cognitive processes. It requires effortful mental processing and is engaged when we tackle complex tasks or engage in deeper analysis and reasoning. Mentalizing in empathy aligns with System 2 thinking, as it involves deliberate engagement and operates at a slower pace.

Just as System 1 and System 2 thinking often work together, mirroring and mentalizing complement each other in the empathic process. Mirroring provides an initial emotional resonance and connection, akin to System 1's rapid responses, while mentalizing adds a deeper understanding and analysis (Sharp and Bevington, 2022), akin to System 2's deliberate cognitive engagement.

While mirroring can be a useful tool for quickly connecting with others on an emotional level, it does have its limitations. Relying solely on mirroring for empathy is like relying solely on intuitive, quick thinking (System 1) in decision-making, which can lead to biases and errors, as pointed out by Kahneman.

To truly enhance our lives and relationships, we should also develop our ability to mentalize, just like how we train our mind's capacity for critical and analytical thinking (System 2). Mentalizing allows us to move beyond surface-level emotions and explore the multiple layers of complexities in human interactions. It helps us understand the underlying reasons behind someone's emotions, motivations, and perspectives. While mirroring offers an initial connection, mentalizing is what we need to have more mature and sustainable relationships.

These are largely simplified analogies, as the mechanisms of empathy are complex and involve interaction between many more cognitive and neural processes. Nonetheless, the comparison of System 1 and System 2 thinking can help us see the distinct nature and complementary roles of mirroring and mentalizing in empathy.

Returning to the objective of our book, one of its primary aims is to support you in developing and expanding your mentalizing skills. By cultivating the capacity to hold multiple perspectives and maintain a nuanced understanding of social dynamics, you can enhance your empathic abilities. This means that even in moments of vulnerability, triggers, or unease, you are less likely to lose your empathy and compassion.

Thus far, we have explored various theories on empathy, mirroring, and mentalization. While these theories may initially come across as detached and academic, they lay the groundwork for the discussions and insights that we will delve into in the later parts of this book.

Having explored the essence of empathy, our next chapter will shift focus to what empathy is not.

3
The empathy illusion

When we say someone 'lacks empathy', we often think of situations where someone struggles to connect with or understand other people's emotions. For instance, they might make insensitive remarks, consistently miss emotional cues, or find it challenging to provide comfort to those in distress. These difficulties in relating and offering meaningful empathy can be linked to various factors, such as cognitive deficits, neurodivergent traits such as autism, or even psychopathy. In reality, empathy exists on a spectrum, and there does not exist a clear, distinct line separating those who 'have' or 'do not have' empathy.

What empathy is not

We all occasionally stumble when it comes to empathy (Müller-Pinzler, 2016; Paulus et al., 2013; Zaki and Cikara, 2015). There are many moments when we mistakenly believe we are empathizing when, in truth, we are projecting our own feelings onto others. This typically happens unintentionally, on a subconscious level.

In academic literature, this phenomenon is known as an empathic error – where an observer experiences an emotion after witnessing a situation, but this emotion does not accurately reflect the true feelings of the person they are trying to empathize with (Brunsteins, 2018; Hawk et al., 2011; Krach et al., 2011; Wondra and Ellsworth, 2015). For example, if we see someone's toes get caught in a door gap, we may feel pain on their behalf. However, they may have a very high pain threshold or be taking a drug that prevents them from feeling pain. In this case, we are simply projecting our inner feelings onto what we see, and even if we think we are empathizing, in the truest sense, it is not empathy. Another example frequently used in research is vicarious embarrassment. A humorous example is that we may notice that someone has left their flies undone and feel embarrassed for them. However, because they are unaware of what is happening, they do not feel embarrassed (Hawk et al., 2011; Krach et al., 2011; Müller-Pinzler, 2016; Paulus et al., 2013). This, again, is not considered true and accurate empathy.

Empathy is not projection

Empathy is often described as the act of 'putting ourselves in someone else's shoes'. While this concept may seem straightforward, it overlooks the fact that we rarely approach relationships, where empathy plays out with a completely blank slate. Our past experiences, whether they involve significant traumas or positive memories, shape who we are today and impact how we perceive and engage in relationships. As a result, our personal histories almost always lead us to view reality with some distortion and project our own emotions onto others. In fact, research consistently demonstrates that the brain networks associated with traumatic memories can trigger intense emotional responses that influence our judgement (Bower and Sivers, 1998; Pally, 1997).

Projection may sound negative, but it is a normal day-to-day phenomenon and, most of the time, benign. In fact, our ability to empathize with others is possible precisely because we bring our own life experiences and stories into relationships. Without these experiences, it would be almost impossible to understand or relate to someone else's inner world. For example, we can only truly comprehend the profound pain of heartbreak if we have personally experienced it, and we can empathize with the anguish of physical injuries because we have felt them ourselves.

While the line between empathy and projection may not always be clear, there is still a way to distinguish between constructive empathy and dysfunctional projections. Essentially, effective empathy involves maintaining a strong sense of our own reality and identity, with clear personal boundaries. It means avoiding confusion between ourselves and others and refraining from using toxic defence mechanisms like projective identification, where we intrusively unload unwanted thoughts and emotions onto others. (We will explore the concept of projective identification further in subsequent chapters.)

When we project, we tend to attribute our own opinions and personal experiences to others without much consideration. In contrast, constructive empathy requires a conscious effort to truly understand and connect with someone else's feelings and perspective. It involves finding a delicate balance between our thinking and feeling faculties, which allows us to comprehend another person's emotions without imposing our judgements or biases too strongly or losing sight of our reality.

Empathy is not fusion or co-dependency

Empathy should also not be confused with a 'psychic merger' or the complete fusion of one's emotions with those of others. You might be or know someone who identifies as an 'empath', which typically refers to individuals who are highly attuned to the emotions of those around them (Orloff, 2017). They also struggle as they seem to 'soak up' emotions from everyone nearby. This can lead to compassion burnout, forcing them to eventually shut down and withdraw. However, with healthy and constructive empathy, you would not get overwhelmed or burn out. Instead, true empathy thrives when you maintain clear emotional boundaries, and connect with others on a deep emotional level while preserving an emotional equilibrium.

Consider the scenario where you are empathizing with someone who is grappling with grief or depression. In constructive empathy, you extend a deeply compassionate understanding of their pain while keeping one foot planted in your emotional reality. This duality empowers you to maintain a steady and reassuring presence, offering comfort and solace to the person in need.

A comparable dynamic can be seen in the bond between a nurturing parent and their infant. When a baby cries, you would want to empathize with their feelings of confusion, fear, or hunger. However, in healthy empathy, you would not let yourself become overwhelmed by those same emotions and lose control. While the baby may perceive the situation as catastrophic, maintaining a dual perspective – acknowledging your own reality while understanding theirs – enables you to provide effective comfort and care as a responsible adult. Imagine if you become 'merged' with the baby's inner world and cry with them! That would presumably not bring any constructive outcome.

On the other hand, emotional fusion represents a form of 'pseudo-empathy' where your emotions become deeply intertwined with those of another, leading to destructive outcomes. This is when empathy becomes distorted and enters the realm of co-dependency. In co-dependent relationships, there is an excessive reliance on others for emotional well-being. In severe cases of chronic co-dependency, one may struggle to experience any emotions and feel empty and numb, unless they are mirrored by someone else.

A clear indicator of emotional fusion or co-dependency is when you feel an incessant urge to 'fix' or 'rescue' someone you care about who is in distress. In destructive empathy, you become as overwhelmed as the other person, almost merging with their experience. This intense emotional response may drive you to desperately want to alleviate their suffering. While your intentions come from a place of genuine concern, this type of empathy is not constructive. Losing emotional balance hampers your ability to be fully present for them, often leading to a shift into problem-solving or advice-giving mode. Paradoxically, this approach can make the other person feel invalidated and unheard, rather than receiving the empathy you intended to convey.

Examples of empathic errors

Apart from the above-mentioned, here are some signs that you may have lost your capacity to empathize constructively:

- **Mind reading**: Assuming you know what others are thinking. For example, you might say things like, 'You must be feeling X', or assume a friend is upset about something specific without them telling you and offer advice based on this assumption. Mind-reading also happens when you over-examine straightforward statements by searching for hidden meanings or ulterior motives that may not exist. As you can imagine, social anxiety and finding it hard to trust people can make us prone to this error.
- **Taking things too literally:** This is when you interpret common figures of speech, idioms, or metaphors as literal statements, missing humour and assuming intention. This tendency often arises when you feel insecure, causing you to revert to a more childlike black-and-white mode of thinking, where you frequently assume the negative to be true in unclear or ambiguous situations.

- **Losing chronological perspective:** This is when you forget about or ignore the timeline of events that may have led to someone's behaviour. For instance, you may become frustrated with a family member for being in a bad mood without considering they had a tough day at work or had spent all day doing housework for you.
- **Lack of consideration for underlying motives:** You may be paying excessive attention to what someone is saying or doing while disregarding their underlying feelings and motivations. An example of this is judging a partner for not expressing 'I love you' frequently without recognizing that they demonstrate their love through different actions.
- **Over-projecting your feelings:** Without realizing it, you may be assuming others feel the same way as you would do. For example, you may assume a friend would be excited about a party because you are, without considering they might feel differently due to their circumstances or personality.
- **Unconscious projection/projective identification:** This is a complex dynamic that involves projecting parts of yourself that you dislike, your shadow side, onto others. This is usually a deeply unconscious process and you are not aware of it happening. For instance, you may criticize a coworker for being disorganized when you struggle with the same issue.
- **Categorizing people:** This is when you start to view others, perhaps momentarily or occasionally, based on race, ethnicity, class, group affiliations, religious beliefs, gender, etc. For example, stereotyping people from a certain background as having specific traits or behaviours without considering their individuality. We all do it to a certain degree, but it is often the

beginning of us losing empathy when considering why someone does what they do.

- **Missing non-verbal cues:** There may be times when you solely rely on what someone says and disregard their body language or tone. For example, believing a friend is fine because they say so, even though their slumped posture and downcast eyes indicate otherwise.

Focusing on constructive empathy

In summary, constructive empathy goes beyond surface-level emotions and involves a deeper, introspective process. Instead of making quick assumptions about someone's thoughts, emotions, or actions, you actively engage in asking questions like 'Why did they say or do that?' or 'What could be driving their behaviour?' Additionally, you consider how your own experiences, emotions and attitudes may influence your understanding of another person's thoughts and intentions. This recognition acknowledges that individuals are separate from you, with their unique intentions and perspectives that may not be immediately apparent.

It is easy to lose our capacity to empathize, or mistake emotional fusion or projection as a form of empathy. However, rather than becoming disheartened, we can feel inspired and motivated by the fact that constructive empathy is a skill that can be cultivated and improved. That means by actively learning, reflecting and practising, we can hone our empathic abilities, and this is exactly what we aim to achieve in this book.

Interlude

Why you may want to stop, empathize, then, create

An itch to create.

A craving for breathing room.

A lingering feeling that you've had enough of the daily grind.

Perhaps you have been stifled to such an extent that you've lost the space to breathe, let alone express yourself and your love for the world.

Yet undeniably, in every human heart lies a deep yearning to be connected, to have a voice, to make a mark, and to create artifacts that echo beyond the confines of ordinary life. When you open your heart, you will find the essence of empathy that allows you to create something that connects you to the rest of humanity.

Empathy is not just the ability to understand and share the feelings of others, it is a profound source of creativity. By deeply feeling and understanding the experiences of others, we can draw inspiration that fuels our creative endeavours. Empathy opens the door to perspectives and emotions that enrich our creative expressions, making them more resonant and impactful.

Your unique expression could take many forms – cooking a meal, taking a photo, crafting an album, writing a book, developing the next computer system, formulating a new math equation, or advancing the next generation of gender theory. Your creative expression is not just a hobby or another 'task' you must do. It is a declaration of your existence, a testament to you being the one and only you.

It starts with an idea, a vision you believe in –

It may enlighten, or it may not.

It may entertain, or it may not.

It may be innovative, or it may be something already done.

But none of that truly matters.

What matters is that you have left YOUR mark in the world.

This knowledge – that you have birthed something into the world, something that might ripple out, may outlast your own life – offers profound comfort in the face of our fleeting existence. It is a potent medicine for our existential angst. But it is not just personally soothing. It is how we heal our collective existence, too.

When you give yourself the space to express, you are harnessing your empathy for universal human experiences in your own unique way. You are imprinting your essence on the world, a task only you can fulfil. Because there is only one you, whatever fruits of empathic creativity emerge when your heart and mind unite is unique. If you had let it slip by, it would be lost forever.

Empathy allows us to connect deeply with others, and from this connection, our creativity is born. It is through empathizing with others' joys, sorrows, struggles, and triumphs that we find the emotional depth to create art, solutions and innovations that truly matter. Empathy fuels creativity by providing the emotional palette from which we draw our most profound and impactful work.

Taking time away from the world, taking a pause, and making time to feel your heart and for your creative expression is not a waste of time. It is not 'unproductive', and it is certainly not selfish. It is, in fact, one of the most generous things we can do.

Surprisingly (or maybe not so surprisingly), getting caught up in a constant dance of co-dependency, where we get sucked into everyone else's demands, judgements, shaming and blaming, does not help humanity one bit. Taking the plunge to walk away from the noise and demands of the outside world, we find clarity and our truth. And it is ONLY from this place that your best gift can be birthed into the world.

This inward turn does not isolate us, nor does it make us selfish. It nourishes us to become the best humans we can be, so we can heal our collective human experience. Perhaps, we are not here just to exist but also to empathize and then create.

Dear ones,

What could you create if you stopped the routine just long enough to listen to your deepest, most empathic inner voice?

PART 3

Empathy at home

Parents with 'too little' empathy

4
Patterns of abusive parenting

Parental empathic failure is a silent pandemic. While it might be deemed inappropriate to say it out loud, the reality is that not all parents can genuinely feel or express empathy towards their children. Society often compels us to uphold the illusion of perfect families and flawless relationships. Those who bravely speak out or unveil the truth face the threats of social ostracism, judgement and ridicule. Consequently, numerous individuals with unempathetic parents silently endure their struggles for years on end.

The taboo of parental empathic failure

Parents who struggle with empathy are often themselves victims of intergenerational trauma, but that does not excuse them from their cruel or harmful parenting practices. Many do try their best to love their children in the only way they know how, but they are unable to break free from behaving in manipulative, narcissistic and controlling ways. Parental empathy deficits can manifest in many forms: Parents can make their child feel like a burden or an inconvenience. They can gaslight, manipulate and guilt-trip their child. They may demand constant attention from their child or invade their privacy. They may constantly invalidate or dismiss their child's feelings. They may verbally abuse their child or call them names. They may favour one child over the others, single out one child to be the family's black sheep, thus sowing the seeds of long-term family conflict and resentment. Some parents may use their children to boost their social status or earn bragging rights. They may pressure their child to live the life they never had, imposing their values to live vicariously through them.

This remains applicable even as the child grows into adulthood. Parents who struggle with empathy deficits may heavily rely on their adult child for emotional or financial support, or they may manipulate and control them by withholding assistance or affection. They may even ridicule or humiliate their adult child because they are envious or view them as a threat.

Despite how dreadful it is to be subject to parental cruelties, children and adult children worldwide are taught to stay silent about these matters, bury them deep within themselves, and never let their trauma see the light of day.

The following chapters, which explore the challenges faced by parents with empathy deficits and their impact, form a pivotal part of this book for a specific reason: our early interactions and relationships, particularly with our parents or caregivers, shape the core of our self-perception, our ability to navigate relationships, and our understanding of empathy. The trauma of growing up with parents who lack empathy, in various forms and to different degrees, can leave enduring marks on our psyche and impair our ability to empathize with others. Therefore, we must address these emotional wounds before we can truly enhance and develop our capacity to empathize with others.

Exploring the effects of parental empathy deficits takes us on a journey into the depths of our personal histories. But we are not only reflecting on the past. We will also build a roadmap for the future. I hope that the information in these chapters will bring you greater self-awareness, self-compassion and practical strategies that will help you harness your capacity for empathy.

Parents play a crucial and distinctive role as the first and most influential teachers in their child's lives. By showing what it means to have empathy, they create a nurturing and secure environment where their child feels acknowledged and accepted. The child is then able to internalize the sense of being empathized with and turn that into a force of self-nurturance that can stay with them for life.

Why parents need to have empathy

Empathetic parents are more likely to offer active listening, provide emotional support and establish appropriate boundaries (Stern et al., 2015). Research consistently shows that children whose parents demonstrate empathy have better emotional regulation skills and develop more meaningful connections with others. On the other hand, when parents struggle with empathy, the impact on their children is deep and far-reaching.

Most prominently, the absence of parental empathy can have detrimental effects on a child's self-esteem and psychosocial functioning. When parents fail to acknowledge their child's feelings and experiences, the child internalizes the message that they are unimportant or unworthy.

Moreover, parents who lack empathy do not serve as healthy role models for social interactions or guides in understanding the emotions of others. As a result, their child may encounter difficulties in forming meaningful relationships and resolving conflicts with others (Meng et al., 2020). Indeed, research indicates that individuals who grow up with parents who are low on the empathy spectrum are more likely to display maladaptive behaviours in adulthood, such as aggression, hostility, impulsivity, risk-taking behaviour and low self-esteem (Bi and Keller, 2021; Feshbach, 1987; Meng et al., 2020).

Empathetic parenting also plays a crucial role in teaching a child how to effectively regulate their emotions. Research indicates that children of parents with empathy deficits often struggle with anxiety and depression, or even develop conditions such as borderline personality disorder or dissociative identity disorders as a result of the emotional neglect they experienced during their formative years.

If you have experienced abusive parenting with parents who lack empathy or have frequent lapses in empathy, please know that having difficulties with relationships or emotional regulation is not your fault, but the natural result of not being provided with the necessary conditions to develop essential life skills.

More importantly, being raised by parents with limited empathy does not definitively constrain your future. By gaining insights and understanding, as you are doing now, you have the power to heal from your past.

'Types' of parents with empathy deficits

To guide our discussion, we will categorize abusive parenting that is associated with empathy deficits into four 'archetypes': the 'Bully Parent', the 'Superficial Parent', the 'Highly Unstable Parent', and the 'Needy Parent'. This approach involves some inevitable simplification and generalizations, but categorization allows us to systematically examine certain behavioural and personality traits. The reality is, of course, far more complex, and not one parent can be reduced into a single 'type'. Your parent may have traits from several categories or predominantly align with one. As you read the descriptions that follow, please use discernment. Take away what resonates with your experiences, and feel free to disregard what does not.

All of these types of parents, who cannot provide consistent empathy for their child, are likely to show some degree of overly narcissistic tendencies, albeit in different ways. 'Bully Parents' and 'Superficial Parents' often show narcissism in more overt and recognizable ways, aligning with the typical understanding of narcissism. On the other hand, 'Needy Parents' might manifest narcissism through an excessive focus on personal issues at the expense of parental responsibilities.

Please also note that it is impossible to diagnose anyone with clinical illnesses such as personality disorders based on descriptions from a book. But if your parents' behaviours match some of these descriptions, you may benefit from reading up on topics including Complex Post-Traumatic Stress Disorder, Borderline Personality Disorder, Narcissistic Personality Disorder, parentification, narcissistic abuse, and gaslighting to see if you can gain further insights.

1 'Bully' Parent

Let us begin by looking at a specific category of parenting behaviours that is associated with a marked deficiency in empathy. Parents who could be categorized as a 'bully' often have a strong need for control and a reluctance to show any vulnerability. The root of their empathic challenge lies in their inability to acknowledge their fragility or to empathize with themselves. Because one cannot give what they do not possess, their empathy deficiency extends to their inability to empathize with others, including their child.

People embodying the 'bully' archetype perceive the world as a hostile, survival-oriented arena where people can be divided into two categories: the strong and the weak. Believing that the only way to ensure their safety is to assert dominance and overpower others, they adopt a combative stance in most interactions.

Bully Parents may behave as though they are entitled to not follow social rules or even the law. They do whatever they want, whenever they want, and resist being subjected to constraints they do not voluntarily accept. Everything must be on their terms. For example, they will decide when and how they will spend time with you, talk to you, and how the interactions go.

While it is generally important for parents to establish boundaries, a Bully Parent tends to become excessively forceful in asserting their authority. They set up a rigid hierarchy in the family structure and may act like they are the family's king or queen.

To the outside world, they come across as someone who exudes confidence and assertiveness; others may even admire their apparent strength. However, behind closed doors, they are emotionally immature and can be pathologically insensitive. For example, they may be extremely self-centred and stubborn, and resist receiving any constructive feedback. They tend to be short-fused, and snap quickly when they are irritated, or when someone challenges their authority.

Their core psychological defence is often denial – they deny others' pain, either by pretending it doesn't exist or dismissing it, as a means to avoid triggering their vulnerability. Years of suppressing their own emotions mean they also struggle to detect and respond to the emotional cues of others. They will mostly be oblivious to your expressions of emotions they most deny in themselves, such as shame and fear. Unless your needs are explicitly expressed forcefully, they are likely to overlook them. Moreover, even if they try to empathize, a Bully Parent likely has a limited repertoire of emotions and the language for feelings. They may recognize only emotions such as anger and aggression but nothing else.

Bully Parents tend to be insensitive not only towards their children but also towards their partners. Growing up, you may have witnessed your other parent being emotionally neglected or even bullied. In such situations, your other parent may turn to you as an emotional crutch, making you take up the role of a pseudo-partner, surrogate spouse, confidant, protector, or counsellor to your otherwise neglected or abused parent. This toxic dynamic is sometimes known as 'emotional incest' and can have a lasting impact on your mental health and how you relate to others in your future relationships.

Occasionally, Bully Parents can seem protective of you, which is sometimes mistaken for empathy. For example, when they see you being treated unfairly by others, they might fiercely stand up on your behalf. However, this behaviour is rarely driven by genuine empathy but stems from their 'me vs. them' worldview, where everyone is either a friend or a foe. They support you in these situations because they have turned you into an extension of themselves. While it may seem like they are protecting you, their primary focus is on blaming and retaliating against the external party, rather than empathizing with your needs. In these moments, you may feel like a mere instrument for them to express their anger towards the world, rather than being recognized as an individual with your thoughts and emotions.

Growing up with a Bully Parent makes it challenging to develop healthy emotional skills. You may have been consistently punished for expressing sad or vulnerable feelings, leading you to internalize the belief that it is unsafe to do so.

While it will take time, conscious effort, and support, it is possible to recover from these traumas. You may or may not be able to find closure with your parent, but the first step is to admit that you were wronged by someone who was supposed to love and protect you. The core themes that may emerge during the healing process from the trauma of having a Bully Parent may include:

- rediscovering or discovering a sense of agency
- finding a path to authentically express emotions
- reclaiming previously oppressed emotions such as anger
- undoing the damage of chronic invalidation.

The ultimate goal when healing from the trauma of growing up with a Bully Parent is to reclaim your sense of power and agency as a healthy adult. We will discuss more of these themes in a later chapter on self-empathy.

2 Highly Unstable Parent

Growing up with a Highly Unstable Parent is a particularly perplexing experience because these parents do show empathy, but only intermittently. They have a hot-and-cold, on-and-off emotional pattern. They can be extremely loving and caring sometimes, but when they are stressed or something triggers them, they 'flip' into a completely different mode and become childish, unreasonable, aggressive, and even violent. Research shows that children with parents who are highly unstable feel like they're dealing with two different people, like Dr Jekyll and Mr Hyde (Glickauf-Hughes and Mehlman, 1998). You never know who you will get next.

While they may not have received a formal diagnosis of any mental disorders, these parents demonstrate emotional volatility ('affect liability' is the clinical term) that aligns with the diagnostic criteria for Borderline Personality Disorder.

Interestingly, newer research has found that many people with traits of this disorder have highly active mirror neurons, a predisposition for emotional empathy (Harari et al., 2010; Sosic-Vasic et al., 2019; Mier et al., 2013). Therefore, when they are in a good psychological place, they can show 'hyper-empathy' and be highly attuned and sensitive to emotional signals. They may appear extremely caring (sometimes overly caring to the point of being intrusive) and focus a lot on your feelings and needs. However, when their trauma is triggered, they flip into a different mode and regress into a child-like state. In this state, they lose the capacity for healthy empathy and are completely unable to think or take any external perspectives other than their own. Their behaviour becomes self-centred, compulsive, and unpredictable, just like that of a child rather than an adult parent.

Most of the time, they cannot pinpoint what triggers a complete meltdown or an episode of emotional crisis, but when it happens, it is as though there is no going back – when they flip into a regressed state, you cannot get through to them no matter what you say or do.

Your parent's instability could leave you feeling insecure and hyper-vigilant even within your own home. The need to be constantly watching out for their next outburst meant that you could not relax, play, or explore the world in a typical age-appropriate way. Your childhood was robbed of its carefree nature as you had to carefully censor your words and actions, always being extremely cautious to deal with or avoid triggering the next crisis at home.

Furthermore, a Highly Unstable Parent may make decisions impulsively and fail to consider the potentially hazardous consequences of their actions. Their frequent risk-taking behaviours, such as reckless driving or promiscuity, can destroy your home life. Growing up in such an environment can mean you are not able to feel safe and secure wherever you go, whoever you are with, even when you have grown up.

Having an emotionally unstable caregiver creates an extremely confusing, back-and-forth dynamic because their lack of empathy is intermittent. When you see their 'good' side, it is hard to relinquish all hope. It is easy to fall into the trap of perpetually seeking the stable parent you want and deserve but cannot find in them. This is entirely natural for a child to do because we all deep down want a loving parent and our inner child could not easily relinquish that desire. However, continuing to try to seek stable love from these parents is like being addicted to a slot machine – you keep trying, chancing, hoping that 'this time' you will get the good parent rather than the vicious version of your parent. You may try again and again to approach and get close to them, desperately wishing for an empathic and loving reaction, only to be met once again with their emotional outbursts and cruel reactions.

This ongoing loop is not just traumatizing but re-traumatizing. When you reach out, hoping for a warm embrace, you may instead find a door abruptly closed, a back turned coldly away, or the hollow disconnection of a dissociated gaze. Just like a wound that is not even allowed to form a scab, your trauma is constantly reopened. Each episode of their explosive outbursts disrupts the protective layer of healing from ever fully forming, leaving all the tender places in your heart exposed and raw – often into adulthood.

Another tendency that these parents may have is withdrawal or dissociation whenever there is a conflict. They might shut themselves off, refuse to respond, threaten to leave and never return, or be physically present but dissociated – displaying a blank facial expression, remaining silent, and becoming 'catatonic'. Experiencing such repetitive 'disappearances' from a primary caregiver can deeply traumatize you and lead to lifelong struggles with a concept known as 'object constancy' – the ability to maintain a mental image of another person or object even when they are not visible.

Disruptions in object constancy can lead to high separation anxiety and a persistent fear of abandonment in your future relationships. The fear of abandonment may mean you find it hard to build trust in intimate relationships or close friendships, have intense anxiety and panic even during brief separations from loved ones, difficulties in accepting your partner's flaws or imperfections, and a tendency to prematurely end relationships to avoid the possibility of being abandoned or rejected.

Because your trust has been broken again and again, relaxing and trusting that others genuinely love and care for you may feel nearly impossible. No matter how minor, any conflict might lead you to assume that the relationship has ended. To protect yourself, you may then end relationships prematurely before you can get hurt; unfortunately, these self-sabotaging behaviours simply reinforce your worst fears and further derail trust in your worthiness.

When trying to heal from the attachment trauma of having a Highly Unstable Parent, it is critical to see reality, trust your experience, and validate your trauma. Just because they sometimes have empathy does not always mean it is adequate and you are not wounded. Moreover, just because other people who only see the surface think of them as kind and loving does not mean they always are.

Again, please remember that your painful childhood experience does not have to define who you are or determine the trajectory of your life. Even if you have been hurt and are now struggling with issues such as insecure attachment and object constancy, breaking the cycle of intergenerational trauma and having healthy and functional future relationships with your intimate partners and children is more than possible.

3 'Superficial' Parent

For our discussion, we will refer to the next group of parents as Superficial Parents, though this does not necessarily mean they are shallow or thoughtless. These parents are primarily characterized by their strong preoccupation with material success and their obsession with upholding a particular image in society. Their priorities often revolve around external appearances rather than emotional connection or understanding.

'Superficial Parents' usually project competence to the outside world. They are the high-achievers, the go-getters. On the surface, they excel both at home and at work. For them, a person's value is judged by their grades, appearance, and talents. They gravitate towards people and institutions associated with wealth and popularity. Unfortunately, as they put material gain and social status over their mental and spiritual well-being, their ability to love and empathize as parents is also compromised.

Many of these parents embody the 'tiger parents' stereotype. They have an authoritarian and demanding approach to parenting, expecting their child to excel academically and in extracurricular activities. They can be extremely harsh if they see you falling behind in school or a talent pursuit. Because they are so desperate to see you succeed, rather than finding out what support you need to thrive, they may resort to punishment and shaming you.

A parent can be both image-obsessed and tyrannical. However, unlike the Bully Parent archetype, a Superficial Parent is abusive in a more subtle way. Due to their difficulty in identifying and expressing their own emotions, when they become frustrated, they resort to escalating their demanding nature, using sarcasm or subtle accusations to send you the non-verbalised, albeit salient message that you are a disappointment. Although the undermining may not be visible, you can palpably feel their disdain.

A Superficial Parent tends to prioritize holding up an extravagant and glamorous facade over building authentic connections with their family. They excel at presenting a captivating image to the outside world but struggle when it comes to emotional openness, genuine empathy, and sensitivity, especially in forming a deep attachment bond with their child. While they may appear charming to others, they can be cruel and dismissive to those closest to them.

Most of these parents' lapses in empathy are driven by their status anxiety. Beneath the surface, they grapple with inner emptiness and the lack of a solid sense of self. Deep down, they feel that they are worthless unless they achieve something grand. Unless proven by external metrics, they feel unlovable and have no meaningful place in the world.

This explains why they panic when you underachieve – they view you as a reflection of themselves and project their insecurities onto you. They desperately want you to appear successful and perfect as if your family is constantly 'on camera'. Regrettably, in this parental dynamic, your individuality and true self are neglected, disregarded, and hardly respected.

Superficial Parents are often unaware of their empathy deficit and inhumane nature. They may genuinely believe they are acting in your best interests. To the outside world, they may even appear as a compassionate philanthropist. For example, they may be actively involved in volunteering, contributing to a church community, or generously donating to charities.

In essence, they have constructed an image of themselves and their family that is devoid of all personal flaws, convincing themselves that these stories are true. Consequently, they treat you in a way that pulls you into their fabricated, inauthentic world, like in the movie *The Truman Show*, while ignoring your genuine needs and struggles. Their cruelty may not even be intentional; they are just so devoid of insight that they cannot even see your pain.

One of the most damaging aspects of having Superficial Parents is not only their lack of empathy for your true self, but also their tendency to overlook legitimate needs, human sorrows, and family problems. This can be particularly harmful when there are issues that require real attention. For example, if you had shown any neurodivergent traits as a child, such as ADHD, autism, or learning difficulties, they are likely to deny or ignore the fact that you are different from the norm. They may disregard your unique needs and push you relentlessly to conform to their agenda and definition of success.

Even if you are grappling with serious conditions like clinical depression, severe anorexia, or suicidal ideation, you may still act as if nothing is wrong to uphold the illusion of a 'perfect family' image. This neglect of your well-being can have severe consequences and hinder your ability to receive the support and care that you need.

Growing up with parents who are obsessed with external success can leave you feeling empty and confused. You are left believing you could only be loved based on your grades and performance, not who you are. If you have never had your feelings empathized, you may lose the ability to have a language for emotions, to feel and express them. You may become uncomfortable with intimacy as you are not used to being seen or heard by others. Unfortunately, this can also cause you to inadvertently push away the conditional love you have always wanted because you don't know how to handle it when it comes.

Growing up with a Superficial Parent can also leave you with a lasting feeling of shame because you were rarely able to meet your parent's success metrics. Even when you accomplished great things, your parent's approval was fleeting. When you had completed one goal, they pushed you to accomplish the next. You may also be left with a painfully heavy amount of unexpressed resentment as you were robbed of a burden-free childhood.

Liberation from the trauma of having a Superficial Parent is realizing that you are now an independent adult and are no longer under pressure to live up to their expectations and can instead define success for yourself. You now can develop a way of life and values. You are no longer responsible for what they think or how they want things done. Ultimately, your healing is about being true to yourself and creating something that makes sense for who you are as an individual.

4 Needy Parent

We do not usually associate narcissistic abuse with Needy Parents because they appear gentle and helpless from the outside. A Needy Parent may seem mild-mannered, but beneath the surface is a strong desire to exert control, often at the expense of their child's well-being. They lack empathy because they are constantly preoccupied with their own emotional needs and prioritize their needs over yours.

Needy Parents grapple with attachment issues stemming from unresolved childhood traumas. Many did not experience nurturing care and trust in a loving parent-child relationship. Regrettably, their unhealed wounds, fear of abandonment, and lack of self-identity can inadvertently turn into suffocating parenting behaviours towards you.

Needy Parents are like children trapped in adult bodies. They are emotionally dependent on you and act in an unreasonably clingy and demanding way. They struggle with boundaries and create emotional drama whenever they sense you want to have a separate identity from them. To fulfil their cravings for attention and affection, they impose irrational demands that restrict their autonomy. As a result, you feel obligated to attend to their needs and constantly ensure their well-being.

Some Needy Parents are so unable to take care of themselves that they can hardly take on any adult responsibilities. They might also be aware of their incompetence in the world (though in other cases, they may be unaware of their limitations and simply act impulsively and recklessly), so they rely on you for a wide range of decisions, problem-solving, and emotional support. This inevitably places a heavy burden on you, creating a dynamic where their needs consistently come before yours, even when you were only a child.

In their possessiveness, they may treat you as if you were their property. In some extreme cases, even objects like your comfort blanket or teddy bear can become targets of their attacks. As you grow older, they become increasingly intolerant of your developing relationships with others, be it friendships or romantic partnerships, fearing that it may diminish their hold on you. Even when you have finally left home as an adult, they may still want to have daily conversations or text-chat with you, wanting you to keep them updated on the details of your life.

In other words, your existence revolved around meeting their needs and validating their self-worth. As long as you fulfilled this role and catered to their demands, they would offer you warmth and support. However, the moment you fall short or disappoint them, they instantly withdraw their empathy and switch demeanour.

On the surface, they may say they are fine with you pursuing autonomy. However, they punish you aggressively when you do so or form a new intimate relationship outside of their control, and start to give them less attention. For example, they might accuse you of abandoning them, become verbally abusive, and attempt to sabotage your relationships and success. Furthermore, they may escalate their neediness in destructive but passive ways, such as making suicide threats, ceasing to take care of themselves, telling you they are becoming depressed, etc.

When you have an emotionally needy parent who is solely preoccupied with their world and feelings, you would find yourself thrust into the role of a parentified child, forced to mature quickly and take on adult responsibilities from a young age.

Parentification is a term used to describe the role reversal between parents and children in which children are expected to provide emotional support and care for their parent, where you have to assume adult roles such as a friend, advisor, confidante, or therapist. Burdened from a young age, it can be difficult now for you to let go of the internal pressure always to be the caretaker or the one holding everything together. This can result in lifelong struggles with co-dependency, perfectionism, and the inability to set healthy boundaries with others while not emotionally draining your resources. You may also struggle to trust others because your past experiences have taught you that no one is there for you, but only the other way around.

Even as a grown-up, you may be stuck in a pattern of trying to rescue your parents. Your unending 'rescue mission' can manifest in various ways, such as continuing to be your parent's financial or emotional caregiver, making decisions for them, complying with their unreasonable demands for frequent contact, and tolerating their intrusion.

Growing up with a Needy Parent, you may find yourself torn between conflicting emotions of love and anger. A part of you clings to hope, unable to let go of the fruitless mission to save your parent from their struggles. Meanwhile, the more authentic part of you is consumed by seething rage, for it recognizes that your life has been held back by a self-absorbed and developmentally stunted parent who has failed to meet your genuine need for empathy.

Identifying and addressing the cause of your compulsion to rescue them can help you reclaim your independence and vitality. You have always been the one who holds the family together, both emotionally and physically. However, as you move into the next stage of your life, you may need to reconsider reallocating your love and resources – for yourself, a family of your own, and a meaningful vocation, rather than remaining stuck in a cycle of co-dependency with an emotionally all-consuming parent. More on how to do this will be discussed in the section on self-empathy.

Breaking out of denial

In this chapter, the invitation is for you to summon your deepest courage to review the empathy deficits you might have experienced in your childhood and acknowledge the trauma you were subject to, even if it is painful and disturbing to do so. Reconciling with the reality that our parents were limited in empathy and, at times, abusive, might be the hardest step anyone has to take in their journey of healing and progressing.

Children naturally look up to their parents, often viewing them as flawless role models. This is not a conscious decision but rather an inherent aspect of a child's emotional development and survival instinct. As a vulnerable young person, recognizing that your parents might have been toxic, dysfunctional, or imperfect was nearly impossible back then because they represented your primary source of stability. The mere thought that your parents could be 'bad' implied that the entire world was a daunting and insecure place. Thus, you had no choice but to fabricate an alternative reality that denies their flaws. You had no other options but to make excuses for their behaviour and even blame yourself for what they did to you.

Nonetheless, as an adult, clinging to this idealized image offers little benefit, if any, and you now pay a hefty psychological price to uphold a false narrative. Continuing to be in denial about your trauma can result in emotional stagnation, internalized anger, a low-grade depression that hums in the background, the tendency to self-sabotage, and a feeling of losing control over your emotions. To move on from your past and thrive, it is important that you bravely confront the reality of who your parents are and the often unconscious, toxic dynamics they have brought into your life.

Your parents may not be inherently 'bad people' and have genuinely tried their best. Their deficiency in empathy could have arisen from factors such as their level of emotional development or intelligence, limited resources, poverty, and trauma, among other unforeseen circumstances. But continuing to claim that your dysfunctional parents are 'good' when they are indeed abusive is not an act of love. Similarly, perpetuating a co-dependent relationship with them is not filial piety or loyalty.

In embracing clarity around the abuse, you give yourself the permission to get on the path of self-discovery and self-compassion. You can start to rewrite your narrative, one that acknowledges the pain you endured but refuses to let it define you. You can learn to develop empathy and compassion for yourself, nurture the wounded child within you, and offer the love and support you have longed for.

While you may never fully understand 'why' what happened the way they did or change the way they are, you can choose to break the cycle and create a different future for yourself. The process of reconciling with your imperfect parents is not about condoning their actions or seeking their validation. It is about reclaiming your power and finding your truth. By bravely confronting the reality of who your parents are, you pave the way for a brighter and more authentic future – one where you can heal, thrive, and create healthier relationships for yourself and generations to come.

5
The ripples of childhood emotional trauma

The impact of growing up with emotional abuse goes beyond childhood. In this section, we will look at the psychological consequences of having parents who are emotionally abusive or lack empathy, and explore how these wounds can affect you. Then, we will focus on how you can empathize with yourself, heal, and find resolutions and resilience from these challenges.

Turning against yourself

Growing up in a home with a bullying, highly unstable, needy, or demanding parent, or where empathy was notably absent, can lead one to live a life of denial.

Our culture often discourages us from acknowledging that we were victims of childhood abuse. We are told to maintain a facade of positivity, to be grateful for everything, and to remain silent about trauma and abuse. The impact of toxic positivity is especially pronounced when the abuse is invisible, which further pushes you into the belief that you do not have the right to feel aggrieved or saddened by your experiences.

When you have nowhere else to turn, the result is often self-blame, internalized shame, and guilt. Instead of directing your anger where it justifiably belongs, you turn it against yourself. This phenomenon, known as 'turning against oneself' (Geiser et al., 2005), is a well-documented psychodynamic observed by therapists and psychologists since the days of Freud. It is particularly prevalent among those who have suffered chronic trauma due to the lack of parental empathy.

As a child, wholly reliant on your parents, you faced the daunting reality of being powerless in an unpredictable and potentially hostile world. To mitigate this fear, you might have found it easier to blame yourself than the parents you had no choice but to be dependent upon. By internalizing the belief that you were somehow at fault – perhaps not good enough or failing to act as a 'good' child should – you created a sense of control over the chaos around you. This self-directed anger offered a semblance of hope. The unconscious rationale was: if you were the problem, then perhaps you could change something to prevent further neglect or abuse. 'Maybe if I was more obedient, more quiet, a better kid . . . I would be loved.'

While this reasoning might seem illogical from an adult perspective, for the child you once were, self-blame was the only way to make sense of the inexplicable injustices you were subject to. It felt somehow more bearable than accepting that those who were supposed to protect and care for you had failed. As noted by psychologist Fairbairn (1952), it seemed better 'to live as a sinner in a world created by God than to live as a sinner in a world created by the devil' (Celani, 2010).

This coping mechanism allowed you to grow up somewhat dissociated from or unaware of the full extent of the harm inflicted upon you. However, this defence is not without its consequences. When you blame yourself for the mistreatment or believe that you deserved it, any righteous anger you feel becomes redirected towards yourself, manifesting as self-directed aggression and shame. With this as a coping mechanism, you entered adulthood burdened by a lingering feeling and the default interpersonal position that everything was your fault.

You might find yourself taking on excessive responsibilities and unfairly accepting blame for issues in your friendships and relationships, even when it is not warranted. It can be easy to harshly judge yourself, believing that conflicts or relationship breakdowns are solely your faults – perhaps because you think you're 'too emotional', 'too selfish', 'too unattractive', or any number of other self-criticisms.

This defence mechanism can be harmful as it wears on your self-esteem and enables people to treat you unfairly. You may even inadvertently attract people with abusive tendencies into your life. Believing that you are inherently toxic or unworthy of love and attention can also lead you to unconsciously sabotage any genuine affection: even when others offer kindness, love, or the attention you truly deserve, you find yourself pushing them away because you do not feel you deserve them.

Depression as internalized anger

In families lacking empathy, anger becomes a touchy subject. You may have a Bully Parent or Superficial Parent who did not tolerate any signs of discontent or disobedience, or perhaps a Highly Unstable Parent or Needy Parent who consumed all the emotional space with their crises or meltdowns, leaving little room for you to voice your feelings or be acknowledged. In such environments, when you experienced mistreatment and felt trapped with nowhere to turn, internalizing your anger was often the only option available. This response, while a survival tactic, can have long-lasting effects on how you handle emotions and conflicts later in life.

Internalized anger, though not widely recognized by many psychologists, is what underlies chronic depression. Internalized anger, though not widely recognized by many psychologists, reveals the complex psychological challenges children can face when they are unable to openly express anger or frustration towards their caregivers. This is often due to a fear of retribution or consequences.

Even when subjected to severe mistreatment or neglect from parents or guardians, the perilous nature of harboring resentment towards one's caregivers can compel the child to redirect those negative emotions inwards. Rather than directing their anger outward, the child may instead turn that anger against themselves, engaging in self-blame as a proxy for the desire to lash out at their caregivers.

The inability to confront one's true emotions towards parental figures, out of a need to preserve those vital relationships, leads to the suppression and redirection of that anger in complex and maladaptive ways.

Freud later expanded on this idea, suggesting that depression is essentially internalized anger (Busch, 2009). This perspective is later supported by numerous psychological research that found individuals with depression often engage in intense self-blame and self-criticism, sometimes to the point of disgust and self-hatred (Anderson and Williams-Markey, 2024).

In psychoanalysis, the phenomenon of internalized anger is associated with the concept of 'identifying with the aggressor' (Frankel, 2002). This is when a part of our unconscious mind adopts the characteristics, attitudes, or behaviours of those who violate our boundaries. This internalized voice, often critical and punishing, morphs into a relentless inner critic, a part of your day-to-day life now.

For example, if your bullying parent publicly humiliates you, calls you names, or punishes you for your exuberance, their words might later be repeated by you in the voice of your inner critic. By internalizing the abusive behaviour of your empathy-deficient parents, you embed them within your psyche. This means that you carry the influence of their actions and attitudes wherever you go.

'Identifying with the aggressor' can still occur even if your parent never directly insulted you. For instance, when your Needy or Highly Unstable Parent consistently prioritized themselves, the message you might have internalized could be 'I am not important', 'my needs do not matter' or 'I am too much for others'. As a result, when you express your own needs, your inner critic chastises you, leaving you with guilt and even the compulsion to self-punish.

Identifying with the aggressor can manifest in adulthood as self-hatred, perfectionism, low self-worth, and other harmful emotional states. When unchecked, this inner critical voice will speak over your logical thought and emotional intelligence. The results may include insecurities in relationships, paranoia or anxiety at work, and chronic depression. It can even lead to suicidal urges in extreme cases (Prysak, 2018).

Understanding that your inner critic isn't inherently 'bad' can help you avoid falling into a deeper cycle of self-blame. This critical voice originally developed out of love, loyalty, and an attempt to help your parents and maintain a connection with them. In the challenging environment of a cold, empathy-lacking household, your inner critic was once crucial for your survival.

However, as you strive to become a functioning, independent adult, this relentless voice of criticism no longer serves its purpose. You are no longer trapped with your parents and you can reclaim your rights to anger. Continuing the 'legacy' of playing small to stay safe does no good for anyone – neither you, nor those around you. Recognizing that you have outgrown the need for such a critic is key to moving forward into a future where you can create a nurturing, 'real' family of your own.

Structural dissociation and feeling empty

Chronic childhood trauma, particularly when it stems from a consistent lack of empathy from caregivers, differs from PTSD, which typically arises from a single traumatic event. Ideally, you would avoid abusers and traumatic environments. However, as a child, physically escaping from abusive or neglectful parents is often not possible. Instead, many children learn to cope by withdrawing psychologically. This involves unconsciously creating a mental 'split'. Within this split, parts of the self that contain deep pain and anger are compartmentalized into a protected inner space that shields these intense emotions.

This compartmentalization is known in psychology as 'structural dissociation'. It serves as a defence mechanism where traumatic responses are segmented into distinct parts within oneself to manage overwhelming emotions more effectively. This differs from clinical conditions such as psychosis or schizophrenia, where you become detached from reality. In structural dissociation, despite internal segmentation, you still have the conscious awareness that you are one person. However, specific triggers can activate various compartmentalized parts, which may feel alien and possess distinct personalities, emotions, and behaviours that can vary in age or even gender (Harris, 2007; Fisher, 2014, 2017).

Structural dissociation can lead to dramatic shifts in how you feel and behave from one moment to the next – you might feel strong and joyful at one time, then suddenly empty and numb, followed by intense rage. These rapid changes can be disorienting and lead to unpredictable mood swings, identity confusion, and a persistent sense of emptiness.

In the original theory of structural dissociation, it is proposed that the psyche can split into two primary segments: the 'Normal Self' and the 'Traumatized Self'. This division helps you navigate life despite the burden of traumatic memories. The Normal Self serves as the facade you present to the outside world – appearing confident, emotionally stable, and in control. This is the self you engage when making decisions, interacting with others, and managing daily activities.

Conversely, the Traumatized Self is an unconscious aspect rooted in your past traumatic experiences. This part of your psyche often remains chaotic and uncontrolled, burdened with unresolved emotional pain from these traumas.

When you rely too heavily on your Normal Self to function and avoid the wounded, hidden aspects of your psyche, polarization can occur. This leads to the suppression of not only painful memories but also basic human experiences and sensations such as hunger, desire, and feelings. While this might help you maintain a semblance of functionality in daily life, it comes at the cost of neglecting essential human needs like emotional expression, play, spontaneity, and intimacy. Consequently, you may experience feelings of nihilism, a pervasive sense of emptiness, and existential boredom.

The more you fear getting in touch with your trauma, the more attached you become to your Normal Self facade, and the more your vulnerable parts may feel alien to you. Feeling numb or avoiding emotions as a coping mechanism might work temporarily, but eventually, your trauma will scream to be listened to. When this happens, the emotional floodgates open, leaving you feeling shocked, out of control, and fearful of what can come out of you. You might then resort to drastic measures to suppress these feelings, such as alcohol and drug abuse, overspending, bingeing, self-mutilation, or other self-soothing, impulsive behaviours. Additionally, maintaining a normal facade can be physically exhausting because it takes considerable energy to constantly push down painful feelings that strive to surface. Eventually, your vitality and motivation to engage with your aspirations, nurture your passions, and pursue your goals may dwindle. This perpetuates a detrimental cycle, diminishing your sense of purpose and the joy you find in life.

Triggered wherever you go

When you were deeply hurt by empathy deprivation as a child, your brain's natural protective mechanism developed a heightened sense of alertness to protect you from harm and prepare you for future threats. This can leave you in a chronic state of hyper-vigilance, which causes you to be tense and react to seemingly innocuous situations that may subconsciously remind you of the traumatic event(s) you experienced.

You may be able to appear high-functioning while operating with your Normal Self, but the truth is that however much you try to deny it, your trauma does not automatically heal itself. Underneath consciousness, you still bring your Traumatized Self wherever you go. Your wounded inner child is constantly on guard despite being hidden deep within your mind, expecting to be harmed or betrayed. Underneath the calm, 'grown-up' surface, your vulnerable part is always on the lookout for danger, criticism, and abandonment, and it struggles to accept love and kindness.

This means you may be extremely sensitive to specific triggers in your daily life. For example, you may find yourself reacting in an unusual and out-of-character manner to certain words, tones, or behaviours that evoke memories of the traumatic event. While you may not be aware of these triggers, when they occur, you instantly lose control of yourself. You may suddenly feel 'taken over' by your wounded self, feeling like a vulnerable child and acting like a raging teenager. You may have an emotional breakdown, panic attacks, or aggressive outbursts. Because your traumatized part is frozen in time, the anger, anxiety, sadness, and shame you feel when you are triggered are all as potent as when you were five years old, trapped in a household with your unempathetic parents.

According to psychologist David Richo (2002), we are frequently triggered when one of our core needs – the 'Five As': attention, acceptance, appreciation, affection and allowing – is not met. Common triggers are events that cause you to feel controlled, abused, humiliated, deprived, neglected, or emotionally invalidated. For example, assume that your boundaries were constantly violated as a child. You might have had highly controlling parents who often invaded your space or dictated your life. This can easily lead to you misinterpreting benign requests from others as an attempt to control you. You may then respond by pushing back too hard or with anger that feels unjustified by the other person.

Unfortunately, when events of various kinds easily trigger you, you can be branded by those around you as 'overly sensitive' or 'overly dramatic', and so on, which hinders your intimate relationships and even your career. It can be devastating to be labelled as 'irrational' for something over which you have little control. People may accuse you of 'overreacting', as if you have a choice. However, if they indeed saw and understood what you have been through and how difficult it was to grow up in a household with little genuine empathy, your hypervigilance and hyper-alertness to threats (of invalidation, of being controlled, and so on) would have made perfect sense. Moreover, if they see that it is not you but the five-year-old in you reacting, they may have more compassion for what you are going through daily.

Stuck repeating the same pattern

Many survivors of childhood trauma find themselves trapped in a cycle of recreating and reliving their past experiences well into adulthood. A good illustration of this is how common it is for children raised in alcoholic homes to somehow, inadvertently, marry alcoholics or someone with an addictive personality. Alternatively, someone whose parent left because of an affair may subconsciously select partners who are unwilling to commit. Or, you may be disturbed by the fact that as days go by, you are seeing more and more traits in your chosen lifelong spouse that remind you of your dysfunctional parents – perhaps they were as emotionally unstable, needy, or cold.

If you find yourself stuck in this predicament, you are not the only one. Despite our awareness that our parents cannot provide the empathy we desperately need, breaking free from abusive, undermining, needy, or bullying parents is a process that can span years and involve numerous failed attempts. It is puzzling how we can repeatedly return to our empathy-devoided parents, fully aware that they will only continue to humiliate, degrade, and inflict pain upon us. For instance, we may still visit them frequently, hoping to receive praise and recognition, but only to be met with neglect, demeaning insults, or more self-absorbed complaints.

Why would we do that? The term 'repetition compulsion' (Corradi, 2009; Levy, 2000) is what psychologists use to describe the compulsion to repeat old relational patterns or trauma. Multiple factors may be involved. It could be our unconscious yearning to stay attached to our parents or the refusal to see the dark reality for what it is. It could also be due to a sense of familiarity. Another theory suggests that seeking meaning after experiencing trauma is human nature. We need answers as to what went wrong and why. This is one of the drives behind our compulsion to revert to the same relational cycle – to make sense of things.

As discussed before, as children, we had no choice but to collude with our parents' denial and projections. We had to find excuses and justify our parents' behaviours. We had to bypass any natural anger or resentment and prematurely jump to forgiveness or false empathy to continue to be their confidant and ally. Even though this survival strategy is no longer applicable in our adult lives, we still act similarly – finding ways to rationalize, justify, avoid our feelings, and protect our parents' failings. Therefore, we keep trying and knocking on the wrong doors until we are so hurt and wounded that we are paralyzed, refusing to acknowledge the tremendous pain and suffering – that our parents cannot love us as we deserve.

Breaking free from an abusive parent becomes incredibly challenging when their empathy deficit is intermittent, as is often the case with Highly Unstable Parents. They may have some normal or even loving behaviour, albeit fleetingly. Psychologist Fairbairn's concept of 'attachment to bad objects' (Clarke, 2018; Ogden, 1983) helps us understand why you may feel a strong attachment to a parent or caregiver who consistently disappoints and hurts you yet provides just enough warmth, support, or care to keep your hope alive, albeit meekly. The erratic and unpredictable nature of their parenting style, coupled with the occasional displays of affection, captivates you. It is akin to the allure of an addictive slot machine, where the occasional wins, combined with your deep longing for love and empathy, keep you hooked. Nevertheless, unfortunately, the mere possibility that love and empathy could 'sometimes happen' becomes enough to perpetuate a destructive cycle of co-dependency that can last for years.

In essence, the root of repetition compulsion is an unconscious resistance to reconcile with reality as it is. In every adult child who has experienced trauma, there is a 'hopeless child' and a 'hopeful child'. Hope is essential to our survival, but it can also be dangerous. Our hopeful optimism can become a master of deception, convincing us that love exists even in those who have never shown any genuine empathy for us. Your unconscious drive to stay in denial, avoiding pain, and the habit of directing anger in rather than out all perpetuate the idea that it was not your parents' fault but yours. The premise is that if you do enough and are 'good enough', your selfish parents may change. The fantasy is that your unempathic parent will someday open up and give you the love you deserve.

However, if you can see things as they are, you will see how hollow this fantasy is. In reality, your parents lack the necessary empathy and cognitive abilities to understand who you are genuinely, so even after all these years, there is little substance to this 'relationship' that you are so attached to.

Repetition compulsion does not just perpetuate the harmful patterns you have with your parents, it can also extend to other areas of your life. One reason you repeat these patterns with others is the unconscious hope that it will be different this time. Since your parents never provided you with the emotional support you needed, you seek it from external sources such as partners, employers, or teachers.

You may, therefore, find yourself in relationships that mirror the dynamics from your childhood. For example, you might end up with a partner who has controlling behaviours reminiscent of your manipulative parents. Perhaps you find yourself staying in a toxic workplace, tolerating abuse because you feel powerless to create meaningful change. Despite these relationships being belittling, humiliating, and abusive, they can strangely feel familiar and even 'comfortable' in a twisted way. By repeating the same behaviours and staying in destructive relationships, you unconsciously try to regain some sense of control. You convince yourself that you can make things right this time, even though you know it is impossible.

Unfortunately, repetition compulsion rarely leads to healing. On the contrary, it often exacerbates the situation. The more you subject yourself to empathy deficits, the more your self-esteem and sense of agency diminish. Eventually, you can lose more self-respect and the ability to stand up for yourself.

Bouncing back

As we explore the impact of growing up with parents who lacked empathy, it is natural to feel unsettled, disheartened, or even despondent. If you were raised in an environment marred by narcissism or emotional neglect, learning to be compassionate towards yourself can seem like an insurmountable challenge.

However, your feelings of unworthiness, your tendencies to diminish your own needs, and even your occasional wishes to vanish are not reflections of your intrinsic value, they stem from not receiving the empathetic nurturing you deserve. Your feelings of unworthiness feel real, but they do not mean the truth. The truth is, you were a secondary victim of your parents' unresolved traumas – bearing burdens that were never yours to carry.

Embracing self-empathy – extending to yourself the compassion and understanding you were denied – will be a pivotal step in your healing journey. It's essential for breaking the cycle of transgenerational trauma and forging a brighter future for yourself and potentially for the next generation.

We will explore some practical steps to cultivate self-empathy in the upcoming chapter.

6
Unconscious drivers of abusive behaviours

While we all use various defence mechanisms to cope with life's challenges, our level of maturity and psychological functioning influence which ones we rely on. In psychology, the concept of the 'hierarchy of defence mechanisms' offers insights into how our psychological health correlates with the specific defences we typically employ (DeFife and Hilsenroth, 2005; Di Giuseppe and Perry, 2021; Drapeau et al., 2003; Tanzilli et al., 2021).

Understanding unconscious drivers

Psychologists have found that people who are less emotionally mature often resort to 'primitive' defence mechanisms, while those who are more psychologically integrated lean towards 'mature' defences. Examples of primitive, maladaptive defence mechanisms include acting out, help-rejecting complaining, passive aggression, splitting (black-and-white thinking), projective identification, projection, devaluing of self or others, and idealization of self-image (Di Giuseppe and Perry, 2021). Conversely, more psychologically integrated individuals are inclined towards mature defence mechanisms like humour and altruism, which are not only adaptive but also promote healthy coping (Vaillant, 2000).

When someone heavily relies on immature defence mechanisms, they lack awareness of their inner world. Rather than confronting internal conflicts and external stressors, they are prone to avoidance or denial. This tendency significantly correlates with a deficiency in empathy.

Understanding certain unconscious defence mechanisms becomes especially relevant when extending empathy towards emotionally immature and underdeveloped parents. By grasping the reasons behind their behaviours and actions, you can lay the groundwork for empathy to grow – not to excuse their actions, but to foster a deeper comprehension that benefits both you and them.

In this discussion, we will focus on two prevalent unconscious drivers often observed in empathically challenged parents: envy and projective identification, which may shed some light on why they behave the way they do (Frederickson, 2021; Kernberg, 1992; Di Giuseppe and Perry, 2021).

Toxic envy

Envy among parents towards their children is a more prevalent occurrence than society typically acknowledges. John Bowlby, the pioneer of Attachment Theory, observes that parents may not always harbour positive feelings towards their children, but certain emotions, such as anger and resentment, are considered taboo in our culture. Bowlby illustrates this with the example of a father who may resent his infant's monopolization of his partner's attention. Unaware of his feelings, his jealousy may stem from unresolved childhood trauma, such as feeling neglected when his younger sibling was born (Bowlby, 1979). He may then attempt to separate the baby from the mother or dismiss the baby's attachment needs, justifying his actions as a parenting technique rather than ones driven by unconscious jealousy.

The truth is that parental emotions are complex and full of ambivalence, not limited to the widely accepted feeling of love. Even the best parents can and will often have feelings of resentment, anger, and even moments of dislike towards their children. It is a natural part of being human, and feeling envy does not negate the profound love a parent can have for a child. In fact, it is entirely normal for parents to experience some inner conflicts. For example, most parents undeniably want the best for their children and are glad to see them with a loving partner. However, the idea of their children leaving home, starting their own families, and no longer needing them as much can also evoke the fear of abandonment and a sense of melancholy.

For parents who did not receive adequate love and care during their childhoods, seeing their children receive the attention and affection they longed for can easily trigger subconscious feelings of envy. They cannot help but compare and realize how they never experienced the same depth of affection their children now enjoy.

Emotions such as resentment and envy are not in themselves evil. Instead of suppressing these feelings and relegating them to our collective shadows, it would be much healthier to acknowledge and manage them constructively.

Psychologically mature parents would have enough self-awareness to navigate these moments of ambivalence. They have healthy emotional outlets and may seek therapy to discuss and process their feelings of resentment and envy, to ensure that they do not turn into harmful parenting behaviours. On the other hand, parents who are emotionally immature and unresourceful may allow their toxic envy to be acted out in actions or words that harm their children.

For example, a Bully Parent will most likely have unconscious envy for your emotional authenticity. They harbour resentment because they were never allowed to be vulnerable or let down their guard. The fact that you can be honest about your own vulnerabilities may threaten them. As an unconscious retaliation, they might punish you for expressing feelings, especially those that garner sympathy or empathy from others. In addition, their attachment to power may cause them to fear that your success and rising self-esteem will threaten their control over you. As a result, however unconsciously, they may criticize you or undermine your confidence to retain their feelings of being in control.

Superficial Parents tend to have a naturally competitive disposition and an incessant desire to emerge as the 'winner' in any given situation or group. They are unlikely to appreciate it when you outshine them. However, since admitting to their envy would challenge their self-image, they are likely unaware of their own competitiveness. Instead, their envy may surface in subtle and unexpected ways. For instance, they might strive to outperform you in an activity or vie for the same awards or recognition you have earned, all while pretending it has nothing to do with you. When you achieve something remarkable, a Superficial Parent might withhold praise, downplay your achievement, pretend that nothing happened, or offer you false compliments that are actually backhanded criticisms. In most cases, their put-downs are so discreet that it is challenging to pinpoint them.

An Unstable Parent may experience envy because you receive the love they never had. Due to the attachment trauma they carry, it requires tremendous effort on their part to be good parents to you. However, beneath the surface, feelings of resentment brew because they have to invest so much energy into parenting you while feeling that they have not received the love they deserve. Buried underneath their parental role is a needy infant starving for attention and that inner child can perceive your attractiveness, power, and abilities as threats. They may also get competitive with you as they fight for their partner's (your other parent's) attention. Not being able to cope with the shadow of their toxic envy, they may resort to their typical patterns, such as becoming emotionally unavailable, oscillating between loving and punishing you, giving you the cold shoulder, being impatient and stroppy, or intermittently withdrawing from your life to retain a sense of control.

A Needy Parent may be threatened by the possibility of your becoming independent and strong because they want to keep you tied to them. Needy Parents affected by toxic envy tend to assume the role of a victim. The hidden message is: 'See how I'm suffering as a result of you. You owe me all that I have given up for you.' They may also use emotional blackmailing or gaslighting to make you feel guilty for thriving without them.

Most parents are not inherently 'evil' and have a loving side. Perhaps, from the healthiest part of their psyche, they want to break the cycle of transgenerational trauma and prevent passing down the painful experiences they endured to you. They hope to create a loving and nurturing home, something they may have longed for but never had in their upbringing. However, inadvertently, emotionally immature parents often find themselves replicating the very behaviours that they suffered under as children – behaviours that were bullying, demanding, cold, and punitive. Tragically, they become ensnared in the cycle of transgenerational trauma transmission, repeatedly reenacting scenes from their traumatic past without even realizing it.

Projective identification

Another factor that can explain some of your parents' abusive behaviours is a complex psychoanalytic concept known as projective identification.

Projective identification is a psychodynamic defence mechanism where someone unconsciously projects their feelings, thoughts, or ideas onto another person. Most of the time, the projector does not even realize they are doing it. Unlike simple projection, projective identification involves a two-way process – the projector does not only project their feelings onto the recipient/victim but also compels the recipient to 'identify with' and internalize the projection.

Pathological projective identification can be highly toxic and unsettling for the recipient. For instance, if someone projects feelings of 'self-disgust' onto you through projective identification, you would feel disgusted with yourself. Since it all happens unconsciously, it is unlikely that you would realize you have been subjected to projection, and you might come to believe that you really are a repulsive person. This is a significant violation of personal boundaries because it crosses the line that should respectfully separate two people.

In the context of home life, parental projective identification is when a parent repeatedly (not just once) transfers and dislodges unacceptable, shameful parts of themselves not just onto but 'into' their child (Reid and Kealy, 2022; Seligman, 1999), forcing the child to then 'swallow' the projected toxic materials. Emotionally underdeveloped parents often engage in projective identification so they do not have to face their shadow sides, which are the parts of themselves they find undesirable.

Your dysfunctional parent may also be unknowingly re-enacting their childhood experiences when raising you. This unconscious repetition compulsion serves to impart to you the same feelings they endured during their upbringing – feelings of worthlessness, shame, and a constant fear of punishment. When your parent criticizes, ignores, or acts in ways devoid of empathy, they effectively transfer their unwanted shame onto you, compelling you to carry and internalize it.

When this happens to you, instead of healing their developmental wounds through personal development, therapy, or addressing their past trauma, they conveniently use you as a way to manage or avoid dealing with their emotional pain. They use various coercion tactics, ranging from abuse to silent treatment or neglect, to persuade you that the relocated fragment of their experience is your own. In other words, when a parent treats you as if you are inherently 'bad', stupid, a loser, or worthless for no justifiable reason, they are most likely projecting a disliked aspect of themselves onto you.

With trained awareness, it is possible to spot instances of projective identification. For instance, a trained therapist will know they have been the target of projective identification by their clients. If they suddenly experience unfamiliar emotions or react in a manner that deviates from their typical responses, they will likely discuss these experiences with their supervisor to check if that has been the case. However, while the therapist can recognize that the patient is projecting, the patient may see their projections as reality. This disparity in perception highlights the complexity of projective identification and the challenge it brings in tackling it.

Parental projective identification is particularly destructive because of the inherent power imbalance of your relationship. Given your parent's authority and your survival need to preserve your attachment to them, it would be close to impossible to resist identifying with their negative emotions and absorbing their projections. If your parent happened to be emotionally unstable, the strength of their projection would be amplified by the level of their emotional charge. This dynamic highlights the difficulty of navigating such toxic dynamics, particularly in childhood when you are still developing your emotional boundaries and self-identity. Through the mechanism of projective identification, for instance, you may absorb their shame and take it in as your own. You would not naturally place blame on them for the trauma you experienced. Instead, you wholeheartedly believe that it was 'your fault' and that you should be ashamed of who you are. Even when their behaviours were the reason you have felt confused, powerless, and undeserving of love throughout your life, you likely have attributed these feelings to your own perceived 'flaws' rather than recognizing their origins in your parents' projections.

This chronic violation of psychological boundaries may have left you unable to establish and enforce limits on what you will accept or internalize even as you grow older. Symbolically, this can turn into mental health challenges such as eating disorders (where you compulsively 'ingest' or 'refuse to ingest' as a way of exerting control), chronic dysthymia (a pervasive, low-grade form of depression that underlies much of your experience), the tendency to blame yourself for everything and be overly apologetic, and, unsurprisingly, co-dependency.

The pressure to conform to your parents' projected perceptions may have led you to believe that your identity is and must always be defined from the outside rather than, emerging from within. This creates identity confusion, wherein you find yourself ensnared by distressing thoughts about who you are, potentially enduring this silent confusion for most of your life without fully understanding its origins.

Understanding how projective identification operates is crucial when it comes to protecting yourself from empathic distress and compassion burnout. When you see and understand projective identification, you can practise disengaging from their abusive behaviours and, instead, perceive them as 'information' about their history, trauma, feelings, and thoughts. You will cease to take things personally and be more resilient not just with your parent but in the world. Going forward, when someone shames you, you'll recognize that they are projecting their shame and it says more about them than you.

Empathy beyond tolerance

Truly empathizing means going beyond what lies on the surface and delving into the invisible dynamics that may be at play between people. To find our capacity for empathy in challenging times, we must use not just our hearts but also our minds, our ability to take different perspectives, and our reasoning skills to understand not just what is happening but why it is happening.

Once you grasp the causes and mechanisms behind your parents' toxic behaviours, you can then use this understanding to gain insight into their inner world. This is the beginning of genuine empathy. Furthermore, this knowledge empowers you to stay rooted in your mental stability, maintain emotional balance, and hold onto your sense of reality, even when faced with projection, gaslighting, or attacks.

Understanding your parents' actions and recognizing that some behaviours arise from toxic mechanisms is not harsh or judgemental. Instead, it can be a way to elevate your relationship to a more mature and realistic level.

This understanding may not necessarily lead to empathy for them. However, it can at least foster empathy for yourself, allowing you to maintain a firm grip on your reality even in the face of toxic behaviours from those around you. This is especially important if you choose to maintain a relationship with your parents rather than cut them off. Seeing reality, even if it is painful, facilitates not only empathy for their suffering but also empathy for your own.

At the same time, understanding the underlying layers and how their defence mechanisms operate does not excuse their bad behaviour. Love is not endless tolerance, unhealthy justification of mistreatment, or denial of the truth.

Very likely, when you can view your family dynamics with intelligent insight, you can reduce instances where you unconsciously transfer or displace repressed anger onto those close to you in your current life. For instance, you may no longer project your repressed anger towards your parents onto your loved ones, your issues with authority figures onto your manager, and repeat your trauma from sibling rivalries onto your friends. These changes in emotional reactivity will greatly enhance the quality of your life, current relationship, and even career potential.

In essence, genuine empathy entails understanding the underlying dynamics of behaviour. This insight enables you to maintain your own well-being while expanding your capacity for empathy within the most challenging family relationships.

7
Understanding parents who have hurt you

To empathize is to understand. When I was grappling with my own parents' limitations, my late therapist offered this poignant reminder: 'To empathize, we must first understand.' Yet, in confronting those who have left us scarred, our default responses often lean towards resentment, judgement, and the urge to punish – an impulse that may inadvertently perpetuate pain for both ourselves and them.

While it's perfectly natural and even necessary to experience healthy indignation, there may come a time when you are ready to break free from the cycle of resentment and regain emotional freedom. Empathy is an invaluable tool in facilitating this transformative process.

It's undeniable that summoning empathy for those who have inflicted pain upon us, especially when they are the ones who are supposed to love us unconditionally, can be immensely challenging. However, if you have chosen to embark on this journey, a first step might be to delve deeply into the origins and motivations that drive their behaviour. This process necessitates a thoughtful exploration of the life events that may have shaped their path to becoming who they are today.

Your parents are likely unaware of how their past influences their parenting choices. They may be compelled to maintain a facade of invulnerability and perfection, primarily driven by a desire to avoid the shame associated with knowing they fall short of being the parents you need them to be. Society also often renders flaws in parenting a cultural taboo, which contributes to their denial. Therefore, it is unlikely that you can gain any useful insights by directly asking or confronting them.

Instead, you may have to consider their lives before you entered the picture, reflect on their challenges during their formative years, the complex relationships with their parents, and any adversities or losses they experienced. By gaining insight into their personal histories, you can transform how you see and approach them, even if, in the end, you decide to distance yourself or maintain no contact.

In this chapter, we will delve into the inner lives of different 'types' of parents, speculating what may have shaped them and led them to become the individuals they are today. These descriptions are based on typologies and may not universally apply. Human psychology is complex and multifaceted; no two people are the same, and no single parent can be neatly categorized into a single 'type'. The categorization into archetypes serves as a tool for our discussion. We encourage you to exercise discretion and retain only the information that is relevant and useful in your unique circumstances.

Understanding 'Bully' Parents

For many parents with bullying tendencies, the world is neatly divided into two camps: the 'strong' and the 'weak'. They believe that power, often linked with physical ability and authority, is crucial for achieving success and staying safe in life.

It's possible that during your parent's childhood or teenage years, they observed or experienced a world where those seen as weak were targeted and harmed, while those with authority and power, like teachers, parents, stronger peers, or older siblings, seemed to prevail as they are. As a young and vulnerable child, they might have witnessed or experienced abuse of power.

One significant aspect often overlooked about your parent with bullying tendencies is the profound loneliness and lack of internal love they endure. Those who are close to them may have become so frustrated by their inability to recognize and respond to emotional cues that they have given up on having deep connections with them. Their incapacity to empathize and engage with tender emotions meaningfully also makes deep friendships nearly impossible. Moreover, they tend to reject love and compassion for themselves. They fear that opening the floodgates to their own attachment needs will weaken them, so they would instead push love away before they feel any tender feelings. When someone is kind and loving to them, they perceive it as a potential threat to their emotional defences and, as a result, push away that person. While they may have acquaintances and friends with whom they maintain surface-level connections, internally, they grapple with feeling painfully alone.

Despite the strength they project, they are unaware that they live in a self-created bubble of delusion, similar to children who wear a cape to play Superman or Superwoman. They 'believe' they have control when, in fact, they do not. They think they can be emotionless and stoic, but they feel desolate on the inside. They thought everyone viewed them as a strong person, but those closest to them often see through them, as in the parable 'The Emperor's New Clothes'.

Your Bully Parent lacks empathy and sensitivity because they are in constant denial of their own softer sides. In every waking moment, they expend a tremendous amount of energy concealing their fragilities. They lack self-compassion because they fear that qualities such as sensitivity and lenience will render them weak. But how could they possibly empathize with anyone's vulnerabilities if they are completely cut off from their own? Consequently, when they see signs of fragility in others, their instinct is to ignore, criticize, or eradicate it.

Empathizing with a 'Bully' Parent

It is entirely valid to distance yourself and cut ties with a parent who consistently mistreats you. However, if you choose to maintain a relationship with a Bully Parent, you may want to look beyond their external facade and into the inner turmoil they may be experiencing. Looking into their past, you might uncover a history marked by abuse, bullying, chaos, and injustice. While their upbringing does not justify their actions, it can provide insight into them. Empathizing with them does not mean accepting or tolerating their abusive behaviour, but rather understanding the deep-seated fears that fuel their actions and navigating them accordingly.

Successfully managing a relationship with a Bully Parent demands a nuanced approach – avoiding triggers for their aggression without appearing gullible. They may get impatient and even lose respect for you if you approach them in an overly 'touchy-feely' manner. To maintain a delicate balance, try matching their energy level by speaking with a voice that is neither soft nor loud, and keep your messages clear and simple.

Psychologically, positioning yourself as an equal, rather than a child or a victim of their bullying, is key. This does not mean trying to counterattack or intimidate them during interactions, but rather projecting confidence in yourself and what you say. If you do struggle with low self-esteem, you may have to work on yourself until you can achieve a true sense of confidence as Bully Parents are adept at detecting false bravery. If they perceive that you're putting on a facade of toughness, they might feel compelled to attack you.

Consider giving yourself pep talks or seeking support from loved ones who remind you of your inner strength. Remind yourself that you are no longer a child under their control. Even if they respond negatively to your kindness, understand that they are rejecting parts of themselves that crave human kindness, rather than you. It is a sad situation for them but it is not your fault. Thus, their reactions do not reflect on you, and try not to feel deflated.

When showing empathy towards them, avoid directly asking about their emotions, as this might make them defensive. Since they may struggle with emotional language, focus on asking about their thoughts or physical well-being instead. They may find it easier to express themselves in these terms.

When you try to be kind to them, opt for simple statements without making assumptions in any way. For example, instead of saying something like, 'You must be feeling incredibly sad', which could trigger defensiveness, you can offer a simple, 'I'm sorry to hear that', and leave it at that. Avoid digging too deeply or pressing for more information, as they might respond defensively and disengage from the conversation. If you can demonstrate strength and confidence without being intrusive, your parent may eventually feel safe in your presence and gradually let go of their defence.

Not all parents with bullying tendencies lack redeeming qualities or are psychopathic. Some feel guilty over their short fuse, and bullying tendencies, and long for a closer, more meaningful relationship with their children. When a Bully Parent heals, they can even evolve into a mature and reliable protector, and channel their feisty nature towards something greater than their ego.

It's not your duty to heal a Bully Parent, but if you feel compelled to express your love and empathy, reaching out and attempting to connect with them despite their aggressive or dysfunctional behaviour can be incredibly meaningful.

Reclaiming your right to anger

Growing up with bullying parents can distort your relationship with anger. You may have learned to suppress your anger and inhibit your ability to express your emotions openly.

As an adult child facing a Bully Parent, it is most essential that you reclaim your sense of agency and personal power. This involves reconnecting with healthy anger and knowing your right to healthy indignation.

In the past, you may have disowned your power because of the fear associated with expressing discontent within your home. This reaction is understandable, especially if the only example of anger you witnessed was aggressive behaviour from your parent. However, anger itself is not inherently aggressive. Anger is a legitimate and natural emotion, and distinguishing between expressing anger assertively and resorting to aggression is crucial for breaking free from the negative patterns learned from bullying parents.

Anger and aggression are not the same thing: while anger is a natural and almost instinctive emotion, aggression is a behaviour that can be chosen or avoided. Anger is not inherently evil or harmful. It, like all emotions, serves as a messenger. It indicates that something in your environment or within yourself needs to be addressed and resolved. When you investigate the root causes of your anger, you gain valuable insights into your values, desires, and the areas of your life that need to be changed or improved.

In her book *The Language of Emotions*, empathy educator Karla McLaren (2023) discusses how anger functions as a boundary-setting emotion. It's not only a natural response to injustice or the neglect of your needs and values but also a tool for identifying personal limits, asserting needs, and ensuring self-protection. Understanding anger is crucial for fostering functional social interactions and nurturing healthy relationships.

If you grew up with a Bully Parent and had to contort or suppress anger for most of your life, rebuilding your relationship may take time and practice. Here is a simple exercise to get you started.

(You will find more extensive exploration on reclaiming your right to anger in Chapter 8, 'Healing with self-empathy', if you feel that this topic is particularly relevant to you. Feel free to jump to or take a deeper dive into that chapter to further understand and address the impacts of this dynamic.

Journalling exercise: Differentiating anger from aggression

The objective is to spend one week exploring and differentiating between anger and aggression, while also identifying healthy expressions of anger.

1 Make time every day to write freely in a journal. Allow yourself a space where you are not judged or censored. If you are stuck, try different writing techniques, such as combining writing with doodling, or pretending you are writing a letter to your past/future self or someone you care about.
2 Throughout the coming week, keep an eye out for situations in which you or others a) feel angry and b) act aggressively. Take note of how the two differ. Observe your own and others' mental and behavioural expressions of anger and aggression. What differences are there in tone of voice, body language and word choice? Write your findings in the journal.
3 Look for and collect examples of healthy expressions of anger in your surroundings. Look for examples of people setting their boundaries, acting in assertive ways, or expressing frustration in ways that promote understanding and resolution. Take note of how they have difficult conversations with strength and clarity, and how they channel their anger.
4 If you cannot find someone like that in your personal or professional circle, you may use characters in television, movies, or fictions you read.

5 Now, broaden your search for healthy role models to include public figures, activists, or historical figures who have channelled their rage into powerful movements or social changes. Analyze their strategies for constructively expressing anger, mobilizing communities, and effecting more significant changes.

What about their approach to inspiring you? Were there any instances, even if they were brief, in your own life when you could or should have done the same?

Identify actionable steps for incorporating healthier expressions of anger into your relationships and interactions.

Understanding a Highly Unstable Parent

As a child of a Highly Unstable Parent, you may have been used as an emotional crutch to prove their worthiness, or you might have played the role of a scapegoat and become the target of their projection (where they project their inner self-hate onto you). You may feel you only exist for the purpose of constantly reassuring them or proving their worth. As long as you continue to fulfil their needs, they offer you warmth and support. However, the moment you let them down, in however innocuous ways, they can become aggressive and punitive. They might accuse you of abandoning them, become verbally abusive, and attempt to disrupt your life. If you are unable to establish boundaries effectively, they may escalate their neediness in destructive or passive-aggressive ways, such as through suicide threats, self-harm, or other harmful behaviours.

In clinical terms, what a Highly Unstable Parent is wrestling with is called emotional dysregulation or 'emotional lability'. This means that they can have extreme or intense emotional responses to things that seemingly are not a big deal, and when they are triggered, they cannot easily bring themselves back to an emotional equilibrium.

Their sense of self can rapidly swing from one extreme to the other, from feeling entitled, excited, and slightly manic to being agitated, depressed, and self-hating. Even when they feel very slightly threatened by the hint of any criticism or rejection, they lose their ability to mentalize or empathize, and regress into a child mode where they can only focus on themselves and their feelings. Underneath their Jekyll and Hyde personas, however, they feel utterly empty on the inside. Sometimes, it may appear as if they are 'creating drama' or 'addicted to conflicts' because that is how they escape the dread of numbness.

Healthy people usually have a robust sense of self that anchors their emotional stability. They know who they are, and they do not require excessive admiration from others to feel deserving. However, an emotionally unstable person often lacks a stable core sense of self and has to seek validation from others to fill the void. Their fragile sense of self makes them see every interaction as a test of their own worthiness. Therefore, even a seemingly harmless remark could set them off – it could be anything from a delayed reply to a funny look from a stranger. Even a minor incident like a small disagreement can become a big deal that shatters their emotional balance.

What lies at the heart of their emotional instability is a deep fear of abandonment or rejection. However, ironically when they respond to conflicts with hostility or passive-aggressive withdrawal, it creates a self-fulfilling prophecy where their behaviours drive people away, which then further reinforces their inner belief that everyone will eventually leave them.

Understanding the above, you may try to remain compassionately detached, not be caught up in their volatility, and see their actions as a reflection of their own unresolved issues rather than anything you have or have not done. Making a conscious decision to stop internalizing their shaming and blaming is a crucial step towards protecting your emotional well-being. Remember, it is not your responsibility to carry the weight of their past or to fix their emotional wounds. By setting boundaries and taking care of yourself, you can start to break free from the cycle and create a healthier dynamic with an unstable parent.

How to interact with a Highly Unstable Parent

It can be extremely difficult to empathize with a Highly Unstable Parent, especially when you are directly subject to their unreasonable attacks. You never know when a Highly Unstable Parent will 'flip', and trying to contain and control the situation – something you've probably done your whole life – might make you feel even more helpless and out of control. When they are triggered, you are communicating not with an adult but with someone who has regressed into a child mode. They can no longer 'reality-test' their beliefs; whatever they FEEL is now taken by them as FACT – for example, if they feel you are abandoning them, they are convinced that that is factually happening. Similarly, a mere glance from a stranger could be taken by them, with full conviction, as signs of mockery and humiliation.

In this situation, the most effective approach is to avoid directly challenging their delusion, but instead use empathy to de-escalate their heightened emotional reactions. Confronting their version of reality is likely to provoke more defensiveness, aggressive reactions, and psychic disintegration. Even when it comes to the point where you have no choice but to address their distorted perceptions, do so with care to ensure that your tone is not perceived as confrontational, sarcastic, or dismissive.

Although it may seem difficult to do so at first, you can still express empathy for them even if, to you, they are completely illogical. This is because validating someone else's emotions does not require you to share their perspective. Even if they are saying something based on paranoia or outrageous assumptions, what they feel is what they feel. It is enough to acknowledge their feelings and understand why they feel that way, without getting into a factual debate with them.

If they are ready to listen, you may even use these moments as opportunities to help them expand their capacity for self-reflection. Ask open-ended questions like, 'How are you feeling right now?', 'What upset you about this situation?', or 'What do you think made this particularly troubling for you?' These questions can help them pause and redirect their attention towards a reflective mindset, rather than focus on externalizing their anger.

If you are the one they are attacking, it could feel impossible to extend empathy to them, and you do not have to force yourself to do so. In abusive situations, it is absolutely appropriate to set firm boundaries or to remove yourself from the interaction.

If you choose to maintain communication, focus on acknowledging their emotions without engaging in a debate about the content of their accusations. Recognize that their feelings of distress are real to them, even if the reasons behind those feelings are unfounded. You can say something like, 'I can see you're really upset', which validates their emotional state without forcing yourself to agree with any false statements.

Responding with empathy and maintaining calm helps you stay grounded in your adult self, rather than getting pulled into emotional turmoil. This approach is not about conceding or supporting their distorted views; rather, it's about protecting yourself and your dignity without escalating the conflict.

Strategies to protect your energetic boundaries

When dealing with parents who struggle with emotional regulation, it's all too easy to be swept up in their emotional turmoils. Maintaining your composure and mental health requires learning how to not become overwhelmed or controlled by their anger or emotional threats – but this is often easier said than done.

The challenge intensifies if your parent is not just physically but also psychologically invasive. They might invade your space by persistently knocking on your door, calling you repeatedly, or trying to reach you through friends and partners. Moreover, in their more irrational and hysterical moments, they may become aggressive, brandish dangerous objects like knives, threaten self-harm or harm to others, throw items, or scream uncontrollably. Their emotionally threatening behaviour can also take a more invisible form, such as using silent protests. They may go missing for days on end, isolate themselves in their room for extended periods, or abruptly leave home – all with the intention of causing worry and distress to those around them as a form of revenge or retribution. These emotionally manipulative actions are not just physically invasive but also psychologically and energetically draining.

They can also infringe on your energetic boundaries by making false accusations and calling you names. For example, they may label you as 'overly sensitive' or blame you for causing disruptions and tearing the family apart despite the fact that they are the ones doing exactly what they accuse you of. These unjust accusations sting because they are false and deeply unfair.

Despite having dealt with their rage and emotional threats your entire life, you may wonder why it doesn't get easier with time but instead gets harder. Even when they are not physically present, their explosive and hysterical states can still distract you. Their emotional threats can disrupt your focus on work, make you feel unable to be present with your partner and children, and even affect your appetite, sleep, and overall mental health.

But this is not your fault – it is simply the way you have been groomed to be. Whether or not it was conscious, they are essentially threatening you to give them the attention they need to fill their inner void. Since 'catering to their threats' is what you have been trained to do throughout your childhood, despite advice from friends and loved ones to simply 'leave them alone', finding the strength to do so can be emotionally challenging.

Seeing the absurdity of their emotionally threatening behaviours is an important starting point; as soon as you become aware of them, you can start to learn and break free from them. Here are some pointers and reminders when you find yourself becoming perturbed by the emotional storms of a highly unstable parent:

Remind yourself 'it will blow over'

When they are having an emotionally explosive episode, it can be reassuring to remind yourself that these outbursts have been a part of your life since childhood and you have survived many of them. Try to stick to your routine as much as possible, even if it is difficult to focus. Maintaining a sense of normalcy can help ground you and provide a buffer against their emotional turbulence.

You may also plan some coping strategies ahead of time to ensure they are healthy and non-destructive. Imagine creating a personal 'protocol' to follow whenever your parent has an episode. In advance, decide who you can turn to for support and what self-soothing techniques you can use. For example, during difficult times, you might grant yourself a day off from work to visit your favourite park or communicate with your partner about needing some space for respite. Planning ahead can help you limit the chances of acting out impulsively and regret engaging in destructive self-soothing behaviours like drinking or overspending.

We humans have a tendency to become deeply immersed in our thoughts, often merging with them to the extent that they feel indistinguishable from our reality (Luoma et al., 2007). This process is known as 'buying into' thoughts (Bennett and Oliver, 2019; Dahl et al., 2014). However, it is crucial to remember that thoughts are not facts, and emotions are transient – they will pass. Just because your emotionally unstable parent makes you feel as though they have the power to ruin your life, this does not make it a reality. Similarly, feelings of guilt or beliefs that you are at fault are not true.

Recognizing the distinction between thoughts and facts can empower you to respond to your emotions and interactions with a clearer, more balanced perspective. Amidst the turmoil, repeatedly remind yourself that as intense as it feels, this too shall pass. It is not permanent, and sooner or later, your parent will calm down, and the storm will subside. Your goal is simply to retain as much inner peace as possible until it passes. When you acknowledge that your thoughts and feelings are just temporary mental events, you create a mental space that allows you to observe them without becoming overwhelmed. This practice helps you maintain your sense of self and autonomy, even in the face of intense emotional manipulation.

At the same time, avoid falling into the trap of over-appeasing your parent in order to calm the storm. This may unintentionally reinforce their unconscious but manipulative behaviours. Instead, calmly, firmly, and confidently maintain your boundaries.

Ultimately, you are not responsible for their dysfunctional behaviour. Their struggles existed long before you were even born, and you cannot change or control what they do. You may feel sad for them and naturally want to help, but even with the best of intentions, you simply cannot. You can offer compassion from a distance, without feeling obligated to sacrifice your own life just to save theirs. You can still care about your parent without allowing their dysfunction to dominate your life.

Try not to resist your feelings

While you can challenge and choose not to buy into your thoughts, managing your emotions requires a different strategy. Paradoxically, the most effective way to deal with unpleasant feelings is to accept and fully experience them. The saying 'What we resist persists' captures the idea that emotions often intensify when we attempt to fight, defend against, or suppress them. Accepting your feelings does not mean indulging in self-pity; rather, it involves acknowledging your emotions without judgement or attempts to change them.

When faced with emotional threats from your parent, take a moment to centre yourself by taking ten deep breaths. Ground yourself in the present moment by engaging your five senses and connecting with your surroundings. Seek out your 'safe space' – whether it's your garden, a nearby park, or the comforting corners of your own bedroom. Feel the stability of the ground beneath your feet and affirm to yourself that you are safe, right here, right now.

Then, practise naming your feelings. See if you can simply identify and verbalize what you are feeling, calling each emotion by its true name without labelling it as 'good' or 'bad'. This practice can help you observe your emotions more objectively, reducing their overwhelming power and allowing you to process them more healthily.

Your emotions will eventually go away on their own if you can learn to 'be with' them rather than resist them. See if you can focus on leading a meaningful life in the interim despite feeling perturbed by your parent's emotional storms.

Sunk cost of the souls: Consider walking away

When faced with unfair treatment, it's natural to seek justice. We often yearn for the wrongdoer to acknowledge their actions and perhaps offer an apology. This need for validation, however, can keep us emotionally tethered to those who have harmed us, trapping us in a cycle of engagement that may not lead to resolution.

In an ideal scenario, expressing your feelings of hurt directly to those who have hurt you can often help you find some emotional closure. However, with an unstable and irrational parent, even your sincere and honest communication may backfire and escalate into further conflict, counterattacks or insults. In such situations, creating some distance may be the most effective way to manage your emotional pain.

If you are certain that a sincere apology will never come, persistently seeking one becomes nothing but a process of repeated re-traumatization. Instead, consider strategic distancing as a powerful act of self-preservation and empowerment. This approach not only safeguards your emotional health but also sends a clear message about the unacceptability of their behaviour.

Deciding to walk away from a dysfunctional relationship, especially one with your family, and the narrative that you have spent your entire life believing in, can be a heart-wrenching and difficult process.

Although 'you are responsible to save me' might have been a fabricated and gaslit story, it was the only one you have known all your life. Even when it no longer serves you, something about it still feels like a familiar home. When combined with the values you hold dear – those of love and loyalty – walking away, and dropping the hope you have invested, could feel like a kind of soul-death.

As humans, we are naturally inclined towards 'loss aversion' – a psychological phenomenon where the pain of losing is often felt more intensely than the joy of gaining. This instinct can make the thought of severing familial bonds seem daunting. You may fixate on the memories, the shared moments, or the hope of what could be, rather than the day-to-day realities of the price you have to pay to sustain the dysfunctional bonds.

Falling into the 'sunk cost fallacy' is human – it is when you continue to sustain the pattern just because of all that you have invested in it – time, hope, love, resources, all the energy you have poured into trying to fix the relationships, your emotional investments, attempts to make it work, endless attempts towards an authentic bond, and the imagination you have poured into building the vision of that ideal family you deserve but never got in reality.

However, it is at this juncture that you may also want to think about the 'opportunity cost' – what you are missing out on by staying in a toxic bond with an abusive parent. Each day spent in a toxic bond is a day not spent living a life filled with love, respect, and tranquillity.

Our time on earth is indeed limited – '*memento mori*'. Considering this may bring sadness and pressure, it is also a necessary and poignant call to action, urging us to live our lives fully and meaningfully, away from situations that drain our spirits and dignity.

The emotional toll of deciding to leave a toxic bond can be overwhelming. It's often easier to succumb to the familiarity of dysfunction rather than embrace the uncertainty that comes with change. However, we must focus not only on what we may lose but also remember that: 1. Staying is also a decision. And 2. There is also a cost to staying.

There might be the illusion that the devil you know is better than the one you don't, but the truth is life has always been inherently uncertain. Just because you choose to stay in a toxic trauma bond with your parent does not mean you have much control over the outcome or have any more certainties in life. In fact, the opposite might be true if the relationship takes away your power and dignity.

You are not alone in this dilemma and millions and billions have walked a similar path. You have not done anything wrong and at every single given moment, even where you are right now, you are doing the best you can with all the resources and knowledge you have. However, that does not mean your next moment cannot be different.

Ultimately, walking away from a toxic situation is not just about ending something and losing something. It is also about cracking open a new door, and this moment may mark the dawn of a fresh start, an awakening, the first page of a new chapter.

Absolutely no one has the power to pressure you to do anything until you genuinely feel ready, but you must remember that your option is to distance yourself from them. There might be a life on the other side of the swinging door waiting for you to grasp it – a life where you are truly valued, respected, and loved.

Experiential exercise: Rediscover your voice

In this exercise, we aim to reconnect with the child within you, who had sacrificed their own spirit to cater to the needs of their emotionally threatening parents. We will use a technique known as the 'empty chair exercise', which is typically facilitated by a professional therapist but can be adapted for personal reflection.

1 **Set up the empty chair**: Place an empty chair in front of you. Imagine your parent sitting in this chair. This setup helps to externalize the conversation, making it feel more real.
2 **Express your true feelings**: Address the empty chair as if the person were really there. Speak out loud, articulating your feelings about the ongoing conflicts, disappointments, and pressures. Allow yourself to express any suppressed emotions. It would be the most powerful if you could speak out loud, but if you do not feel comfortable doing that, you can write your thoughts in a journal or letter.

3. **Time-travel advocacy**: To go even deeper, consider a unique time-travel experience within your imagination. Picture yourself as an adult, now equipped with the wisdom and experience you've accumulated. Imagine going back in time to advocate for your younger self. Reflect on what you, as a child, truly needed to thrive – emotional support, understanding, validation – and why these needs were critical.

   With this powerful adult perspective, confront the imagined parent in the chair. Speak up for your younger self, articulating the needs and emotions that were overlooked or disregarded. Finally, someone is speaking up for your wounded, vulnerable self, and that is you.
4. **Reflect and heal**: After you've expressed everything, take some time to reflect on the experience. How did it feel to voice these thoughts? Did new insights or emotions emerge? Consider writing down any revelations or feelings that came up during the exercise.

Understanding Superficial Parents

Understanding and empathizing with a Superficial Parent can be challenging. You may naturally want to avoid them, as their hypocritical behaviour often leads to unpleasant interactions. At their core, they are someone who has abandoned their true selves to serve an external facade, thus, your interactions with them can feel insincere and empty. When you're dealing with someone who is disconnected from their authentic self, it is easy to unconsciously mirror their internal conflicts: you might find yourself wanting to distance from and reject them, just like how they treat themselves.

You have the option to walk away at any time. But if you choose to keep a relationship with them, the key to summon compassion and empathy for them is to focus on the person inside rather than the facade they unconsciously put up.

Seeing beyond their facade

At the root of your parents' shallow behaviours is the unconscious fear that they have nothing to show and that they are not even worthy of existence if they do not prove themselves through external accolades. This may sound extreme, but a Superficial Parent's inner panic and insecurity can be this intense, and it is most likely rooted in a childhood in which they were not allowed to be their natural self.

It's possible that as children, they were primarily valued for their achievements and abilities, rather than for their inherent worth. If their own parents – in this case, your grandparents – only offered praise for successes and met failures or emotional vulnerability with indifference or punishment, it would have deeply influenced their self-perception. Children naturally seek parental approval, and when approval is contingent on performance, they learn to continuously chase external validation. This pattern, once established, persists into adulthood and shapes how they present themselves to the world. In other words, their current superficial demeanour and focus on maintaining appearances could be a deeply ingrained strategy to receive the affirmation they've been conditioned to earn since childhood.

As a young adult, your parents may have concentrated all their energy on serving their egoic self to survive, rather than nurturing their authentic self. The more they concealed their true identity, the stronger their belief grew that their genuine, unadorned selves were unlovable and worthless, and thus should be hidden from the world. Suffering from a severe but invisible case of Imposter Syndrome, they feel compelled to rely on external possessions, a glamorous appearance, a falsely positive attitude, and public accolades as a shield against their deep-seated insecurities.

Fearing devaluation, they pour their hearts and souls into projects, work, and maintaining appearances that serve to impress others, often at the expense of giving themselves the time and space to explore their internal emotions or connect meaningfully with loved ones. What began as a survival mechanism has evolved into a personality marked by insincerity, self-absorption, and competitiveness. As a workaholic and a relentless 'doer', they are so drained by a life driven by fear that they have no energy left to engage with what's truly happening around them, much less recognize and respond to your needs for empathy and parental guidance.

But imagine how daunting it is to live with a deep internal void every single day: they look in the mirror and see nothing, so they desperately pile on external materials to prove that they exist. Every mistake is interpreted as a failure by them, and the mere thought of failing can elicit paralyzing feelings of shame and the fear of inner emptiness. Recognizing this enables you to perceive the inherent vulnerability that lies beneath their outward display of confidence and extravagance.

Despite their harsh actions towards you, internally, these parents are not typically sociopathic but rather, they are profoundly fragile. They likely have delicate emotions and can be extremely sensitive on the inside.

Though it may be challenging, try to draw upon the strength from any positive memories you may have, where moments of their warmth and sensitivity were evident. Consider also visualizing them as their younger selves. What images come to mind when you think about their inner child and their experiences growing up?

Sadly, healing for your parents will not occur overnight. Perhaps the greatest gift you can give them is a quiet presence – which they rarely have – and to be with their inner emptiness with deep patience and empathy, even only in an unspoken way.

Connecting with a status-obsessed parent

For much of their lives, your parent may have overlooked their basic human needs for rest, restoration, and connection, behaving more like a 'robot' tirelessly executing tasks, rather than a 'human' with emotional and physical needs.

To encourage positive change without seeming overbearing, you can express your concerns and compassion about their neglect of self-care and the potential risks of burnout. Signs of impending breakdown, such as irritability, changes in eating and sleeping patterns, and paranoia, can be subtle indicators to watch for. You can help increase their self-awareness by gently pointing out these signs, but be cautious about how and when you do this. Highlighting their needs, even with the best intentions, might be perceived as implying they are flawed or needy, which could trigger their deep-seated fears of being judged or ridiculed.

Your parents may be aware of their own needs, but they also know how to mask it. One of the most profound ways to love them is to help them understand that interdependence (not to be confused with co-dependency) is a natural part of life. Perhaps, after a lifetime of relying solely on themselves, they can now learn to express their needs and ask for help from others.

Giving them genuine compliments can help soften them to receive your empathy. However, any compliments or gratitude you express must be genuine, or you will be complicit in their bubble of self-deception that says 'everything is great', which can later lead to your own resentment and thus compassion fatigue. Physical contact may also be an effective way of getting past their defences, as it is an unspoken, direct right-brain-to-right-brain way of expressing empathy without explicitly demanding that they drop their public persona.

Indeed, you may want to be realistic with your expectations when you express genuine care towards your parent; they may refuse help because they have spent their entire lives believing that solving problems on their own will make them appear more competent and capable. Unlike Bully Parents, they may not lash out or walk away, but they may quickly revert to their theatrical facade, and you will receive a 'play act', or a standard 'scripted' response to your empathy.

If you were raised by a Superficial Parent, you might have developed a pattern of seeking approval from others, which can make it particularly tough when your attempts to show empathy or offer help are rejected. Remember, you are reaching out not for the sake of changing them but for your own integrity. You are no longer there for their approval, and your sense of self has transcended beyond what they know. If they refuse your kindness, it is on them, not on you.

With age, your parent may be forced by circumstances to relinquish their need for control. If they are able to use their midlife turn as an opportunity to grow and change, you will notice them expressing affection and emotions more spontaneously and openly. They will start to accept themselves as they truly are, moving past the emotional deception that underlies their outward confidence and cheerfulness.

Initially, their attempts at emotional expression may be awkward, and they might still try to 'look good' in your presence. However, as they gradually lower their defences, you both have the opportunity to introduce humour and playfulness into your relationship. This shift allows for a connection to their gentler, kinder side to emerge naturally, fostering a healthier and more genuine bond.

Reflective exercise: Articulating your values

The primary objective of this reflective exercise is to identify and articulate personal values independent of external influences.

1 Consider the principles that have influenced your life thus far: Which values were highlighted or played down during your upbringing? For instance, the importance of education, the significance of financial matters, and other examples that come to mind.
2 Now, recall some 'high points' of your life, those instances when you felt genuinely 'in the flow', at peace. With yourself, or fulfilled. Identify the values that played a role in these positive experiences.
3 Reflect on your most significant achievement and ponder the qualities that deeply resonate with you on a personal level. In essence, explore what matters most to you.
4 Imagine an ideal future scenario where external expectations and limitations no longer apply. Picture a life free from financial constraints and the opinions of others. In this liberated space, contemplate the person you aspire to be and the core values central to that vision. Consider values such as integrity, compassion, courage, creativity, autonomy, and connection as you shape your ideal self. If it would help, you may refer to the Values List at the bottom of this chapter for inspiration. To help this process, you may also explore the following values-based questions:
   - What principles do you want to guide your decisions and actions?
   - If you had unlimited resources, how would you spend your time and energy?
   - What causes or issues do you feel passionate about?
   - What behaviours or qualities in others do you admire and find inspiring?
   - In what situations do you feel most authentic and true to yourself?

   If you've identified more than seven values, consider refining this list. Review the values you've pinpointed and determine which ones are particularly important or resonant. Are there values that, if compromised, would cause significant internal conflict? Narrow down to 3–5 core values that hold the greatest significance in shaping your beliefs and guiding your decisions.

5 Finally, create your Personal Values Statement: Condense your important values into a short, clear statement, using simple language that captures what you truly believe. For instance: *I commit to being honest, caring, and true to myself. These values guide everything I do because they represent who I am and who I strive to be.*

6 Finally, think about aligning your daily choices with what matters to you. Set goals that match your values and build real connections that reflect your true self. Every now and then, review and update your values statement as you continue to grow and evolve.

Values list

Here is a reference list of values for you to consider. Feel free to choose from these or create your own using words that resonate with you. After all, using your own words is the most powerful approach.

Achievement
Adventure
Authenticity
Balance
Belonging
Boldness
Comfort
Compassion
Connection
Courage
Creativity
Curiosity
Determination
Empathy
Fairness
Faith
Family
Freedom
Friendship
Gratitude

Growth	Personal Development
Happiness	Quality
Health	Recognition
Honesty	Resilience
Humility	Responsibility
Independence	Security
Inner Harmony	Self-discipline
Integrity	Service
Joy	Simplicity
Kindness	Spirituality
Knowledge	Stability
Leadership	Success
Learning	Teamwork
Love	Tolerance
Loyalty	Trust
Open-mindedness	Understanding
Optimism	Unity
Patience	Wisdom
Peace	Well-being
Perseverance	Wealth

Understanding Needy Parents

You may think of your Needy Parents as children trapped in adult bodies. Their clingy, demanding, and controlling actions do not stem from them being inherently terrible people but rather reflect their psychological immaturity. They struggle to make independent decisions and often rely on you for reassurance. They find it challenging to establish healthy boundaries and create drama whenever they sense that you may want to pursue a separate identity from them. They want you to take care of them in their old age, as well as solving their many day-to-day problems. To fulfil their intense cravings for attention and affection, as their child, you might feel responsible for attending to their needs and constantly ensuring their well-being.

In this chapter, we will explore some potential root causes and mechanisms that drive your parents' behaviours, namely, the deep fear of abandonment, a sense of inadequacy, and an insatiable need for validation. This need can be traced back to their past, often rooted in childhood experiences that had left deep emotional scars. By understanding the roots of your parents' childlike behaviour and the impact of their past traumas, you can better navigate these complex dynamics and support them while preserving your sense of self and well-being.

Understanding Needy Parents: A compassionate lens

ENMESHMENT AND CO-DEPENDENCY

Fundamentally, a Needy Parent engages with those in their life through a pattern known as 'enmeshment'. The term originates from family therapy models developed in the 1970s, notably through Salvador Minuchin's introduction of structural family therapy in 1975. Enmeshment describes a condition in which individuals find it challenging to distinguish themselves from others. This often results in a diminished sense of self-identity, an over-reliance on others for emotional fulfilment, and difficulties in recognizing and prioritizing their own thoughts, emotions, and needs (Minuchin et al., 1975; Green and Werner, 1996). As a relationship pattern, enmeshment is when one or both people involved feel like they cannot survive or find purpose without constant interaction with each other. In severe cases, when a person is alone, they become overwhelmed with feelings of emptiness, confusion, and a deep questioning of one's meaning of existence.

In a parent–child dynamic, enmeshment often evolves into co-dependency. As your parent lacks a robust sense of self-identity, they overcompensate by merging their identity with yours (Bacon and Conway, 2023). From a young age, they might have inappropriately shared their personal troubles with you. They disclosed excessive details about their life challenges, including their emotional and marital issues, which at your young age is emotionally burdening. You may notice that they frequently use 'we' or 'us' when discussing problems that actually concern only themselves. For instance, they might say, 'Your father keeps cheating on us. He is doing this to hurt us. He has betrayed us,' among other sentiments. Through this type of language, they not only attempt to draw you into their personal issues, and create a sense of 'fusion', but they also show a lack of empathy and consideration for you as a separate being.

Your parent might have adopted a facade of helplessness as a coping mechanism. For example, they may appear more helpless, emotionally unstable, and incapable when they know someone is there, hoping that you or someone else will come to their rescue. But when actually left alone, they suddenly become more self-sufficient than they initially let on. This is not always a conscious attempt to manipulate; it has become such an ingrained coping mechanism for them that they do not even know they are unintentionally dramatizing things to get their needs met.

CHILDHOOD EXPERIENCES THAT MIGHT HAVE SHAPED THEM

Enmeshment often emerges as a relational pattern that is passed down through generations. For example, your grandparents might have expected your parent to always be available to listen to and solve their problems and to remain closely connected throughout their lives. Growing up with such role models, your parent now comes to expect the same level of constant availability and involvement from you.

Another scenario might be that your grandparents had created an overly sheltered environment. They might have tried to shield your parent from life's challenges, inadvertently disempowering them and hindering their independence. This overprotection led to the formation of unconscious, limiting beliefs that now shape your parent's self-image, interactions, and behaviour. Some of these beliefs may include: 'I am incapable of handling life's complexities on my own', 'I must rely on others for protection and support', and 'My safety depends on staying closely connected to others'.

On the other hand, from the lens of Object-Relations theory, a branch of psychoanalysis, we may assume that some experiences of parental loss or perceived rejection have disrupted the development of healthy attachment patterns in your parent, resulting in a persistent need to cling to others.

Suppose your grandparents were not consistently available or emotionally responsive to your parent's needs during their upbringing. When support from caregivers is unreliable, children learn to take desperate measures to ensure they receive attention and care. The unpredictability can lead children to adopt controlling behaviours to secure the care and support they need, laying the groundwork for future co-dependent and unconscious manipulative tendencies.

As a child, your parent might have lived in constant fear that their parent could disappear, leave, or abandon them at any moment. This trauma can be so powerful that it becomes 'frozen in time', stuck in their unconscious memory alongside the fears of a scared child. As a result, they become extremely sensitive to any signs that people close to them might leave, feeling deeply threatened by the prospect of being alone. These fears can explain why, during your formative years, you attempted to exert control over your choices, relationships, and daily routines to maintain your reliance on them. As you matured and sought independence, they may have resorted to manipulation, guilt-tripping, and dire warnings out of desperation.

In addition to neglect, your parent's neediness may be rooted in an excessively critical upbringing. If a child is raised in an environment where caregivers are unreasonably critical or punitive, they may internalize severe self-criticism and develop an intense fear of 'getting things wrong'. The ongoing need for approval and fear of rejection can persist into adulthood, resulting in a pattern of submissiveness and a reliance on the judgements and decisions of others.

In simpler terms, your parent got 'stuck' in their emotional development. They are still trying to fill the void left by their difficult childhood. When their needs are not met, they may resort to dramatic measures, such as emotional outbursts, tears, or anger. These behaviours are often unconscious attempts to keep you close and attentive to their emotional needs, similar to how a young child might act out to get what they need.

What about you?

Growing up as a child of needy and dependent parents can potentially mould you into someone who consistently places others' needs before your own. This self-sacrificing pattern is linked to a phenomenon known as parentification.

From a young age, you might have learned to suppress your concerns and emotions to support your Needy Parent. This could involve denying, avoiding, or disconnecting from your feelings, particularly regarding emotions like anger. Your emotional needs might have been overlooked as you were preoccupied with catering to your parent's needs.

Either due to your natural sensitivity, competence, or sibling order, you may have had to forgo your own developmental tasks to take on the role of a surrogate parent for your parents. Anecdotally, it appears that the oldest child is often burdened with responsibilities and chores, known as logistical parentification, while the youngest child is more likely to become an emotional counsellor, confidant, or 'ally' for one or both parents, known as emotional parentification.

As a result, you miss out on enjoying extracurricular activities, developing social skills, making friends with peers, and exploring your sexuality and personal interests. Instead, you consistently prioritize the desires of others over your own, which can lead to a point where you feel lost about what you – the real you – genuinely want or need.

Now, as an adult, focusing on your needs might feel selfish, and even saying no to unreasonable demands can trigger overwhelming guilt.

The expectations placed on you to be consistently supportive and present for your parents were unrealistic, as no one, whether child or adult, can fulfil such a role. Repeatedly trying to 'rescue' your parents from their misery but failing can lead to chronic feelings of inadequacy and shame.

Growing up parentified likely has an impact on your current relationships as you may suffer from what is known as a 'rescuer complex'. This complex manifests as an overwhelming and compulsive urge to constantly assist, mend or save others, often to the detriment of your physical and emotional well-being.

You may find yourself repeatedly drawn to partners who, consciously or not, act just like your Needy Parent. Their neediness may not be so apparent from the get-go. However, as the relationship develops, you often find yourself the higher-functioning partner and financially, physically, or psychologically taking care of your other half. You have to step in and make decisions for them, or they just would not take responsibility for their choices.

Repeatedly getting into lopsided relationships, unfortunately, reinforces your unhealthy relational pattern, where you perpetuate the cycle where you continue to disregard your well-being, convinced that it is your responsibility to provide support and care to those around you, with your own needs taking a back seat.

Another common coping mechanism that often emerges from this experience is conflict avoidance. You may go to great lengths to maintain harmony, even if it means silencing your authentic voice and suppressing your desires and needs. This could be as minor as not expressing where you want to eat or as significant as denying your sexual desires.

This behaviour arises from a desire to shield yourself from the discomfort associated with confrontation, which you might have unconsciously associated with your Needy Parent's emotional outbursts or demanding behaviours. While it feels natural to put others' needs before your own in your adult relationships, this self-sacrificing behaviour can also lead to feelings of being unappreciated and taken for granted.

Over time, these strategies can lead to a struggle to assert your boundaries, express your desires, or prioritize your well-being. They become ingrained patterns that influence how you navigate your relationships and personal life. Moving forward, we will explore strategies for healing and reclaiming your identity and self-worth within these dynamics.

Releasing the burdens that are not yours

SETTING BOUNDARIES

To set boundaries with emotionally needy parents is not an easy task. To do so reasonably, realistically, and empathically, start by introspectively identifying what is it that you, as a unique person, require for your well-being, rather than relying on clichés or what others might suggest.

To start, you have the power to choose the frequency, duration, and nature of your interactions. For instance, if your parent tends to make unannounced visits to your home, you can communicate your preference for advance notice before any visits. If face-to-face meetings become emotionally overwhelming, consider alternative ways of staying in touch, such as texting or phone calls. If your parent bombards you with phone calls or messages daily, you can state your preference for less frequent communication. If your parent offers unsolicited advice on your life choices or criticizes your decisions, you can politely tell them that though you appreciate their attempts to help, you will make choices based on your own judgement.

To reinforce your boundaries and convey your commitment to them, you must also establish clear and appropriate 'consequences' for instances of boundary violations. These consequences should be fair and directly related to the specific situation. They are not meant to punish but to reinforce your message and intention. For example, if your parent consistently invades your privacy by going through your personal belongings, you can restrict their access to your personal space. This might mean keeping certain rooms locked or setting clear rules about which areas of your home are off-limits during visits.

If your parent oversteps boundaries by excessively probing, you may need to start withholding certain non-essential information from them, including details about your whereabouts, availability, and schedule. This is not about secrecy but about reinforcing the importance of your personal space and autonomy. Remember, you are a grown-up with your own life, and you are not obligated to share every non-essential piece of information about your life with them. By setting these boundaries and consequences, you help ensure that your relationship with your parent respects your independence and personal space.

When setting boundaries with a Needy Parent, be prepared for a battle of wills. They may attempt to persuade you that boundaries are unnecessary, emphasizing that you are not 'enmeshed' but just 'close'. They might argue that, as your parent, they have the privilege to be privy to every aspect of your life and express their views however they want and whenever they want. They may also reframe their intrusion as a form of love and care.

Some pitfalls to avoid are the temptation to explain or justify yourself, to overshare your feelings, or to tell them how much they have hurt you. Naturally, if you feel you have been unfairly treated, you want to seek balance and justice and communicate your needs. However, do not forget your enmeshed parent is in a completely different mental space from you. While you want them to see and understand your point of view, their capacity for empathy is limited. All they see is that they are losing control over you, and the only thing they can focus on is their panic. Offering justifications can leave you in a vulnerable position for judgements and counter-arguments.

If they respond to the boundaries you set in punitive and vindictive ways, you can calmly and assertively say, 'I have already explained this to you. You may disagree, and I do not need you to agree.' Focus on communicating your boundaries without delving into lengthy justifications or oversharing. Remember, it is not a discussion, not a negotiation, and you do not need their approval for the boundaries you have set.

They may be receptive and grow from your new, mature way of communicating, or they may remain stuck and act punitively against it, but their reactions should not deter you either way. Their reaction does not change the reality that the enmeshed and dysfunctional dynamic does not serve either of you. What you must consistently bear in mind in this process is that you are doing what is kind for both of you – despite what they say, what you are doing is not cruel or abandoning, but mature and necessary.

If your parent is unwilling to change, you may have to shift your focus to building your emotional resilience and strength. With a strong sense of self, you can hold your head high and know you are doing the right thing – not just for you, but for both of you.

GETTING OUT OF THE RESCUER CYCLE

A truth that you must bear in mind in this process is that it is not and never should have been your responsibility to continually fix their problems or clean up after them.

Despite their childlike behaviour at times, your parent is, in fact, an adult who has managed to survive in their way up to this point in their lives. Regardless of their current physical or psychological condition, it was their own choices, actions, or lack thereof that brought them to this stage in their life. Irrespective of cultural values and societal norms that suggest otherwise, it is not your obligation to rescue your parent.

To escape the trap of being their perpetual rescuer, see if you can explore whether your parent has other support networks or family members who can help. Consider guiding them towards exploring additional avenues of support, such as broadening their social connections or even accessing government assistance programs. Have them assume responsibility for their well-being, so the weight of responsibility does not rest solely on your shoulders.

Even if they cannot attain complete self-sufficiency overnight, both you and them ought to recognize that you cannot forever serve as their caregiver. The situation is not sustainable and the longer you delay helping them gain independence, the worse the ultimate outcome might be.

CHALLENGING THE FAMILY NARRATIVE

Deciding to set clear boundaries with your family or demanding parent involves more than just external actions, it is also a psychological journey. You might have to confront and question deep-seated family beliefs that view setting boundaries as wrong or that dictate you must always protect, assist, or avoid upsetting your parents.

This process requires challenging the conditioning you have received from your family. It is a transformative but demanding path that asks for your willingness to reshape long-held perspectives.

Those closest to you, especially your parents and siblings who have relied on you as the caretaker, may resist healthy changes. They might even use shaming and guilt-tripping to try to pull you back into the familiar but dysfunctional status quo. This resistance can turn into tension, conflicts, and emotional upheaval. But try to remember that, much like any storm, this tumultuous phase is temporary. It is often better to endure temporary discomfort than to perpetuate a pattern that you have now come to realize is toxic and unsustainable.

See if you can reshape your mindset and view the family resistance and chastising not as signs that you are doing something wrong, but as an indicator of progress. Even if your role within the family shifts from being the 'golden child' to the 'black sheep', and you are labelled as disloyal and selfish, you can hold firmly to the understanding that these labels stem from your own dysfunctional beliefs rather than reality.

You do not necessarily have to confront your family directly, but you have to, at least in your own mind, challenge the false narrative you once believed. Clear-eyed acknowledgment of reality can transform your love from a fairy-tale-like, perhaps somewhat naive view, into a more mature and integrated perspective. The process of reckoning involves embracing the complex nature of human relationships, and acknowledging that imperfections coexist with virtues. While admitting their imperfections might initially cause feelings of guilt, doing so does not mean you're betraying your family.

Enduring a period of 'growing pain' as you establish and enforce boundaries is a small price to pay compared to a lifetime of unhappiness resulting from overextending yourself. Eventually, your determination to set and maintain boundaries will yield positive outcomes. Ultimately, the intent of your action is not to hurt anyone, you are simply reclaiming the birthright to autonomy and respect.

Breaking cycles of transgenerational enmeshment

In the course of family life, relationships undergo shifts and transformations. Establishing boundaries with parents marks a pivotal moment in transcending your relationship. However, given the uncertainty about what lies ahead, it's natural to feel anxious and uneasy about it. You do not have to be certain that you are doing everything right; the key is to muster the courage to begin. The journey of setting boundaries is a dynamic process, a bit like the exploration of uncharted territories. New paths will reveal themselves along the way, and each discovery will contribute to your strength.

Embracing this process involves navigating through the storms of resistance with resilience and conviction. Recognize that the initial pushback is a natural response to change, especially when challenging long-established patterns. Keep your focus on the broader picture and the positive impact that setting boundaries can have on the overall well-being of both yourself and your family.

The significance of this transformation goes beyond liberating yourself from the stifling patterns of enmeshment and co-dependency. It holds the potential to break the cycle of transgenerational trauma that may have endured within your family for generations. Your actions today wield transformative power, capable of reshaping the future. This provides not only liberation for yourself but also an opportunity for your entire family to experience a healthier and more balanced family dynamic.

By standing firm in your pursuit of healthier dynamics, you can become a catalyst for positive change, leaving a lasting legacy of strength and resilience for generations to come.

Reflective exercise: Addressing the fear of regrets

The fear of regret is often a significant psychological hurdle when it comes to establishing boundaries with a Needy Parent. This fear might arise from worries about harming the relationship, being seen as unkind, or dealing with guilt over prioritizing your needs. To strengthen your courage and assertiveness, you may have to take a strategic approach that involves mental rehearsal, reframing, and the use of effective self-talk.

At the moment, you may be asking yourself:

- 'What if, when they pass away, I am burdened with regret for not doing more for them?'
- 'What if I regret causing them emotional pain and feeling like I have abandoned them?'
- 'What if I am haunted by overwhelming guilt and unending remorse?'

These unspoken questions can haunt you like a specter lurking in your mind. The fear of regret often originates from a mix of imagination, societal expectations, and, at times, explicit threats from them, such as:

- 'You'll regret not appreciating everything I've sacrificed for you when I'm gone.'
- 'After all I've done for you.'
- 'Remember, I won't be around forever.'

Despite acknowledging the rational truth that you are not obligated to bear the burden of caring for your parents or rescuing them from their lifelong sorrows, you may still find yourself susceptible to this emotional blackmailing.

To directly confront the fear of regret, instead of letting it linger in the background, initiate a Socratic method of inquiry. Start by asking yourself: What exactly do I fear I would regret?

Take a moment to reflect on the nature of this relationship. Have you genuinely experienced a meaningful connection with them, or is it more of an idealized vision of a parent-child bond? Is it perhaps a childlike illusion based on portrayals in fairy tales, the media and other families rather than a tangible reality?

As you delve deeper, you may realize that there is little substance beyond an enmeshed, dysfunctional relationship fraught with daily grievances. Due to their psychological limitations, an authentic and meaningful parent-child bond was never within reach. It might have been a fantasy of your inner child, reluctant to let go of the idealized image of having a nurturing parent.

In contrast, consider equally valid questions that arise from a standpoint of self-respect:

- 'What if I deeply regret compromising my well-being and sacrificing my happiness to please my parents?'
- 'What if I regret staying entangled in transgenerational trauma, failing to break free for my own sake and the potential future of my own children and family?'
- 'What if I realize it's too late to rewrite the story of who I am beyond being a 'good child' to them?'
- 'What if, by not investing so much time in their unreasonable demands, I could have achieved more in my career, found my soulmate and relished my freedom?'
- 'Will I come to regret my compromises, realizing the toll they took on my self-worth, identity, and ability to genuinely relate to others?'

By posing these questions, you can recognize that your intention to set boundaries with your parents stems from a deep longing for personal growth and authentic connection, rather than a desire to hurt or abandon them.

Rather than yielding to fear of potential regret, you can also confront it directly and equip yourself to address it: try to envision a scenario where your parent is no longer present, and contemplate how you would acknowledge your actions, your good intentions, your integrity, and how you would dispel any potential regrets. As a mental exercise, craft a reflective script for your future self.

Here's a sample of what that could look like:

> 'I recognize and honour all I have done with my parents throughout my journey. Despite the challenges and limitations, I have consistently shown love, respect and understanding towards them as flawed human beings. I tried to maintain a connection, even when it was tenuous and emotionally challenging.
>
> I invested considerable effort, time and energy to foster an authentic relationship, gracefully navigating through the most challenging times. Despite their protests and attempts to manipulate me with guilt-tripping, I set and upheld boundaries. This act of self-preservation was courageous and necessary for our well-being.
>
> Given my circumstances, I want to remind myself that I have done my best. I faced my fears and took steps towards personal growth and independence. I chose to honour what is best for myself and my parents. I showed resilience, strength and unwavering commitment through it all.
>
> Therefore, I reassure myself that there is no reason or room for regret. I approached this journey with integrity and love. I am proud of the choices I have made and the progress I have achieved. I deserve to acknowledge my bravery and embrace the peace of knowing I have done everything within my power.
>
> I will continue to navigate this path with compassion and self-assurance, knowing I have taken the necessary steps to honour myself and my parents. I release any lingering doubts or regrets, knowing I have done my best.'

8
Healing with self-empathy

'I hope you heal from the things no one has ever apologized to you for.'

Anonymous

In the previous chapter where we discussed ways to empathize with your parents, we lightly touched upon safeguarding yourself, reclaiming your emotional rights, and navigating their challenging behaviours while maintaining your boundaries. In this section, we will delve much deeper into the healing process required to address the wounds inflicted by abusive and unempathetic parents. This emphasis is essential because the ability to empathize with others is closely linked to your capacity for self-empathy. Without addressing your own wounds, attempting to empathize with your parents may just result in a form of 'intellectual' or 'spiritual bypassing'. Therefore, please take time for the processes laid out in this chapter, and give yourself and your healing the time and attention they deserve.

Empathizing with yourself when your parents cannot

The process of developing self-empathy has many layers and complexities. While in reality it is far from linear, for the sake of discussion we will conceptualize it into six steps: 1. Validate 2. Grieve 3. Feel 4. Trust 5. Release 6. Act.

Self-validation and grieving are the initial steps to developing self-empathy. Even if those around you had not given you the time and space to speak your truth, you owe it to your younger self to recognize the horror of growing up with unempathic parents, free of illusions or the need to justify their actions. This can be painful at first because it is common for those of us who have been traumatized to use denial and suppression as coping mechanisms for trauma. But seeing the truth for what it is is a foundational step, as it frees you from the gaslit narrative that you were to be blamed for their lack of empathy.

Following that, in Step 3 we shall look at how having parents who deny and invalidate you can affect your own relationships to emotions. We will concentrate on anger, a complex and multifaceted emotion. You will discover that contrary to popular belief, anger is not a 'bad' emotion but one that can also bring vitality, strength, and freedom.

In the final few steps, we will focus on ways to move forward in life, and how you may see any mid-life or quarter-life crisis as a transformative opportunity. Even if you are currently feeling lost and despondent, you can realize at this critical juncture that your happiness and authenticity should never be compromised to appease a bullying, narcissistic, or emotionally needy parent. You are not your parents, and you do not have to carry their dysfunctional beliefs. You have the agency, and perhaps even the responsibility, to choose a path free of any intergenerational trauma. Moving forward from there, you can truly reclaim the 'second half of your life' as yours.

This process will not be easy, and there may be moments of doubt and uncertainty. However, if you can trust that within you lies the strength and desire for a life that is liberated from past burdens, you will no doubt move forward with grace.

Six essential steps to self-empathy

The following six steps provide a roadmap to help you understand and nurture your own feelings. You may find yourself revisiting some steps as you grow and learn. As much as possible, embrace the process with patience and compassion for yourself.

1 Validate
2 Grieve
3 Feel
4 Trust
5 Release
6 Act

1 Validate

RESIST SPIRITUAL AND INTELLECTUAL BYPASSING

The wounds inflicted by emotionally unsupportive parents run deep, often prompting us to use coping strategies such as denial and suppression to protect ourselves. However, when we try to 'forgive' prematurely, or when we are stuck in an endless loop of trying to 'make sense of our parents' trauma', we are not moving towards genuine empathy for our parents or compassion for ourselves, but simply engaging in what is known as 'spiritual bypassing', or 'intellectual bypassing'.

Spiritual bypassing

'Spiritual bypassing' is a coping mechanism wherein we try to shield ourselves from disturbing thoughts and feelings by immersing in spiritual dogma, religious clichés, or seemingly 'spiritual' activities such as meditation, mindfulness, and self-improvement. For example, you may have been taught by a spiritual teacher or have interpreted religious scripture to suggest that you should suppress and hide your anger and that you have no choice but to stay loyal to your parents, even when they are abusive. In such cases, even when your heart is not ready, you might adopt the belief that 'we must forgive our family' prematurely, using it to bypass the deep-seated pain of betrayal and unresolved resentment.

Growing up with dysfunctional parents requires you to grieve the pain rather than bypass it. Perhaps no one has ever told you this, but it is not only acceptable to feel sad, angry, and resentful about your experiences – it is crucial. Grieving is a gradual process, not something to be hastily 'done and dusted with'.

Some people claim that their trauma can be completely resolved through a single spiritual awakening in meditation, or after only one session of psychedelic substances like magic mushrooms, but many later find that the effects are fleeting. For authentic healing, even when such an 'awakening' occurs, it has to be followed by a period of reality-checking to consolidate one's insights and learning. While these transcendental experiences can provide glimpses into alternate states of consciousness and temporary relief, the real work involves a consistent commitment to introspection, self-awareness, self-compassion, and self-love.

The path to healing and acceptance is not a straight line. It includes periods of progress and setbacks, as well as periods of clarity and confusion. It necessitates perseverance, patience, and the willingness to confront the difficult emotions that arise along the way. For most people, this is a cyclical and complex process that can take years. However, this should not be a cause for discouragement, the journey itself can be incredibly gratifying and fulfilling.

Intellectual bypassing

In addition to spiritual bypassing, it's not uncommon for individuals who have experienced trauma from unempathetic parents to resort to rationalization and intellectualizing as ways of coping. In this form of 'intellectual bypassing', there is a tendency to overanalyze facts, rely on theories, and articulate truisms as a way of navigating and distancing oneself from the trauma. Some examples may be using statements such as 'no one is perfect', and 'there are people who suffer worse' to justify what happened and to distance yourself from feelings of sorrow and resentment. For example, you might say, 'Feeling upset won't change anything' or 'My parents did the best they could.' 'They have been through trauma and are helpless, so I can't fault them'. 'I had a decent childhood in comparison to many', 'They will never change, so what's the point of revisiting the past?' These statements may not be factually untrue, but they are irrelevant in the context of trying to heal from your pain.

With intellectual bypassing, you may appear to be adept at 'talking about your trauma', you might even have told your story to numerous therapists, but you do so as if they were fiction written by someone else rather than your living history.

Those of us who are intellectually inclined may become engrossed in the pursuit of understanding the 'why' behind our experiences with dysfunctional parents. While gaining insight and making sense of our past can be beneficial, we must also recognize when this intellectual pursuit becomes a way of avoidance. In some ways, being stuck in an endless loop of 'trying to understand' why you were not cared for as much as you deserved, why your parents abused or neglected you, and why they acted selfishly can be a refusal to grieve rather than an attempt at genuine empathy for yourself. Instead of dwelling on the 'why', at some point, we have to accept that unfair, unjust, and cruel events can happen, and we may not be able to figure out the reason behind them.

The most difficult challenge is accepting that what has happened cannot be explained by reasons. As humans, we like to think we have control over our lives and should take responsibility for what happens to us. However, the reality is that there may be far more factors beyond our control. The truth is that you did not choose to be born into this world. You had no say in who you were born to. You did not choose your trauma, it was passed down to you.

Ultimately, you may have to come to terms with 'what is' – accepting that the world is not always fair, that you didn't win the 'birth lottery' to have empathic parents, not because you were 'bad' or being punished by a higher power, but simply because of the unpredictable, sometimes illogical nature of life.

VICTIM ONCE BUT A 'VICTIM NO LONGER'

The stigma surrounding the term 'victimization' may be a sign that many of us, and possibly society as a whole, have participated in trauma bypassing. In recent years, with the proliferation of self-help, motivational speaking, and the social pressure to adopt 'positive thinking', the word 'victim' has become a sensitive one.

If you admit, or even suggest, that you were victimized, you may face judgement from society or well-meaning friends who will try to talk you out of your 'victim mindset'. In today's society, phrases like 'I am not a victim' and 'I refuse to be victimized' have become mantras. The word 'victim' seems to imply that you have resigned yourself to a life of passivity or surrender. Furthermore, admitting that your parents or caregivers have harmed you is frequently interpreted as ingratitude, narcissism, or immaturity. None of these assumptions, however, is necessarily correct. Unfortunately, this extreme rejection of any notion of victimhood deprives you of the fundamental right to speak the truth of your victimhood.

Intellectual or spiritual bypassing or premature forgiving will not set you free. Your suppressed anguish had to come out somewhere, and it frequently manifests as physical illness or misdirected rage. Spiritual and intellectual bypassing may lead to a tendency to blame yourself for everything, even things over which you have no control. As a result, you deny your truths, suppress your pain, obliterate your personal history, and suffocate your soul.

A healthier approach is to simply reconcile with the fact that, in certain circumstances, you were unequivocally victims of the circumstances, of fate, of situations over which you had no control. During your vulnerable infancy, you were thrust into families marked by abuse, neglect, or violence. Your parents showed bullying tendencies, excessive neediness, emotional immaturity, and instability. As an innocent child, you had no means of escape; you were a victim, and nothing you did caused or justified what you endured.

At the same time, of course, admitting what had happened to you does not bind you to that identity. You might have been hurt by things beyond your control, but you now have the power to walk away and heal. Also, life is not simply black and white, it has shades of grey. Recognizing that you were the victim of your parents' limitations does not negate the good they may have done or erase any gratitude you have. 'Holding both truths' is a sign of psychological and spiritual maturity. In other words, you can admit to being a victim while also acknowledging the love and positive experiences you have had.

More often than not, it is your resistance to the trauma rather than the trauma itself that perpetuates your pain. While the word 'acceptance' may appear passive to some, it is, in fact, the most proactive first step you can take to address the root of the problem. Once you have accepted your victimhood, you can stop resisting the truth and fighting the emotions that come with it. This frees up the energy to take responsibility for your future and pursue your dreams.

To summarize, admitting to being a victim once does not result in a life sentence. In fact, it is the doorway to liberty. You can be a 'victim once' but a 'victim no longer'. Like phoenixes rising from the ashes, you can be very proud of who you are.

Experiential exercise: Honouring your younger self

The goal of this reflective exercise is to help you recognize and validate the pain your younger self had felt as a result of emotionally unsupportive parents. Through this, you will learn to embrace your authentic emotions and empower your inner child to share their story without denial or suppression.

Set aside a quiet, comfortable area where you can concentrate without distractions. Prepare a notebook or a journal as well as a pen.

Close your eyes, take a few deep breaths, and imagine adopting an attitude of 'surrender' towards the present moment. Allow yourself to release tension, let go of control, and be present in the here and now.

Now, visualize your younger self as a child again, and try to recall and feel the emotions you have once experienced when denied, punished, or dismissed by your unempathetic parents. You may use your memory of one or two specific incidences to bring your memories to life.

Now, imagine talking to your younger self, asking them about what happened, and having them narrate their story as it unfolded. Approach this process slowly and delicately, recognizing that your younger self may feel guilty about speaking negatively of their parents or fear repercussions. Create a safe and compassionate space for them and assure them that this is a secure environment and that no one will ever discover what they have told you. Encourage your younger self to be honest with themselves about their emotions and experiences, no matter how difficult or painful.

Now, open your eyes and start writing a letter to your younger self.

Begin the letter by using their preferred nickname. Then, tell your younger self that you see and understand their suffering. Assure them that their feelings are valid and that being hurt, angry or upset about their experiences is absolutely okay.

In your letter, make a heartfelt promise to your younger self that you will no longer spiritually or intellectually bypass the pain they went through. Assure them that you will face the truth bravely and compassionately without denying or suppressing any part of the story, even when they are ugly and violent.

You may also promise to respect their authenticity and validate their truth, even if others try to deny or dismiss it. They can always come back to you and tell you their story repeatedly.

You can also tell your younger self how you have grown throughout the years. Let them know how they can survive hard times and what it means to practise self-compassion.

Finish the letter by expressing gratitude and love to your younger self. Thank them for their bravery and strength in the face of adversity. Assure them that they are loved and worthy.

Finally, when you are ready, read the letter to yourself silently or aloud. Allow yourself to experience any emotions that arise from this process.

Keep the letter somewhere safe so you can refer to it whenever you need to reconnect with yourself. Use the letter to remind yourself of your commitment to recognizing and honouring your truth and empower yourself to share your story authentically.

Ultimately, you must find your own authentic words for this to work. To help you get started, here are some examples of what you might say:

- 'As I write this letter, I want you to know that I see you, I hear you, and I understand the pain you endured.'
- 'I know that there were times when you felt unseen and unheard, when you had to hide your emotions to protect yourself. But I want you to know that you no longer have to carry that burden alone. We can do this together.'
- 'Throughout the years, I have grown and changed. I want you to know that your strength and resilience have shaped the person I am today.'
- 'You are a true survivor, no matter what others say.'
- 'Thank you for holding on, for never giving up.'

2 Grieve

MOURNING THE PARENTS YOU NEVER HAD

Many of us bear the scars of not just one-off but repeated wounds inflicted by dysfunctional parents. Maybe your inner child thought that if you tried harder and loved them more fiercely, your parents would finally reciprocate. If you have an emotionally unstable parent, whose empathy is partially and intermittently given, setting boundaries can be especially challenging. It is easy to fall into the trap of false hope, knocking on the same door repeatedly, but getting the same pain and disappointment every time.

When caught in the cycle of co-dependency, you might feel the need to keep trying to make them recognize your true self, beyond the image they want you to be. Despite your strong desire for a real connection, you never quite achieve it. Their hearts stay closed, and even when they make an effort, true attentiveness is lacking. They continue to impose their expectations on you and expect you to conform. Their selfish desires still come first, yet they insist on portraying a picture-perfect family.

You have hoped against hope, not because you were foolish or stubborn. It is human nature, and we all do it. The undying longing for the perfect parents is woven and imprinted in our DNA. From a young age, we catch a glimpse of what could have been – from fairy tales to ancient folklore, we see this collective yearning for a nurturing presence, unconditional love, and solid parental guidance. Sadly, when you have unempathetic parents, your childhood becomes a swinging door between the bitter reality and the sweet fantasy: you see the Fairy Godmother, but all you have is the Wicked Witch.

When you find yourself trapped in an endless cycle of trying to make the impossible happen, it might be time to embrace the timeless wisdom of reckoning with reality for what it is, and confront the 'one hard thing' you have been avoiding: grieving for what you never had, and may never get.

'What do you mean by grieving?' you may ask. 'Am I not already sad enough, and have been grieving all my life?'

In the realm of psychoanalysis, there is a theory that says depression is a form of denial – the refusal to deeply grieve (Freud, 1924; Burch, 1989). Instead of accepting that they will never be the parents you need them to be, you might have instead numbed your emotions, withdrawn from meaningful engagement with the world, and let hopelessness stop you from trying anything that might lead to more disappointment. The lingering low-grade depression becomes a self-blinding shield that protects you from the unbearable weight of unmet longings and shattered dreams.

When you resist the transformative power of conscious grieving, you end up in a constant loop of passively responding to each disappointment, and allowing yourself to be triggered time and again by your parents' unempathetic actions.

By refusing to enter the deepest grief, you may 'win' the battle of temporarily numbing your feelings, but you lose the war – you are inadvertently prolonging your suffering. In other words, your depression is a way of preserving the fragile psychological equilibrium, albeit at the cost of joy, authenticity, motivation, spontaneity, and life energy.

In contrast, truly grieving is an act of courageous confrontation – an intentional journey into the depths of your psyche. Through conscious grieving, you peel back the layers of denial and delve into the rawness of your emotions. You hold space for yourself to truly weep, scream, write, draw, punch – whatever it is that you need to do – to grieve the loss of a cherished fantasy, a profound longing for the archetypal perfect parents that you have yearned for but never truly experienced.

FREEING YOUR SOUL REGARDLESS OF JUSTICE

Grieving also means you ultimately have to accept that you may not be able to persuade them to change their views or treat you fairly. Accepting does not mean you like it or approve of it, it is simply a way of freeing yourself. Just as you can't control the weather or world events, you cannot force them to see things differently. But you do not need their approval or apologies to lead a full life.

Seeking recognition from someone who refuses to accept responsibility for their actions can be a never-ending cycle of disappointment and frustration. They are unable to provide the understanding and closure you seek, leaving you feeling even more betrayed and trapped in their emotional web.

To free yourself, your beliefs about fairness and justice may have to be challenged: life is not always fair, and people may not always act justly, even when they are your parent. But by grieving what you never had and will never get, you can start to release the emotional burden associated with expecting fairness in every situation. You can then direct your energy and focus towards things that you can control, such as your own choices, reactions, and gratitude for who and what you do have in your life now.

However hard it is, you may also have to give up on the idea of ever getting an apology from family members who collude with your parent's fabricated narrative. Rather, concentrate on what you know to be true and have people who would be willing to listen and believe in your side of the story. To counteract years of gaslighting you might have been subject to, you may have to retell your side of the story and emotional experience again and again until it feels more 'real'. Eventually, your authentic truth will replace the lies (that you are the 'sick one', that you had a 'perfect family', or a 'happy childhood', etc.) you have been told all your life.

They may continue to frame you as the 'bad' one, the 'black sheep' of the family, and accuse you of being cruel or abandoning them. Even if they persist in thinking they are right and you are wrong, you have the right to ignore their accusations, keep them out of your life, and protect yourself.

Remember, you are no longer that vulnerable child under your family's control. You can remind yourself of your current reality, including your financial, emotional, and spiritual independence.

You have the right to shift your attention to what truly matters in your life. As much as possible, channel your energy into nurturing your relationships, advancing in your career, and pursuing your aspirations and dreams.

Grieving yields its fruits when you finally surrender your fantasy of the perfect parents as a distant mirage and bravely embrace the imperfect reality as they are. And once you have truly grieved what could never be, you may also arrive at a profound realization: when it comes to your parents, you have exerted your utmost effort, that it was never your fault, and you have no regrets. Then, you free yourself from the unfulfilled expectations that have held you captive, opening up new possibilities for a different future.

There is no magical way to do this, and grieving the parents you needed but never have could be the most difficult thing you ever have to do. But here is an exercise you may try to start the process:

Experiential exercise: Dual memory boxes

This exercise involves creating two memory boxes that serve as tangible representations of your relationship with your parent. One box provides a space for acknowledging any gratitude and shared experiences, while the other box allows for the exploration of pain, longing and unmet needs.

This activity is essentially a 'sorting process' that encourages you to work through ambivalence and move beyond black-and-white thinking. Through this nuanced exploration, you see your parent more clearly as who they are: a complex, flawed human being.

This exercise may help you mourn some of the unmet needs, the longing for consistent love, and the aspects of your relationship that may have fallen short of your desires. Hopefully, it also paves the way for a more compassionate and realistic view of your parent, which would ultimately free you from the endless loop of resentment and confusion.

Start by preparing:

- Two sturdy boxes or containers
- Some art supplies (such as markers, paint, or collage materials)
- Photographs, objects, letters, or other artifacts that hold significance about your parent.

Instructions:

1 **Set the intention**: Begin by setting an intention to approach this activity with self-compassion. No matter what emotions emerge, try to not fall into blaming and

shaming yourself. Embrace the understanding that it is natural to hold a mixture of positive and painful emotions regarding your relationship with your parent.

2 **Revere what exists**: Start with the first box. Decorate its exterior with colours, images, or symbols embodying any pleasant memories associated with your parent. Curate a collection of photographs, objects, or written memories that symbolize the love, kindness, and cherished moments you have experienced with your parent. Deliberately arrange these items inside the box, taking the time to reflect upon each one and the emotions they stir within you. You may even craft a heartfelt gratitude letter or a series of affirmations articulating your appreciation.

   It is okay to skip Box 1 if you do not think there is any merit to your parents' actions and you cannot recall any good memories. Do not force it. In this case, skip to Step number 3.

3 **Acknowledge your longings and unmet needs**: Transition to the second box; this is the space where you will explore your unfulfilled desires, longing, and the ache associated with not receiving what you yearned for from your parent. You may express your anger and disappointment by tearing up some papers or other actions that feel right.

   Inside box 2, select some symbolic objects, evocative images, or words that represent your unmet needs and unresolved resentment. Some examples may be magazine cut-outs of words and images, broken dolls, colours that symbolize your hurt, torn photos, or anything your intuition guides you to pick up. Grant yourself the space to acknowledge and sit with the deep feelings this process brings up.

4 **Reflect and validate your feelings**: Pause and look at the contents in Box 2. Imagine how you might feel if this was made by another child and the compassion you may feel for them. Affirm and validate the pain, longing, and unmet needs within you.

   If you feel ready, see if you can write an angry letter to your parent, fearlessly conveying your honest emotions and the profound impact their actions or absence have had on your life. This letter will not be sent, but it is where you safely contain all your anguish, resentment, and rage.

5 **Integration and self-compassion**: Now, position both memory boxes side by side, and in front of you is a powerful visual representation of the complexities of your relationship with your parent. See if you can embrace the duality of your experiences, recognizing that it is possible to hold both love and pain within your heart. Cultivate a deep sense of self-compassion and acceptance as you navigate the complexity of such mixed feelings, and understand you are not 'weird' to be feeling this way – it is a part of the human condition.

6 Finally, you may find a sacred place to house both memory boxes and revisit them when you want to add or take things out. If you find it too disturbing, and discarding the artifact feels more right to you, you can do that too.

It is normal to experience a range of emotions as you engage with the memory boxes. If, at any point, the emotions become overwhelming, consider seeking support from a therapist or a trusted individual who can provide guidance and understanding along the way.

3 Feel

WORKING ON YOUR RELATIONSHIP WITH ANGER

Consider how you currently deal with difficult emotions. How do you usually react to feelings of vulnerability, sadness, or fear? As we emerge from the shadows of growing up in an empathy-deficient home, reclaiming your right to feel is an important aspect of your healing journey. Anger is particularly relevant because it is complex and is often the biggest taboo in dysfunctional homes.

During your childhood, your parents were your primary caregivers, forming the foundation of your world. Considering the possibility that your parents are 'bad' could imply that the whole world is a frightening and insecure place, a notion too threatening to accept. Faced with mistreatment, you had to choose between two possibilities: either your parents were incompetent or abusive, or you were to blame. Unfortunately, due to the need for emotional survival, many children had no choice but to resort to the latter: they internalize, swallow, and suppress their anger. The fear of rejection and the potential loss of their love became powerful motivators for you to direct all blame towards yourself.

Moreover, as a child, you may have faced punishment for showing anger, leading to the ingrained lifelong belief that expressing this emotion was unacceptable. Consequently, whenever you feel resentment or anger towards your parents, an overwhelming sense of shame and guilt follows.

Yet, a distorted relationship with anger can hold you back from moving on in life. As an adult, you might struggle to assert your needs and establish healthy boundaries with others. The fear of conflict or the possibility of facing rejection or abandonment when expressing anger could make interpersonal relationships excruciatingly painful. The inability to take up space holds you back from your own creativity and vitality. Therefore, healing your relationship with anger is a fundamental step in recovering from the wounds inflicted by an unempathic parent.

CONSIDER THE MULTIPLE FACETS OF ANGER

In a previous chapter on parents with bullying tendencies, we explored the distinction between anger and aggression. In this chapter, we will dive into an even more nuanced understanding of anger. While anger is frequently demonized, when we look deeper we discover that it is also a source of admirable traits such as integrity and respect, as well as many other life energies like joy and drive.

In this journalling activity, you will explore different facets of anger and consider how it can be utilized constructively. For now, we are engaging with this topic on an intellectual level, so please don't pressure yourself to undergo a significant emotional shift or to immediately shed any shame or guilt associated with anger. After all, suppressing anger may have been a crucial survival tactic during your upbringing, and it's natural that some part of you may find it challenging to simply let go of this mechanism.

Journalling exercise: The many faces of anger

Reflect on the following passages and see if you can see some truths in them. Then, write your responses to the prompts in your journal.

1 **Anger aligns us with our values:** Anger can teach us a lot about ourselves and our core values. It manifests itself when our beliefs about what is important to us are violated. We can be angry at ourselves or others, but in either case, the outpouring of rage fuels our desire to stand up and fight for what we believe is right. For example, if you value timekeeping or punctuality, you

may become irritated if you are repeatedly inconvenienced by others who disregard your time or cause unnecessary delays. It is infuriating when colleagues consistently arrive late for meetings, or appointments begin late due to others' negligence. Or, suppose you believe that everyone deserves good health and nutrition. You may become frustrated with schools that provide unhealthy snacks to students, angry with companies that prioritize profits over consumer well-being by engineering hyper-palatable food, or even angry with yourself if you consistently make choices that do not align with your nutritional goals. In other words, anger is a powerful emotion that, when channelled correctly, compels us to take a firm stance and take action to correct what is out of alignment.

- When was the last time you were enraged because you witnessed or experienced someone who violated your beliefs and values?
- What did you do, and what does that reveal about your core values and principles, or things in which you have a strong belief?
- Moving forward, how can you use anger to motivate yourself to stick to your core values and beliefs?

2 **Anger brings us vigour**: Our bodies and minds release energy when we get angry. It makes us feel alive, reminds us of what is important in life, and motivates us to take action. Research has validated that the energy generated by this state of heightened arousal is an essential part of being human and suppressing it can lead to ill health (Begley, 1994; Hosseini et al., 2011).

Indeed, many people have discovered that suppressing their anger saps their life energy and zest for life, holding them back from finding their own voice and claiming their place in the world. Reflect on the following:

- How does anger make you feel in your body?
- Do you tend to internalize it or transform it into something else (such as depression or shame), or can you tap into the burst of energy anger provides?
- Consider a time when you were able to channel your rage into positive action and progress.

3 **Boundaries and self-protection**: Anger also prompts us to take action to enforce healthy boundaries and protect ourselves. Noticing feelings of anger arising – even when it is just showing up as mild irritation or frustration – can be a valuable cue that our boundaries have been crossed. As a physical example, if someone invades your personal space without your consent, such as by standing too close or touching you inappropriately, it can make you feel uneasy. Whereas interpersonally, anger should also come out when someone consistently disrespects your opinions, values, or boundaries or when you are interrupted, belittled, or dismissed. Furthermore, when someone betrays your trust, manipulates you, or coerces you into doing things you dislike, it is natural for anger to be triggered.

Many people who grew up in a narcissistic home may have never learned to recognize and feel anger. You might have buried these emotions so deeply within yourself that you are disconnected from your own anger. In such cases, it becomes important to start the journey of re-learning how to notice subtle signals from your body that indicate anger might be coming up. In our bodies, anger may manifest as increased heart rate, muscle tension, or a sense of heat or energy building up. By becoming attuned to the body's signals, you can begin to identify the initial stirrings of anger and work with it before it escalates beyond your control. You may also need to rewire how you relate to anger;

instead of immediately turning it into shame, self-blame, or fear, understand that anger is a natural emotion that arises in response to a violation of boundaries.

If you can learn to notice anger emerging in your body, and then couple anger with appropriate assertiveness skills, anger can guide you to communicate your needs and expectations. It can give you the courage to stand up for yourself, express your opinions, and find your place in the world.

- Can you recall a time when you could palpably feel the signals of anger surging up in your body?
- In what personal or professional contexts have you used anger as a tool to assert your needs or boundaries? How did it impact the outcome of the situation?
- Did you encounter any blockages? Consider the influence of your childhood conditioning, which may have been shaped by schools, churches, or parental figures, and how it may have hindered your ability to harness and express anger effectively.
- Recollect an experience where you successfully and assertively communicated your boundaries without veering into aggression. How did you navigate that situation, did you manage to strike a healthy balance between standing up for yourself and respecting the other person's perspective?

4 **Empathy and compassion**: Anger can also serve as a catalyst for deepening your sense of empathy and compassion towards others. When you witness or personally experience someone enduring pain that resonates with your own experiences, you may get angry on their behalf. This anger then becomes a fuel for profound empathy.

Empathy sparked by anger can propel you to become an advocate for others' rights, to speak out against oppression, and to actively contribute to the creation of a more compassionate and equitable society. When channelled in a healthy way, anger is a driving force for change.

- Take a moment to contemplate moments when anger has ignited your empathy for others. How has experiencing anger transformed your understanding of their pain and challenges?
- Reflect on specific situations where anger has driven you to show kindness, understanding, and support to those in need. How have these actions contributed to creating a more fair and compassionate world?

Through this series of journalling exercises, I hope you've come to realize that contrary to the popular conception of it being solely negative, anger also encompasses facets such as integrity, energy, activism, and drive. Each of us experiences and expresses anger uniquely, but none of that needs to be violent or aggressive. Moving forward, it will be beneficial to contemplate how anger unfolds in your own life and how these dimensions align with your personal journey.

LETTING YOURSELF FEEL ANGER

Now that you have gained an intellectual understanding of the nature and facets of anger, you may feel more ready to embrace and experience it without denying, suppressing, or recoiling from it. Initially, you may have a limited capacity to tolerate anger, so you must give yourself grace, time, and patience as you gradually develop a healthier relationship with this emotion.

Expanding your tolerance for anger involves a process of self-reflection, emotional awareness, and developing a new set of coping strategies. You can learn to become aware of your triggers and patterns related to anger, empathetically validate your emotions without judgement, and then cultivate assertive communication skills to express your needs and set boundaries respectfully. While this is a complex topic on its own, here are some basic steps to consider as a starting point:

1 **Notice that you are feeling anger**: When you feel anger emerging in you, pay very close attention to how anger feels in your body and the thoughts and emotions that come with it. As much as possible, stay present and observe what is happening inside you without resorting to dissociation or avoidance. You may have to use some grounding techniques, such as breathing and anchoring yourself in physical sensations without getting overwhelmed. One example might be to pause everything you are doing and engage your mindful awareness: 'I notice a tightness in my chest and a racing heartbeat. I am having thoughts of frustration and a surge of anger. There are sensations and thoughts related to anger passing through me.' Consciously observing and describing your experience will help you slow down and allow you to create a space between yourself and the anger. This way, you can train yourself to respond constructively rather than react impulsively.
2 **Validate your anger**: Instead of trying to dismiss or suppress your anger, validate it as a valid and natural emotion. Recognize that your anger is a valid response to the mistreatment or abuse you may have experienced. Offer gentle reminders to yourself, such as, 'It is absolutely normal to feel angry. Anger is a normal human emotion, and it serves a purpose in expressing my boundaries and protecting myself.'

   You may also want to remind yourself that your punitive parent is no longer present and that it is safe to feel and express your emotions now. In the past, expressing anger may have been met with dreadful consequences, but now you have the freedom to acknowledge and validate your anger without the fear of retribution.

3 **Resist the urge to 'control' feelings**: Anger, like all emotions, is transient and impermanent. Instead of getting caught up in the specific thoughts and details of your angry state, remind yourself that emotions come and go. They are not permanent or absolute truths.

   It is tempting to want to 'control' how you feel, but any attempt to do so will only make things worse. Anger can be compared to a murky swamp. Imagine yourself standing at the swamp's edge, observing its stagnant waters. Instead of impulsively jumping in and thrashing about, you can remain on solid ground, allowing the swamp to settle naturally. By staying grounded and observing your emotions from a safe distance, you create space for clarity to emerge. Just as the swamp settles on its own, your feelings will also find their balance as you allow them to flow without judgement or resistance.

   By keenly observing your anger, you will notice its natural ebb and flow. Just as waves rise and fall, emotions arise and pass away. Approach your anger with curiosity. Observe it without judgement or the need to hold on to it. As soon as you become aware of anger, anger is already on its way out. This recognition may help you to become less weary of anger, as you know that if you allow yourself to feel it, it will naturally dissipate over time.

   If you can relinquish your need to 'control' anger, you may paradoxically find that it has less control over you.

4 **Recognize your larger self beyond anger**: Remember that anger is present within your current experience, but it is not the totality of who you are. You are more expansive and multidimensional than that. Anger is a state, and there is no such thing as an 'angry person'.

Engage in constructive self-talk to reinforce this understanding. For example, you can say to yourself, 'I observe the presence of angry thoughts, but anger is not me and it does not have to consume or define me. These thoughts will pass.' Alternatively, you might affirm, 'I notice I am having some vengeful thoughts, yet they are just thoughts. I am not obligated to act upon them or let them rule me.'

By recognizing that anger is not the defining characteristic of your being, you open yourself up to a wider perspective.

5 **Define your values and take decisive action:** Anger helps you clarify your values and help you move forward in life. Irrespective of your past experiences, you can align yourself with what truly holds significance in your life now. For instance, if honesty and authenticity are important to you, you will use anger to say no and set boundaries when faced with abusive or manipulative people. Likewise, if independence and autonomy are significant values to you, you can use healthy anger to resist your parents' attempts to control your life. The more you can express anger healthily, the more you will trust yourself with anger, and the more it will become your ally. Remember, anger is not a threat, it is a tool. Focus on using anger to harness your strengths, honour virtues, and align yourself with values that bring you closer to who you want to be in the world.

The above pointers provide a starting point for reclaiming your relationship with anger. Working with anger can be a lifelong process, and it takes time and practice to undo years of social and familial conditioning.

An additional benefit of having a good relationship with anger is that you will gradually become less afraid of other people's anger. Extending from that, you will be less conflict-avoidant and thus generally less socially anxious. When others get frustrated at you, you will not feel the need to run away or retaliate. Instead, you can remain present, actively listen during conflicts, and have open dialogue that deepens relationships. In other words, tolerating and normalizing anger in a relational context can bring profound changes in your life as it offers you freedom and relief.

To sum up, reclaiming your right to anger does not mean acting aggressively or becoming consumed by negativity. Anger, in your raw and honest form, is pure energy. It acts as a messenger by demanding your attention. It is here to reveal the wounds inflicted upon you, the boundaries violated, and the injustices thrust upon you. Through healthy anger, you can claim your place in the world, find your voice, assert your worthiness, and declare your right to be seen, heard, and respected.

4 Trust

YOU ARE NOT YOUR PARENTS

Many of us who grew up with unempathic, abusive, or narcissistic parents carry an unspoken worry – that we will become like our parents, perpetuating their dysfunctions and behaviours.

This fear is often unconscious, lurking in the background but holding us back from living fully. It can become a voice in our heads, a nagging doubt that whispers in our ears, telling us that we are somehow toxic, will harm those around us, or that we are not cut out for parenthood.

We may become hyper-vigilant and anxious, harshly scrutinizing every thought and action of our own, second-guessing and questioning our motives, and constantly worried that we are hurting those we care about.

When we are haunted by the fear of becoming like our unempathic, immature, and maybe narcissistic parents, we usually resort to three coping mechanisms: surrender, avoidance, and overcompensation.

1 **Surrender**: Some people 'surrender' to the fear of becoming like their parents. They become so overtaken by fear that they allow the sense of learned helplessness to govern their lives.
2 **Avoidance**: Others may strive to avoid any event that can trigger this dread. They distance themselves from others and avoid situations that remind them of the relational wounds. They go about their regular lives as if they had a joyful and 'normal' upbringing. They may suppress their true feelings and deny their longing for a family, for the fear of finding out that there is no way out of the vicious cycle of abuse and neglect.
3 **Overcompensate**: Others may overcompensate, expending all of their life energy to ensure that they are nothing like their parents. They may try to be overly empathic and caring, shouldering the emotional problems of others but ignoring their own. They may believe that they must continuously prove their value as a 'good person', so they people-please, become co-dependent, and measure their self-worth on what they do but not who they are.

If you identify with the above, it is not that you knowingly adopt these unhealthy coping mechanisms – but the fear of one day becoming like your parent or the thought that you share similar traits can be so overwhelming that you have no choice but to resort to helplessness, avoidance, or overcompensation to cope.

Unfortunately, none of these coping strategies works in the long run. Surrendering to the idea and fully believing that you are doomed to be just like your parents can make you feel stuck in life, unable to move forward with your goals and pursuits. Avoidance isolates you, as the underlying assumption that you are toxic or unlovable is never addressed and may even be reinforced as you ruminate. Overcompensating may appear productive at first, but it can lead to burnout and ultimately prevent you from being loved for your authentic self. Crafting your life in such a way that you run and run from any possibility of being anything like your parents is, ironically, yet another way of remaining bound to and controlled by them.

Nevertheless, having unempathic parents does not mean you will repeat history. In reality, the opposite is often true. You may have spent your entire life trying to make up for what is missing in your family, rescuing your parents from their miseries, and protecting your siblings from volatility. You might have been groomed as the emotional caretaker of everyone in the family, the one who had to keep the peace and make sure everyone was okay, and that has given you extraordinary sensitivity, empathy, and resilience.

In addition, because you have suffered invisible trauma yourself, you have developed a deep compassion for others who are also invisibly wounded. Abuse is not always physically recognized by society, and you know all too well what it is like to be in pain and not have anyone to turn to. Therefore, you know how much it means to be there for someone and hold the space. All these qualities make you markedly different from your parents, who have limited ability to empathize.

It may take time and some inner work, but eventually, you can fully see how unlike your parent you are. Yes, unfortunately, due to the lack of a role model, you may have adopted some of their negative patterns and mindset. Perhaps you have let some of the transgenerational shame seep into your psyche. Nevertheless, even if, at times, you behave in similar ways or share similar traits, it does not mean you are just like them.

Furthermore, you do have the power to choose. You can take proactive steps to ensure that you do not perpetuate negative patterns from your past – you can find recourses, you can learn, you can find mentors and spiritual parents, and you can surround yourself with very different people. By being honest yet compassionate with yourself, you can begin to heal and grow into the person, friend, partner, and parent you want to be.

It takes courage and immense bravery to confront your fear and face how your past has shaped you. By recognizing the patterns passed down to you, you can start to break free from them. You have the power to live your life in a different way, one that is defined by empathy, kindness, and compassion.

Reflective exercise: 'A letter from the future'

1 Find a quiet and comfortable space where you can focus. Take time to reflect on and make a list of situations where you notice differences between yourself and your parents. How do you view things differently? How do you deal with events – pleasant or unpleasant – differently? Explore your values, beliefs, and aspirations and how they are distinct from those of your parents.
2 Close your eyes and take a few deep breaths to centre yourself. Imagine your future self – a wiser and more evolved version of who you are now. Perhaps this can be you ten years from now. Reflect on the qualities and traits you can see in your future self. Consider the progress you want to make in breaking free from negative patterns and transforming into the person you aspire to be.
3 From the position of your future, wiser self, write a letter to your current self. Start with something like 'To the person I once was'. In the letter, describe your life in the last ten years – use your imagination for this. Highlight the choices you have made that demonstrated your commitment to living a fulfilling and authentic life, and

how it is very much unlike the life your parent had lived. Give specific examples where you have shown resilience, courage, and personal growth. You may detail how you have broken through chains of transgenerational trauma and how proud of those achievements you were.

4 Express your hopes and aspirations for your current self. Offer advice and reminders on how to stay true to your values and trust in your journey.
5 Take a moment to visualize your future self sealing the letter and handing it to you, symbolizing the connection between your present and future selves.
6 Open your eyes and reflect on the insights and guidance you received from your imagined future self. Consider how you can apply this wisdom and make choices aligned with your desired future. If possible, come up with 3-5 action points for the coming week.

5 Release

LEAN ON SOMETHING BIGGER THAN YOURSELF

Recovering from the wounds caused by insensitive parents can be a daunting and isolating journey. Seeking solace in something greater than yourself can be immensely useful in the healing process from such wounds.

Adopting a 'spiritual' perspective does not necessarily mean holding particular beliefs or adhering to a religion. It simply means recognizing that a greater force is at work in the background, one that can guide and comfort you. It can be a sense of oneness with a higher power, the natural world, or a universal energy.

Empathy and interconnectedness are intricately linked within the realm of spirituality. When you recognize that there is something beyond your ego-driven identity, you come to understand that all beings – those you love, those you despise, and those you feel indifferent towards – share a fundamental unity. Renowned spiritual teacher Eckhart Tolle introduces us to the concept of the 'pain body' (2004) to help us understand and rise above personal suffering. The pain body is an accumulation of lingering emotional pain from collective past experiences stored in the body and mind. It acts as a field of energy that thrives on negativity and, when triggered, can lead to intense emotional reactions.

The key to using spirituality to heal is to realize that your childhood trauma is a part of the collective human suffering. Of course, your painful history is real, and it deserves to be recognized for what it was. However, it is not personal and you have not been 'targeted'. Your sorrow is embedded in and a reflection of the collective pain experienced by humanity. When you see this, you can cease being overly identified with the narrative you might have felt stuck in. You can become aware of what you are going through and even feel sorry for yourself, but you do not have to drown in it or perpetuate any shame associated with it.

You may also consider adopting 'spiritual parents' as a healing approach. If your biological parents have failed to provide the love and support you deserve, the concept of spiritual parents offers an alternative path. They are your chosen family. Your spiritual parents may be real individuals, such as wise friends or mentors, or fictional characters, like heroes in stories, who embody the qualities lacking in your biological parents – qualities like genuine empathy, compassion, and understanding. For instance, you might discover a supportive teacher or mentor who listens without judgement or find solace in the wisdom of a favourite author or artist. The key is to identify those who symbolize the attributes you long for, regardless of their age or gender.

For many people, being with nature can also offer a deeply healing and revitalizing encounter. Nature has a unique ability to reestablish our connection with the interconnected web of life. Take in the vibrant colours, listen to the calming sounds, and feel the gentle caress of the wind. By immersing yourself in basic elements such as the earth and the woods, you might see your inner strength and resilience reflected in the vastness of the natural world. Time in nature can remind you of your inherent power, expansiveness, and untapped potential, even if your parents may not fully recognize these qualities.

Your spiritual journey is unique and personal, so feel free to tailor and personalize these suggestions to match your preferences and beliefs. Hopefully, you can find a way to fortify a more empathetic understanding of yourself, those around you, and all sentient beings.

Reflective exercise: Finding your spiritual parents

First, take a moment to consider what you need and desire in an archetypally ideal parent. Are you seeking emotional understanding, wisdom, or specific skills? What have you craved all your life that was lacking in your childhood? For some, it may be intellectual stimulation, while for others, it could be emotional attunement.

Next, embark on a quest to find real-life mentors who exemplify the qualities you desire. Explore your community for wise friends, mentors, or spiritual leaders whose principles align with your aspirations. Build connections with potential spiritual parents by attending events, following their work, and initiating direct conversations with them.

Expand your exploration by finding solace in the works of authors, artists, musicians, and creators who ignite inspiration within you. Reflect on the elements of their work that you can integrate into your personal journey. This deep dive into different forms of art and expression can provide unexpected insights and emotional support that align with your inner needs.

Explore fictional characters from literature, movies, or mythology who embody the qualities you seek in a spiritual parent. Identify characters that have made a lasting impact on you, considering how their traits or journeys resonate with your own aspirations and challenges.

Once you've identified potential spiritual parents, whether real or fictional, delve deeper by reflecting on what specifically attracted you to them. Was it their wisdom, compassion, or perhaps the embodiment of strengths and resilience you aspire to cultivate? Consider if they possess qualities you've longed for but found lacking in your own upbringing, or if they represent the person you could potentially become.

If they are real individuals in your life, engage with them directly: talk to them, spend time with them, and ask questions to gain deeper insights into their experiences and wisdom. If they are fictional or historical figures, immerse yourself in their works, explore their teachings, and engage with interviews or documentaries about their lives. This can involve reading their books, listening to their music, viewing their art, or watching films and plays about them.

Focus on the journeys, teachings, and challenges these mentors faced, paying special attention to how they discovered strength and wisdom in the face of adversity. This understanding can provide a blueprint for navigating your own hardships. Finally, distil the wisdom and teachings that resonate with your own healing and growth journey, integrating these lessons into your life to foster personal development and emotional fulfilment.

6 Act

RECLAIMING YOUR TRUE SELF

Growing up with parents who prioritized their needs over your feelings can significantly impact your sense of self. Being raised in an environment where your needs and desires are neither understood nor acknowledged often leads to the formation of what psychologists term a 'false self'. This term doesn't imply intentional dishonesty on your part; rather, it describes an unconscious psychological defence mechanism.

If you had a Needy Parent, you might have taken on the role of an emotional caregiver, neglecting your own needs to meet everyone else's. Alternatively, if you had a Superficial Parent, your False Self might have constantly sought perfection, seeking validation from others at the expense of your well-being. While other children freely pursue their desires and find joy, your False Self is preoccupied with what you 'should' be doing. Instead of exploring your passions, you felt compelled to act like the obedient child your parents groomed you to be.

To maintain the False Self, you had to suppress certain aspects of your personality. This could involve hiding your feelings, denying parts of your sexuality, or compromising your values and beliefs. In other words, you had to trade spontaneity and authenticity for the possibility of being loved.

Initially, your False Self may have served you well as you were rewarded for being responsible, hardworking, reliable and industrious. However, as you reach a certain point in your life, you may suddenly feel restless and dissatisfied. Life may become empty and unfulfilling, and the prospect of continuing this way is daunting. This is commonly called an existential crisis or a quarter-life/midlife crisis.

A crisis occurs because your true self cannot be suppressed indefinitely. After a significant amount of time, perhaps ten or twenty years, your soul demands to be heard. Your crisis may be felt as chronic depression or emptiness. Even if everything appears fine, a constant dissatisfaction gnaws at you. Your crisis may also materialize as a failed marriage, severe illness, an affair, or workplace burnout. Something within you yearns to 'break out'.

Jungian analyst James Hollis provides valuable insights into the nature of a midlife crisis. He notes that the first half of our lives primarily focuses on survival – adapting, gathering resources, and seeking acceptance within our community. However, our purpose and priorities shift in the second half of life – it becomes a time to explore the depths of our being and reclaim our true selves.

Emerging from this crisis demands a courageous willingness to challenge ingrained patterns of thinking, being, and doing. People in your life, including parents, siblings, and long-time friends with fixed mindsets, might struggle to support your newfound life choices. Some may even object to or resist the changes you are implementing. Therefore, a pivotal developmental task in this journey is what psychologists refer to as 'individuation'.

In individuation, instead of seeking approval from external sources or parental figures, you learn to recognize your self-worth and assert your needs and values without fear or guilt. Start by considering what genuinely brings you joy, and a sense of purpose, and aligns with your unique values. Reflect on how these might differ from collective mindsets, conventional wisdom, or your culture's perspectives. If there's a fear of outgrowing your parents or friends, remember that pursuing your path honours your true self and you are not doing it to hurt anyone. As the saying goes, people may stay in your life for a season or a reason, and embracing personal growth is a natural part of this evolving matrix of connections.

Answering the summons of your genuine, authentic self, long suppressed, marks a crucial milestone in healing from an empathy-deprived childhood. Summoning the courage to pursue your renewed passions may prove difficult after a lifetime of conforming to others' expectations. Yet, the fulfilment and joy derived from staying true to yourself will soon surpass any external validation or approval, propelling you forward in this second half of your life.

Journalling exercise: Unveiling the mask of your False Self

Create a list of traits that characterize your 'False Self'. Be radically honest with yourself to unearth the behaviours, thought patterns, and personas that you have adopted to gain validation and acceptance. For example, reflect on how you have become an emotional caregiver or an endless seeker of perfection.

Let the emotions flow as you recall the interactions with your unempathic parent that had created the False Self. Allow yourself to fully feel the weight of their needs and how those were prioritized over yours. Explore the moments when your authentic self was dismissed or ignored. Write down these experiences with honesty and vulnerability.

Then, write about the restlessness, dissatisfaction, and yearning that have pervaded your being in the last 10 or 20 years. It is time to acknowledge the profound impact of living in your False Self and the toll it has taken on your spirit. In this process, always remember, that adopting the False Self was an inevitable outcome of having unempathic parents – it was not a conscious choice on your part. You did your best to survive, so there is no reason for self-blame, guilt, or regrets. Embrace the pain as a catalyst for change, as a call from your true self urging you to break free from the confines of inauthenticity.

Finally, list five action points – of the smallest things you can do in the next few weeks to align your actions more with who you authentically are, rather than who you were conditioned to be.

MOVING ON IN LIFE: FURTHER READING AND REFLECTION

If the above resonates with you, or you feel you are currently going through a healing/meaning crisis, you may want to spend some time reading up on the concept of the False Self/True Self (Winnicott), midlife crisis, individuation, and parentification. Here are some classic works on these topics:

- *The Drama of the Gifted Child: The Search for the True Self* by Alice Miller (Basic Books, 1997) explores the impact of childhood emotional neglect and how we can develop a 'False Self' to please our parents or caregivers. The book offers insights on how the emotionally gifted but burdened ones can reclaim their true selves.
- *Finding Meaning in the Second Half of Life: How to Finally, Really Grow Up* by James Hollis (Avery, 2005) explores the psychological and spiritual challenges that we can face in the second half of life. As a Jungian Analyst, Hollis delves into the topics of existential crisis, midlife transitions, and spiritual transformations that occur during this stage.
- *Falling Upward* by Richard Rohr (SPCK Publishing, 2013) challenges the conventional notion that the second half of life is a time of decline or stagnation. Instead, he argues that this can be a time for profound spiritual awakening.
- *The Artist's Way: A Spiritual Path to Higher Creativity* by Julia Cameron (first published Souvenir Press, 1994) is a popular guide on how to reconnect with one's artistic spirit. It offers a 12-week program to help us remove creative blocks.

Summing up: What self-empathy really means

At its core, self-empathy means becoming your own ally instead of the enemy. It involves empowering yourself, validating your unique experiences, and showing compassion towards your past and present selves. This also involves embracing your past, letting go of guilt and blame that does not belong to you, acknowledging and honouring your emotions, and breaking free from the cycle of inherited trauma.

To move on, rather than holding out hope that justice will come or constantly trying to change your parent and family, you may have to reconcile with the reality that they may never change. The reckoning experience involves pain and grief, but it will liberate you from the cycle of disappointments that happens when you hold empty hopes.

You cannot change the past, but you can be wholeheartedly accountable for your mindset, your actions, and where you go from here. By recognizing how past deprivations may have led to projecting emotions onto others – such as rage, disappointment, and fear – you gain clarity. This lucidity allows you to redirect these sentiments to their rightful place, thereby improving your relationships, enhancing your capacity of empathy towards those in your life now, and giving you a more fulfilling future.

Genuine empathy and compassion are not saying to your unempathic parents: 'Nothing wrong happened; you are excused from everything you do.' Instead, it is saying: 'You have flaws as parents, and I was hurt by them. But I can choose to forgive, even if I may never forget what happened', or 'I still love you, even though sometimes I cannot fully trust you.' If that is not possible, you can also say, 'I choose to honour myself by walking away.'

You had the option of living a life of denial, suppression, and misdirected rage. You could have squandered the rest of your life, lashing out at those you love without knowing why.

You could have insisted on being 'never a victim' and go through life with false stoicism and spiritual bypass. You can, however, choose not to do the above.

In the end, it is not your wounds that define you. What you choose to do with your injuries and how you move forward from them shape who you are.

This journey is going to involve back and forth, but the point is not to 'arrive' somewhere but to honour yourself along the way.

As you break the chains of transgenerational trauma, you also create a ripple effect. It does not even mean you have to become a parent, but by emerging as a resilient soul who also speaks the language of invisible trauma, you are in a unique position to offer deep empathy to others in pain.

Since we live in an interconnected world, if you heal and manifest emotional maturity and resilience, the peaceful energy that you hold will ripple out to the communities and the world at large

So, please be reminded once again, that:

You are not your past.

You are not your trauma.

You can emerge from the other side,

You can create new legacies of empathy for yourself and others.

You can become who you are meant to be, whether it is despite or because of your trauma.

Interlude

From 'why' to 'yes'

Enduring the weight of adversity, we often find ourselves ensnared in an endless cycle, ceaselessly seeking answers to the haunting question: 'Why?'

'Why was I born into this family with these parents?'

'Why me?'

'Why was I the chosen target of bullying and abuse?'

'Why was I the black sheep of the family?'

'What did I do wrong?'

'Why was I abused, neglected, used, manipulated?'

'Why didn't they accept me for who I was?'

'Why was love not unconditional?'

Asking 'why' can be a double-edged sword. On one hand, trying to make sense of our trauma can be a part of healing. On the other, the relentless search for answers can become a form of intellectual bypassing, a way to avoid confronting the raw emotional truth of our experiences.

We find ourselves entangled in a web of analysis, attempting to rationalize what is essentially an emotional journey, unwittingly distancing ourselves from the emotions that demand our gentlest empathic attention. Busying with the 'why', we skim the surface of our feelings, sprinting away from the depths where our pain and vulnerability reside.

When faced with the tragedy of a wounded childhood, it's natural to seek meaning or an explanation. It's human nature to look for a 'why' to regain a sense of control and order in our lives. So we start analyzing – we analyze our past, our parents' histories, our ancestral wounds, and even whether or not we did something to offend the higher power. This quest for answers can also take a harmful turn when we become trapped in a cycle of blame. We might begin by blaming ourselves, convinced that we were a 'difficult child' whom our parents did not love. Or that we were a 'bad partner' so our loved ones left us behind.

At this juncture, turning our gaze inward, and harnessing not our analytical skills but the heart wisdom of self-empathy, is the pivotal point that will save us.

When we practise self-empathy, we allow ourselves to feel compassion for our own suffering. Instead of harshly judging our reactions or blaming ourselves for our circumstances, we begin to understand and accept our feelings as valid responses to our experiences.

Empathy allows us to see our pain in the context of our humanity and the shared human experience. One of the most challenging aspects to accept, especially in the face of great injustice, is that life doesn't always follow a clear, logical plan. We like to think we have control over our lives and can assign credit or blame for what happens, but the reality is that many things are beyond our control. We did not choose our birth, nor could we prevent the generational trauma that existed long before our arrival in the world.

The 'why' may never find complete answers, but empathy reminds us we are not alone. While the 'why' may forever remain elusive, we can mourn in solidarity.

Instead of fixating on 'why', there comes a point where we must embrace the realization that life brings both fairness and injustice, kindness and cruelty. It's our rite of passage as adults to integrate both, enabling us to navigate life's uncertainties without falling into a cycle of blame or conspiracy.

Acceptance does not mean endorsing abuse or giving up; rather, it's a path to liberation and the creation of a new life story. Saying 'Yes' to life invites us to stand at the intersection of our past and future with open arms, ready to receive the beauty that lies ahead. It empowers us to step boldly into the unknown, declaring, 'Yes, that happened, but it wasn't the end of my story.'

You recognize the pain as part of your story, not as something that defines you, but as a thread that shapes and strengthens you. Life comprises both joyful and agonizing experiences, and each thread contributes to the richness of the whole. Saying 'yes' to life involves embracing the entirety of your existence, both light and shadow.

By accepting 'what was', you liberate yourself from the burden of ceaselessly seeking explanations. The energy that frees up helps you move forward.

When you embrace 'what was', you stop running from your history and attempting to rewrite your past; instead, you author your future.

By relinquishing the compulsion to dissect and analyze every detail of your pain, you understand that your worth isn't determined by the answers you find or the questions you ask but by your capacity to navigate adversity with grace, empathy, and resilience.

Even when justice wasn't pursued, you possess the power to rise above and reclaim your dignity.

By letting go of the need for clear explanations of 'why', you create space for the mysterious beauty of life. In this sacred space, you honour your intrinsic worth.

PART 4

Empathy at home

Parents with 'too much' empathy

9
Can you have too much empathy?

When it comes to parenthood, empathy is usually deemed as a highly desirable and necessary quality. However, in this chapter, we will explore a provocative question: is it possible to have too much of a good thing? Is a parent's self-perceived empathy always based on authentic emotional connections, or might it sometimes stem from projection or excessive identification? In this chapter, we will explore the nuances of what defines 'good empathy' in the realm of parenting, and unravel the complexities surrounding these themes.

Empathy is commonly regarded as a positive quality, the bedrock for virtues like patience, compassion, and forgiveness. While the prevailing view is that there is no such thing as too much empathy, research suggests otherwise (Hodges and Biswas-Diener, 2007). While empathy forms the basis of compassion, its misuse has been associated with 'cruel and irrational actions' (Bloom, 2017). In certain situations, empathy can contribute to burnout and exhaustion and was found to be an ineffective motivator for prosocial behaviours. Unregulated empathy can also cause many unhealthy symptoms, including caregiver burnout, vicarious trauma, and compassion fatigue. For instance, studies indicate that excessive empathy among firefighters can lead to more traumatic events and psychological distress (Wagner et al., 2019). In other words, when it comes to empathy, it is not a case of 'the more, the merrier', but rather something that must be regulated, managed, and accessed at the appropriate time.

The phenomenon where a person's empathy becomes excessive and burdensome can be described as 'engulfing empathy' or 'encroaching empathy'. In this pattern, the typically positive trait of empathy becomes detrimental. This occurs when a person becomes so absorbed in and shares the feelings of others to such an extent that they become ungrounded in their own reality. Consequently, this can lead to emotional exhaustion, a loss of personal identity, and a sense of being overwhelmed or suffocated by the emotional demands of others.

In the context of family and close relationships, excessive or misused empathy can cause someone to over-identify with their loved ones, where they experience their partners' or children's emotional pain as if it were their own. When they start to assume responsibility for the other person's emotions and problems, empathy crosses the line of love and care and becomes co-dependency.

Is it even 'empathy'?

Most psychology researchers agree that genuine empathy has at least three essential components. Firstly, there's the emotional response, often automatic and influenced by our mirror neurons (refer to Chapter 1). Secondly, the cognitive capacity to consider the other person's perspective. Lastly, the ability to regulate one's own emotions and maintain boundaries (Decety and Hodges, 2006; Ickes, 2001; DeWaal, 2002). People struggling with encroaching empathy might be strong 'feelers' (the first component of empathy), but are weak in the cognitive and emotional self-regulation aspects (lacking in the second and third components).

When a parent is 'overly empathic', to the point of exhaustion or losing themselves, it is likely due to their lack of energetic boundaries and an inability to separate their experience from that of their children. One example is when they witness their children's pain or distress, they experience an immediate and intense emotional and physical response that is disproportionate to the situation. This can lead to long-term consequences, from physical tension and insomnia to psychological symptoms such as irritability, chronic anxiety, and the loss of joy and motivation.

The concept of 'boundaries in the mind', developed by Ernest Hartmann (1991), describes how a person interacts with other people and elements of the world, specifically in how they deal with energies and perceive the tone of their surroundings. According to researchers of this theory, the robustness of a person's boundaries determines which stimuli come in or are kept out and how they manage their own and others' emotions. One might assume that unregulated, engulfing empathy is likely common among people who have 'thin boundaries'. To illustrate, here is a quote from Hartmann:

> 'There are people who strike us as very solid and well organized; they keep everything in its place. They are well defended. They seem rigid, even armored; we sometimes speak of them as "thick-skinned." At the other extreme are people who are especially sensitive, open, or vulnerable. In their minds, things are relatively fluid . . . such people have fragile boundaries.'

Parents prone to engulfing empathy are often plagued with anxiety. They may be overly vigilant, constantly scanning their child's environment for potential threats or signs of distress because they cannot bear to see them in pain. For instance, if their child experiences a minor setback, such as not performing well on a school assignment, parents with engulfing empathy may become paranoid about the impact of this setback on their child's self-esteem or future success. They may become tremendously anxious and jump into action to try to rectify the situation. Consequently, they become overly protective. Even though their intention is to keep their children safe, engulfing empathy can actually hinder the youngster's ability to grow up resilient and capable of handling problems independently.

Many people with dysregulated empathy have heightened sensitivity to threat signals, which can be attributed to both nature and nurture factors. It may stem from their inherent wiring or as a response to past traumas they have experienced. Neurologically, they may have a hyper-responsive limbic system, particularly the amygdala, while their prefrontal cortex function may be underactive or underutilized. Due to their heightened awareness, they can better recognize and respond to potential threats in the environment. However, at the same time, they have an attentional bias towards threats and are more likely to perceive danger in everyday situations when there is none (Bar-Haim et al., 2007; Reinecke et al., 2010). This causes them to, without meaning to hurt their child, behave in paranoid and controlling ways.

It is not uncommon for someone who struggles to regulate empathy to lose themselves in parenthood. They may lose sight of who they are as an individual, forget who they were before having children, no longer have the energy to connect with their partner and friends, and lose their sense of self. This is dangerous because as their children leave home, they would lose their sense of meaning and purpose in life. They may then flounder to control people around them even more or resort to drugs, alcohol, food, extremist ideologies, and even religious cults to fill the void.

Empathy vs fusion

Genuine empathy necessitates a 'dual awareness': it involves not only sharing and understanding the experiences of others but also recognizing and maintaining a clear sense of self. In other words, while we empathize with others, we must simultaneously acknowledge that we are separate individuals with our own distinct thoughts, feelings, and experiences. As the father of humanistic psychology, Carl Rogers stated:

> 'The state of empathy, or being empathic, is to perceive the internal frame of reference of another with accuracy and with the emotional components and meanings which pertain thereto as if one were the person. . . . , *but without losing the as-if condition.* (Carl Rogers, 1995, p. 140)

The focus of this quote should be on the last part: 'without losing the as-if condition'. That is, we recognize that the emotional pain we are experiencing is not our own but that of another person (Bird and Viding, 2014; de Vignemont and Singer, 2006; Jackson et al., 2005; Lamm et al., 2016).

In the case of engulfing parents, they rely heavily on their reflexive and automatic mirror neurons to perceive and internalize their children's emotions. However, they lack the self-awareness necessary to differentiate their own emotions from those of their children. As a result, they struggle with regulating the emotions they absorb, leading to a state of emotional overwhelm.

The experience of engulfing parents might be more accurately described as 'emotional contagion' rather than a fully developed and mature form of empathy (Waal and Ferrari, 2012). Emotional contagion is a process by which an individual automatically mirrors and absorbs the emotions of others without necessarily understanding or empathizing with their perspective.

Some scholars argue that emotional contagion is a primitive and immature form of empathy, as it lacks the cognitive and self-reflective components necessary for a more advanced understanding of others' experiences. Others contend that emotional contagion does not fully meet the criteria to be classified as empathy, as it does not involve a genuine understanding or concern for others' well-being.

Even if we consider engulfing empathy as a valid type of empathy, it tends to be neither useful nor productive. Practical empathy relies on the cultivation of mentalizing, which involves considering both one's own thoughts and feelings as well as those of others.

Mentalizing is a crucial skill that allows individuals to understand and interpret the mental states of others accurately. Strong mentalizing abilities empower parents to perceive their child as an independent individual with distinct thoughts, feelings, and motivations. This skill is particularly crucial for effective parenting as it enables parents to comprehend their children's perspectives and emotions without imposing projections and mental distortions.

For instance, when a child cries, emotionally mature parents can acknowledge their own mental state while also tending to the child's needs. This dual awareness enables them to respond as responsible adults who can provide comfort and soothing to the child. Instead of becoming overwhelmed by the child's distress or getting lost in a sense of helplessness, they maintain their role as the supportive caregiver.

In a moment of distress, what a child needs most is a parent who firmly holds their place as the grown-up in the room, offering comfort and a sense of calm. Imagine the confusion and distress a child might feel if their parents became so consumed by the child's emotions that they started crying together! This would only heighten the child's anxiety and sense of insecurity.

Genuinely empathetic parents skilfully navigate their child's world while preserving their own identity and using their empathic abilities appropriately. They strike a balance between understanding their child's emotions and maintaining the stability and reassurance that the child needs. This perspective aligns with extensive research in mother-infant studies and mentalization-based interventions, which emphasize the importance of parental emotional regulation and the ability to provide a secure base for the child (Sharp and Fonagy, 2008).

When someone struggles to draw a clear energetic boundary between themselves and others, it actually undermines their ability to have true empathy (Engelbrektsson, 2020; Krol and Bartz, 2022). This is how empathy researcher Karla McLaren (2013) puts it:

> 'If your experience of empathy is primarily unregulated Emotion Contagion, such that you act as an emotional sponge, to the point where you become overwhelmed by the emotions of others, you'll probably be unable to provide much support to them. . . . you'll shut down.'

Apart from emotional shut-downs, and abrupt withdrawals that disrupt the child's attachment, empathic burnout can also cause these parents to resort to passive-aggressive, controlling, and manipulative behaviours. It is not that empathy-dysregulated parents deliberately choose to do so or harm their child; instead, they lack the emotional capacity and mentalizing training to channel their emotional empathy correctly and at an appropriate level. Ironically, their hyperactive 'pseudo-empathy' depletes their resources so much that it leads them to act in ways that contradict their original intentions to love and help their children.

Parents with engulfing empathy

Engulfing empathy can hurt any relationship, from romantic relationships to teams in the workplace. However, it is especially impactful in parenting because the parent–child relationship shapes the child's worldview and ideas about relationships and the world, often for life.

In psychoanalysis, there exists a concept known as the 'too-good mother' (Ashley, 2002; Bohm, 2017; Shields, 1964). This phrase is often used to describe a caregiver who becomes excessively attached and preoccupied with their child. (Note that despite the traditional language used in the psychoanalytic literature, the term 'mother' in this context can refer to primary caregivers of any gender.) A 'too-good' parent is highly attuned to their child's emotional state, to the point of being overly focused on it. While this heightened sensitivity may seem positive at first glance, it may stop them from providing the necessary structure, boundaries, and guidance crucial for the child's healthy development.

Some parents are more anxious than others, and they may resort to overprotection as a way of coping with anxiety (Bögels and van Melick, 2004; Brenning et al., 2017; Clarke et al., 2013; Creveling et al., 2010; Thomasgard et al., 1995; Turner et al., 2003). Unfortunately, overprotection is based on the parents' needs rather than the child's; it is more of a form of control than it is an expression of love.

When parents overly empathize with their children without allowing them the space to develop independence and skills, they inadvertently infantilize them. When children are shielded from difficulties and denied the opportunity to learn from their mistakes, they may be deprived of the opportunities to develop resilience (Affrunti and Ginsburg, 2012). Studies after studies have shown that anxious parenting can negatively impact children's sense of control, self-confidence, and independence, leading them to see themselves as less competent and experience more anxiety (Affrunti and Ginsburg, 2012; Chorpita and Barlow, 2002; Hudson and Rapee, 2005; Costello et al., 2008). Over-protective parenting can also create a perception in children that the world is dangerous, reinforcing avoidance behaviours and limiting their opportunities to face challenges and acquire important life skills (Manley, 2017; Rapee, 2009). In other words, excessive coddling may contribute to the development of a dependent personality, wherein they become heavily reliant on others for decision-making, feel insecure or helpless when alone, struggle to assert their own opinions and needs, and experience intense separation anxiety in their relationships.

Furthermore, overprotective parenting often coincides with permissive parenting, especially among parents who struggle to assert themselves and set boundaries. When there is a lack of boundaries, children may encounter difficulties in adhering to rules, managing their impulses, navigating complex situations, and experiencing emotional dysregulation later in life (Jinnah and Stoneman, 2016).

While it is crucial for parents to empathize with their child's pain, there comes a point where they must move beyond mere empathy to assert their authority and set boundaries. For instance, when a child throws a tantrum and refuses to go to school, an excessively empathic parent may become overwhelmed by the child's distress and yield to their demands. In contrast, a healthy empathic parent would recognize the child's emotions while also setting clear expectations. They may say something like: 'I understand that you are upset, and I am sorry that you do. However, it's still important for you to go to school because (provide a logical explanation of the reasons).

In other words, empathy is not a merger, nor is it dependency or the compulsion to rescue. As a parent, one must balance one's empathetic instincts and exert discipline when needed, even if it may not always feel pleasant. When parents lose themselves in giving to and living for others, they paradoxically lose the ability to express genuine empathy.

To summarize, empathic parenting is not overparenting. In contrast, effective parenting requires the ability to establish healthy boundaries, differentiate oneself from others, and regulate emotions. These qualities distinguish genuine empathy from toxic emotional engulfment masked as empathy. Merely experiencing emotional contagion or mirroring without the ability to respond appropriately does not qualify as good empathy. As we shall see next, the impact of a parent's empathy dysregulation can go beyond personal burnout and affect the overall dynamics of the family system.

10

Recovering from empathy suffocation

Growing up with engulfing empathy

Growing up with engulfing empathy can be a confusing and challenging experience. When parents become excessively involved in their child's life, it may appear to outsiders as a manifestation of love and care. Unfortunately, society often praises and values the seemingly selfless acts of these parents, which can easily overshadow their underlying emotional immaturity. However, this type of parenting often stems from the parent's emotional immaturity and unresolved issues, which creates a stifling environment for the child.

If you have had overprotective parents, it can be challenging for you to feel your suffering is legitimate or that you can blame them because it may appear that everything they did was for your benefit. While others may view them as considerate and gentle, you know deep down there is something not right about the smothering nature of your relationship. Unfortunately, the discrepancy between the outward appearance of your family dynamics and your internal experience may make it challenging for the trauma you have endured to be recognized and for you to trust your own experience.

This chapter explores the complexities of what it means to grow up in such an environment, its impact, and the path to recover from the trauma of growing up with engulfing empathy. Only when you have found healing for yourself can you transition to the next chapter, where we will explore how to extend self-compassion towards yourself and develop empathy for your parent. Our ultimate objective is to find an equilibrium between acknowledging and validating your experiences, providing room for processing any anger or resentment you may carry, while also nurturing your capacity for empathy towards them.

Did you grow up suffocated?

Here are some signs that you might have been impacted by having grown up with a parent with engulfing empathy:

- You do not have a strong sense of self, and you are often unsure of your likes and dislikes, desires and needs.
- You have yet to learn what your goals or purpose are, and feel dissatisfied and lost in life.
- You often feel lost in unstructured environments, where you are left to your own device to decide how to use your time.
- You feel powerless in general and have little confidence in your sense of agency, power, or ability to solve life's problems.
- You feel the compulsive need to consult with others before you make a decision, no matter how minor.
  You have difficulty trusting your own judgement and intuition, often second-guessing yourself and seeking reassurance from others.
- You have difficulty expressing your own opinions or disagreeing with others, as you fear disapproval, rejection, or conflict.
- Even if someone mistreats you, the prospect of confronting them overwhelms you. You either delay a potentially tricky conversation for as long as possible, or you avoid it entirely.
- Saying 'no' feels impossible, as you bend over backward to keep everyone happy, even if it means sacrificing

your own needs. You find it hard to express anger or frustration, as you fear upsetting others or appearing ungrateful.

- You tend to put on a smile and hide your true feelings, especially negative ones, to maintain a facade of harmony.
- You have little psychological defence against (even unjustified) criticisms. When you are accused, you are immediately convinced that others are correct and that the problem must be yours.
- You tend to take on excessive responsibility for others' emotions and well-being, feeling compelled to fix their problems or ensure their happiness.
- You find it difficult to be alone. When the people you care about are not physically present, you worry that they will never return or eventually leave or reject you.
- You gravitate towards partners who are controlling or overly involved, unknowingly recreating the dynamic you had with your parent.
- You are overly attached to your parents and feel obligated to keep them updated on your daily activities, call or text them daily.
- You worry about things that most would not worry about, and others tell you that you tend to catastrophize.
- You are constantly afraid that something terrible will happen, and you will be powerless to prevent it.
- The thought of growing old on your own is terrifying to you. You fear being alone, so you may lower your standards and stay in an unhealthy relationship.
- You struggle with self-compassion and tend to be overly self-critical, holding yourself to unrealistic standards and berating yourself for even minor mistakes.

If you identify with many of the signs listed above, you have likely been affected by growing up with a parent who exhibited engulfing empathy. This experience can shape your life in various ways, influencing your sense of self, relationships, emotional well-being, and overall outlook on life. The following are some ways in which a parent's engulfing empathy can influence a child's emotional and psychological development:

Dependency

When you have a parent who lacks boundaries and tends to over-focus on your feelings without offering the necessary structure or discipline, you are deprived of the opportunity to individuate and grow a sense of self. Just as someone can be groomed as the family's 'clown', mediator', or 'golden child', you might have been made to take on the role of the 'eternal child' of the family – someone who was never allowed to grow up and strike out on their own; like the 'Peter Pan' character, you were forced to play the role of a perpetually dependent and immature teenager.

Paradoxically, overbearing parenting often goes hand-in-hand with a lack of mirroring. In attachment theory, 'mirroring' refers to the caregiver's ability to reflect and validate the child's emotional experiences by attuning to their feelings and responding in a way that acknowledges and validates those emotions. When there is a lack of mirroring, the caregiver fails to accurately perceive and respond to the child's emotional needs, which can lead to insecure attachment (Fonagy and Target, 1997; Taipale, 2016). This, in turn, can result in difficulties developing a strong sense of self and trusting one's own emotions and instincts later in life.

Just because your parent appears to be 'excessively empathetic' does not mean they have truly understood your needs and were there to provide the mirroring you needed. Instead, they might have projected their anxieties onto you, offering a distorted form of empathy through projection rather than accurately reflecting your emotions. Coupled with their controlling nature, this can hinder your ability to cultivate a stable sense of self. Consequently, when you find yourself alone, you may experience a haunted sense of emptiness.

Dependency is a trait that develops in the background, and you may not recognize the problem until it causes significant problems in your relationships. You could, for example, be highly successful at work and appear mature and solid, but revert to a childlike dependency in other areas of your life, such as in intimate relationships. When you get together with someone, you find yourself becoming overly anxious, unconsciously expecting your partner to take the place of your parent or to take care of you the same way your parent did. When your anxiety is triggered, you may lose your ability to function, become disoriented, lose your sense of self-confidence, and feel like an abandoned lost child. Without understanding what is happening, unfortunately, your partner may also accuse you of being excessively needy and clingy.

On top of that, perhaps your parents had never modelled how to say no and set boundaries, so you do not know how to express your feelings, assert your needs, and stand up for yourself even when you are mistreated. You might never have learned how to claim your rightful space in the world, such as speaking up, expressing feelings in a conversation, and allowing yourself to be seen and heard in public spaces; so now, even when allowed to be seen and celebrated, you do not know what to do with it. This can hold you back in your career or stop you from being socially capable. Eventually, your experience can solidify the belief that you are incapable of being on your own and that you would not be able to find love outside of your family.

Co-dependency

When your parent is constantly anxious and watching over your needs, attempting to meet your desires before you even express them, excessively asking about you, reading into you, and refusing to separate from you, what looks like empathy on the surface becomes nothing more than a boundary intrusion. Whether or not you were aware of it at the time, you were suffocated by inappropriate intimacy and a false sense of support. The outcome of such upbringing is usually not 'healthy dependency' and appropriate individuation but a coerced form of co-dependency.

Co-dependency is a dysfunctional relationship in which one person relies on the other to an excessive or unhealthy degree to meet their psychological needs. Your parent might have pushed you into an enmeshed relationship, where your thoughts, feelings, and needs become merged with theirs. When you are feeling down, they cannot bear to witness it without leaping in with solutions. Conversely, when you see that they are sad, the weight of responsibility to rescue them falls on your shoulders – even when you were only a child.

This enmeshed dance, though seemingly normal when it is all you have ever known, is far from natural. To make matters worse, you might find yourself burdened with a peculiar obligation – proving your parent's parenting skills by reluctantly accepting and responding to their intrusive 'help'. If their self-worth hinges on your compliance, rejecting their interference in your life can provoke a storm of passive-aggressive or outright aggressive reactions. In their reality, your affirmation of their parenting skills becomes their shield against their loneliness and emptiness. Playing the role of a dependent child becomes their lifeline to navigate the challenges of an empty nest. This toxic burden is illustrated by psychologist John Bowlby's observation back in 1979 (again, back then, the word 'mother' was often used to denote all primary caregivers):

> '. . . the mother impelled to possess her child's love who, by her endless self-sacrifice, tries to ensure that her child is given no excuse for nay feelings other than those of love and gratitude. This mother, who at first sight appears so

> loving, inevitably creates great resentment in her child by her demands for his love, and equally great guilt in him through her claims to be a so good a mother that no sentiment but gratitude is justified (Bowlby, 1979, pp. 18–19)'

Since your parent lives vicariously through you, you may feel compelled to share every detail of your life with them. Even when you are not seeking advice, withholding information from them can leave you feeling restless and guilty. Despite your adult self-consciously recognizing the absurdity of these feelings, the inner child who was so loyal to your parent may even feel as though you are betraying them when you allow new people into your life or embark on a new relationship.

However, you must remember that the deprivation of your opportunity to grow was not your fault. As a child, you could not have known better, and the responsibility of maintaining appropriate boundaries should have fallen on your parents, not on you.

Internalized anxiety

Growing up with a parent who constantly projects their anxieties onto you can lead to the development of an unconscious belief that the world is inherently unsafe. This belief can fuel a persistent, heightened fear of impending disasters beyond your control, causing you to focus on life's negatives, such as pain, death, loss, conflict, and resentment. You may find yourself constantly worrying about making mistakes, facing betrayal, or anticipating things going wrong in various aspects of your life, including job security, health, and external threats like accidents or disasters.

If you have experienced anxiety for as long as you can remember, it could be the result of having internalized your parent's belief that the world is a dangerous place. For example, if your parent repeatedly warned you about the risks of trying new things or always seemed to have excessive concern about your safety, you might have grown up believing that the world is full of hidden dangers. This belief can manifest in various ways, such as a reluctance to take risks, a tendency to overthink and catastrophize situations, or a constant need for reassurance.

Moreover, your parents' coddling may have instilled a lasting sense of powerlessness and diminished your confidence in your ability to cope with stress, make decisions, or solve problems independently. This further reinforces your reliance on others for emotional support and guidance, perpetuating the cycle of anxiety and dependency.

Considering the hidden dynamics: It was never you to begin with

While you may have spent a long time beating yourself up for the situation you are in, here is an alternative perspective to consider: it might not have been you to begin with. Although traditional psychology seldom addresses this dynamic, there is a strong possibility that you are not genuinely dependent on your parent. Instead, you are taking care of their need to be needed.

You did not enter the world as a co-dependent person. You came into the world with a desire for individuation at a certain age. However, perhaps because you were unconsciously aware of your parent's need to be needed, you sacrificed your need to individuate to accommodate their dysfunctional trait. Children who are highly perceptive and naturally empathetic are particularly prone to this predicament.

You may have had a parent whose life lacked meaning and passion, and for whom parenting was their only job. If you, as a sensitive child, could sense this, you would have done everything you could to make them feel like they were 'good', helpful, and strong parents. You 'pretended' to need them so that they never ran out of something to do, someone to advise, serve, or rescue. In both overt and subtle ways, your parent conveyed that their entire existence revolved around you. It might be hard to admit it, but you can see that they appeared to thrive when you were facing challenges and required their support. They found joy in playing the role of your hero and rescuer, as that seemed to be their exclusive identity and reason for living. You felt obligated to tell them every detail of your life and seek their advice on everything; this way, they could feel valuable and relevant, and continue to live vicariously through you.

Even as an adult, to protect them from the inevitable 'empty nest', you may have sacrificed your own need to individuate and stayed home longer than you would have had to. You have put aside your own need for independence, or even downplay your capabilities so they would not feel threatened. It was not that you truly needed their protection, but you recognized that assigning them the role of protector or caregiver provided them with a sense of power, and you knew they needed that.

From a psychodynamic perspective, your parent had attributed their insecurities and reliance onto you, essentially projecting their inner child's needs onto you. This phenomenon can be understood through projective identification, a complex psychological process. Projective identification occurs when individuals project their own unacknowledged emotions, desires, and vulnerabilities onto another person and combine them with behaviours and actions that subtly coerce the other person to participate in the projection. In the context of your parent, they might have projected their deep-seated dependency and insecurities onto you, assigning you the role of the needy child. You were then made to believe you were the dependent one when they were the dependent one. Their actions were not malicious or intentional, they stemmed from their unresolved emotional wounds and patterns developed in their upbringing.

Perhaps, over the years, you have forgotten that this 'needy child' role was scripted into your life arbitrarily. This deep-seated identification with this role may have shaped your perception, making you believe in your helplessness and dependency.

Realizing what might have happened can be unsettling. Yet, the truth is what will set you free. Remembering who you are without their fearful and needy projection will set you free from the prison of a narrative that was not yours to begin with. It opens the door to reclaiming your independence and making choices based on your desires and capabilities.

Moving on with healthy distance

Given the nature of your parent's behaviours and the dynamics at play, keeping a healthy distance from them may be the only viable option.

Changing a family dynamic established over a long period is notoriously challenging. When a parent acts as though they cannot survive without being attached to you, your inner child would feel very bound by the obligation to stay loyal to the family script. It may be time to reframe and rethink what a healthy change could mean for your parent and your entire family, despite their apparent resistance.

Deep down, your parent may be aware of the toxicity of their compulsive need to infringe on your life, and they may feel guilty about it. However, their psychological immaturity and weakness have trapped them in a self-inflicted predicament, making it difficult for them to break free from these patterns.

It is possible that a healthy, adult part of your parent genuinely hopes for you to live an independent and fulfilled life without co-dependency. Although their anxiety and limitations hinder them from effectively communicating this or paving the way for you, your parent very likely still wants the best for you.

In other words, when you summon the strength to create a healthy distance from your parents, who are emotionally incapable of doing so, you are taking the lead and doing for them what they cannot do but wish they could. While the child in you feels terrible about abandoning them, the healthy adult in you knows this is the right decision for you and the whole family in the long run.

Closing thoughts: It's time to free yourself

When you have grown up with parents who act in engulfing and overbearing ways, the journey to becoming your person and establishing healthy distance could be the most challenging yet critical change you ought to make.

If you have spent your life under the weight of your parents' constant concern and intrusion, the idea of having a 'sense of self' might seem foreign or even intimidating.

It is not easy to identify your emotions and empathize with your suffering if you have spent years being an emotional crutch to your parent and rejecting your uniqueness and sense of self.

There might be parts of yourself that you do not like or struggle to change. Nevertheless, rather than blaming yourself or drowning in guilt, take a step back. Reflect on how your upbringing has influenced your current behaviour patterns.

At some point in your late childhood or early adolescence, you have internalized the threat that you would be abandoned and left entirely alone if you did not relinquish your independence and merge with one of your parents. So, to keep the bond with your caretaker strong, you did the 'sensible' thing and abandoned your individuality. This was not your fault but the only thing you could have done to survive. Therefore, to move forward, you must start by being gentle and forgiving with yourself.

If you can take time and summon compassion to reflect on what you have been through, you will begin to see your challenges not as a personal character flaw but as a result of unfortunate circumstances you were thrust into as a young, innocent child.

Your co-dependency with your parent was once essential for survival, but today, it no longer serves its purpose. As an adult, your parent is no longer the dominant figure in your significantly broader and more enriching life.

Being an adult involves accepting responsibilities and obligations, but it also brings satisfaction and fulfilment that you may not have thought possible. With time, you will come to appreciate the rewards of being an individualized, independent adult. This includes the opportunity to celebrate achievements and learn from setbacks when you give yourself the time and space to do so.

Independence and a strong sense of self do not equate to loneliness; quite the opposite, they pave the way for healthy, mutually beneficial relationships. Reclaiming your independence is especially vital if you want to build meaningful relationships with others as a true grown-up.

When you decide to change, you must take a leap of faith into the unknown. But keeping your end goals in view can motivate you: the fruits of successful transformation include discovering your hidden skills and abilities, cultivating fulfilling adult relationships, dissolving irrational fears, and realizing your long-cherished ambitions.

Establishing distance from your parent and gaining independence is not an act of rebellion or abandonment, but rather a proclamation of your self-worth. Their needs are not your responsibility, and their inability to help you build a strong sense of self does not mean you do not deserve to have it.

You can begin by taking small, manageable steps towards authentic change. Transforming yourself does not have to be radical or overwhelming. Start by nurturing independence in your daily life, beginning with making decisions on your own, and then trusting that they are right for you.

It may take time, but as much as you can, try to work on reclaiming your sense of independence and identity with excitement for the new life that awaits you.

11
Empathizing with engulfing parents

Finding the middle ground between protecting your child and encouraging their independence is one of the most challenging tasks of parenting. However, there are additional challenges for parents with compromised emotional boundaries. These parents can often become overbearing and controlling, projecting their own unfulfilled needs for love and connection onto their children. Even if they do not mean to, their co-dependent tendencies can cause them to traumatize their children.

Something does not feel quite right

Parents with engulfing empathy are not inherently bad people. However, it's important to recognize that, in some cases, their apparent kindness may underlie emotional challenges or unmet needs. They may appear compassionate on the surface and genuinely believe they are loving and caring. While their intentions may be sincere, their outward empathy often stems from a deep, unsatisfied need for love rather than a natural and spontaneous place. Their apparent kindness can have a neurotic and suffocating quality, which their children are acutely aware of.

Their actions are often driven by the desire to be seen as a 'good' and caring person, which means they can be particularly charming and flattering in social settings. They might also overestimate their ability to genuinely understand and empathize with others, leading them to take pride in their seemingly good intentions. This pride can result in a misguided belief that they are truly empathetic, when in reality, they may be projecting their feelings onto others. At times, this can make those who are close to them feel as though they are part of a narrative the parent has crafted, more a character in a story that may not fully reflect the shared reality.

By understanding their psychology, you can maintain compassion for them while also attending to your needs for boundary-setting and self-care. While understanding their psychology is important, it is equally crucial to prioritize your well-being and growth.

It can be challenging to empathize with them if you are still processing feelings of resentment, establishing your individuality, and working towards a healthy distance from them. Therefore, please be mindful that anything that has to do with empathizing, forgiving, and rebuilding a relationship with them is best done at a stage when you have healed from their chronic engulfment and feel solidly grounded in a renewed sense of self.

In this section, we aim to understand the minds of parents who have become dysregulated in empathy and boundaries. The insights we discuss provide a deeper understanding of their way of being. We also explore how we might help them integrate areas for growth and development, which can hopefully be beneficial to your family dynamic as a whole.

What makes them lose themselves

People with engulfing empathy are often preoccupied with the needs and emotions of others. This tendency can result from multiple factors, including innate temperament, an overactive nervous system or mirroring system, and early life conditioning.

Your parent might have experienced developmental trauma that demanded them to play the 'giver' or 'caregiver' role in the family. They may have had to take on chores and responsibilities that were too heavy for their age just to gain their parents' and siblings' love and approval. In this context, love became synonymous with selflessly giving to others, even if what they gave was not reciprocated.

Because they were groomed to put everyone else before themselves, they were never encouraged to express their feelings, so they internalized the message that doing so would make them appear 'too needy'. Through experience, they learned that they could only receive positive attention and affection if they made other people happy. As a result, they became lifelong over-giver and felt guilty whenever they focus on meeting their own needs.

They may not have been neglected physically, but they might have been neglected emotionally. As a coping mechanism, they hyper-focused on what was happening around them rather than on themselves so that they could project their needs outward and divert attention away from their trauma and pain.

During adolescence, when they should have been consolidating their identity, they lost themselves in the orbit of other people's energy and needs. This caused a halt in their psychological development, where they did not successfully individuate and only hinged their sense of self on serving others.

Sometimes, there may be an entirely unconscious and unintentional 'hidden agenda' behind their actions: they hope that by giving enough love and attention to others, they will receive the same in return. In other words, your parent has an underlying belief that if they are extremely empathic and helpful, others will eventually reciprocate. They are not being intentionally manipulative, they simply automatically give, and are not aware that they expect the world to function in the same way they do. Unfortunately, most of the time, those around them may not recognize the hidden message behind their generosity, which can reinforce their underlying belief that people are disappointing and that they are unworthy of love. This dynamic can create a cycle that inadvertently mirrors and perpetuates their childhood trauma that only they care about and others do not.

They might not realize it, but as their mind and body inevitably become fatigued from over-giving, they will break down one day. Suddenly, they are overcome by the feeling that they have sacrificed everything, but no one seems to be reciprocating to the same degree. This 'breaking point' can happen at any time and surprise them and those around them. When they finally burn out due to their own making, they may feel an unexpected surge of resentment and a compelling sense of entitlement. Suddenly, they swing from being subjugated to unreasonably demanding the time, affection, and attention of those close to them. This is ironic because, after identifying with the unrealistic archetype of the 'all-sacrificing parent' their entire life, when they burn out, they morph into martyrs and traumatize their children by being possessive, overbearing, and controlling.

Moving from engulfing empathy to real empathy

Parents with engulfing empathy often operate within their blind spots. While they may occasionally recognize the warning signs of burnout, they struggle to understand how their seemingly well-intended behaviours can negatively impact those around them.

Of course, despite their psychological blindspot, there is a genuinely loving and empathic person inside. If they can work through their trauma and establish healthier boundaries, they have the potential to make a real difference in their community, especially in a world that is becoming increasingly divided.

As their child, it is not your responsibility to change your parents' deeply ingrained behavioural patterns. However, if you can cultivate understanding and compassion for their struggles, you may be able to support them on their path to growth. By maintaining healthy boundaries and modelling self-care and emotional regulation, you can create a positive ripple effect within your family dynamic. Ultimately, if your co-dependent parent can break free from their lifelong dysfunctional patterns of being excessively other-focused, everyone in the family will benefit greatly.

The following are a few suggestions for what you can do to extend empathic support to them.

1 Helping them see their needs

Your parents' struggle with recognizing and addressing their own needs likely stems from their upbringing. The fear of becoming 'too much' for others is deeply ingrained, yet it is paradoxically paired with the unfulfilled yearning for love and connection.

Throughout their lives, they have wanted someone to intuit their needs and proactively care for them. Yet simultaneously, there is a fear of potential rejection if they were to openly acknowledge this longing. This internal struggle is so delicate and painful that, more often than not, they avoid contemplating this dilemma. Instead, they drown themselves in caretaking tasks or preoccupy their minds with concerns for others.

While helping your parent examine their subjugating behavioural pattern can be beneficial, it's crucial to proceed with care to avoid triggering their defences or shame.

Likely, your parents constantly feel under-appreciated, like a background hum that never quite goes away. Therefore, a good starting point is to express your understanding of how disheartening and frustrating it must be when their love is not reciprocated.

Start by encouraging them to embrace their basic needs for rest and self-care. In areas where self-neglect is evident, whether physical or otherwise, prompt them to contemplate steps for treating themselves with kindness, just like how they would treat a cherished friend. Often, it is easier for them to envision care and compassion for others, and from there, perhaps they can move on realizing that they, too, deserve such consideration.

2 Giving purposefully and with boundaries

Overly empathic people typically have a highly developed feeling function, but it may not be balanced by the skill of discernment. One thing that can help is for them to balance their innate empathy with the skill of critical judgement, which would enable them to continue honouring their inclination to give, but only with intelligence and thoughtful consideration.

Given their heightened sensitivity and inclination to absorb the emotions of others, it becomes essential for your parent to develop the skill of differentiating between their own feelings and those of the people around them. Then, they must learn to identify the responsibilities that genuinely belong to them and those that do not. Additionally, they should be mindful of the delicate balance between generosity and naivety, recognizing that the latter is not a virtue.

You might also remind them that just because they love giving does not mean they can assume that others will value their contributions. You can advise them to ask permission before offering help. Without directly confronting their pride, get them to wonder if they are truly indispensable in all the events and things they have committed. Is there work that they could delegate to other people? Could their efforts to help backfire? Can they ask for permission before offering their assistance? Then, see if you can bring them a new perspective. You could, for example, bring up the concept of 'love languages' and point out that perhaps, because everyone expresses and receives love in their unique way, the person receiving their acts of service and compliments does not want them in the way they give them. Alternatively, you can remind them that some people need more time to be ready to deal with their problems even with the best-helping hands. Some people may feel uneasy receiving help when they have not asked for it. Others may be offended or feel intruded upon.

They often do not realize how inappropriate some behaviours can be. You may find it surprising that what seems like common sense to you, such as understanding interpersonal boundaries or recognizing when certain flattery can come across as insincere or exaggerated, may be unfamiliar territory for them.

For these parents, growth and change involve finding a balance between their empathetic nature and developing discernment and critical thinking skills. By doing so, they can become more well-rounded individuals, capable of navigating emotional complexities without feeling overwhelmed and of respecting the boundaries of others.

3 Moving beyond repression

People with engulfing empathy often have a dysfunctional relationship with their own feelings of need. They've somehow come to believe that maintaining relationships in their lives necessitates the suppression of their own desires and always putting others first.

Being habitually self-suppressing, your parent may find being with their own emotions intimidating and unimaginable. It is unsettling for them to contemplate what they need or how they feel.

To nurture personal growth and foster genuine empathy for themselves, however, your parent must ultimately learn to redirect their attention inward and cultivate an awareness of their inner world. A simple yet impactful way you can encourage this shift is by sincerely asking them how they feel. Initially, they might provide default responses such as 'I'm fine' or 'I'm good'. Try to delve deeper into their emotions by expressing genuine interest beyond a generic 'How are you?' and encourage them to open up and explore more nuanced feelings. Convey through your words and actions that 'difficult' emotions, such as anger and disappointment, are welcome. Clarify that you don't categorize feelings as good or bad and that every emotional experience is valid and should be accepted. Emphasize that you want to hear their truth.

In the process of befriending one's feelings, some principles and practices from the Buddhist wisdom of mindfulness can be helpful. Given its popularity, there are abundant resources that you can introduce to your parent. By cultivating mindfulness, they can learn to accept and become more attuned to the full spectrum of feelings with equalized attention, without needing to hold onto some and run away from others.

If your parent can stop judging their feelings, they will also stop acting out in unconscious, dysfunctional ways, such as not expressing their wants and later punishing you for not mind-reading them, or engaging in other passive-aggressive behaviours. This shift could lead to more open and honest communication and more genuine relationships.

If your parent has reservations about anything that appears 'religious', there's no need to explicitly introduce Buddhism or even the concept of mindfulness. Instead, you can serve as an example by embodying it. In your conversations, maintain a neutral and receptive stance, use your body language to communicate openness and curiosity, and imagine yourself as a neutral observer of whatever arises. This approach aligns with the principles of right-brain-to-right-brain communication, which has been scientifically validated (Schore, 2008). By embodying mindfulness and maintaining a neutral and receptive stance, you can engage in a non-verbal exchange that resonates with your parent on a deeper level, gradually helping them internalize such wisdom and incorporate it into their life.

4 Relearning boundaries and saying 'No'

Your parent's boundaries were likely violated throughout their childhood, so it will take time for them to relearn what appropriate boundaries mean and look like.

You can support them in understanding that saying 'no' lovingly and respectfully does not have to result in tension and hostility. Let them know that saying no, setting limits, or maintaining emotional distance do not constitute rejection or abandonment.

After a lifetime of helping others, they probably feel exhausted and crave more self-care. You can encourage them to honour this need and start by establishing small, practical boundaries. For example, they can set aside specific times for rest by putting away their phone and making a point not to respond to any external requests.

You may also encourage them to experiment with solitude, even if only for brief periods. Emphasize that being alone does not automatically lead to loneliness. Help them see that the more they focus on and care for themselves, the more others will appreciate them. Although it may seem counterintuitive to them, maintaining appropriate distance between people can strengthen and deepen meaningful bonds.

5 Learning to be loved for who they are, not what they do

The most significant breakthrough would happen if your parent could reconnect with their authentic selves and cultivate self-love based on who they are, rather than solely on their actions for others. Ultimately, they might only feel secure in breaking free from their pattern of self-subjugation and over-empathizing once they realize that they can still be loved and valued even when they are not actively engaged in acts of service.

Unfortunately, the notion that they can be loved without constantly striving may have never occurred to them. They may not have recognized that they can be a source of joy and companionship simply by being themselves, rather than consistently striving to help and give.

Perhaps you can remind them of the immense value they bring through their mere presence and existence. Explicitly highlight their positive qualities, such as intuition, playfulness, a sense of humour, and a warm demeanour. If it feels authentic for you to do so, you can even praise their charisma, practical communication skills, remarkable loyalty, honesty, and willingness to make sacrifices for loved ones.

They are indeed great at connecting with people and serving others, but that does not have to define their entire identity. Encourage them to shift their focus inward and recognize who they are apart from their selflessness. For example, they may have a creative side that has been set aside for years. By directing their attention inward, they may be able to rediscover hidden talents and interests that bring them fulfilment and joy.

Ultimately, what will change things for your parent and the entire family is when they finally accept that they are loved simply for being themselves, not for what they do for others.

Managing relationships with parents with engulfing empathy

Dealing with overly giving and self-subjugating parents requires patience, understanding, and a gradual approach. A key aspect of supporting their growth involves deeply understanding their experiences while also modelling healthy behaviours such as setting boundaries, fostering authentic connections, and recognizing their inherent value. However, it's crucial to prioritize self-care throughout this process.

It can be tempting to become entangled in co-dependency and take on a 'rescue mission' to fix their dysfunctional patterns. Nonetheless, by maintaining intact boundaries and prioritizing your own well-being, you can provide the necessary support to your parents. Remember that self-care is essential not only for your own sake but also to ensure that you are in a position to truly help them.

Thankfully, as we have discussed in the last chapter, recovering from having an engulfing, overly empathic parent is very much doable. Once you have had time to recover from the effects of being over-suffocated your entire life, you will be able to relate to them as a mature adult instead of a helpless child who is stuck in an unhealthy, love-hate, push-pull dynamic.

12 Parenting on the empathy tightrope

So far, we have delved into the consequences that arise when we have imbalanced empathic energy. As parents, balancing empathic energy means striking an equilibrium between understanding and responding to our children's emotions while providing guidance and structure. It means neither overwhelming them with excessive coddling nor withholding the warmth they need to feel seen and understood. In this chapter, we shall discuss how we can achieve such a balance by drawing from the insights of Carl Jung and his concepts of the feminine and masculine aspects within ourselves.

Integrating masculine and feminine in parenting

In Carl Jung's theory, the animus represents the masculine functions in our psyches. It includes qualities such as assertiveness, logic, and independence. On the other hand, the anima symbolizes the feminine aspect, embodying traits like intuition and emotional sensitivity. Note that individuals can possess characteristics of both animus and anima, regardless of their sexuality or gender identity.

Archetypes are universal patterns in myths, stories, and religions across cultures. The mother archetype is characterized by traits such as caring for others, sensitivity and nurturing qualities, whereas the father archetype is linked to attributes like strength, protection, and guidance. In reality, we all have an inner father and an inner mother. However, depending on our temperament and societal influences, one archetype may dominate.

Representations of the sacred maternal archetype in popular culture and folk traditions show us how important feminine qualities are when it comes to bringing up a child. For instance, characters like Cinderella's benevolent fairy godmother symbolize nurturing presences offering warmth and comfort. Traditional myths and indigenous spiritualities likewise portray the divine mother, Mother Earth, as symbolic of bounty, fertility, and caring for her offspring. Mary, revered as the mother of Jesus in Christianity, represents compassion, devotion, and unconditional love. In Buddhism, Kwan Yin shows empathy, understanding, and unconditional love. These depictions mostly highlight qualities significant for children's socio-emotional growth. However, relying solely on feminine traits is not enough when it comes to parenting. To achieve a balance, we must also cultivate certain paternal guiding principles alongside maternal qualities.

The masculine function is closely linked to the ego and rational thinking. People with a dominant masculine function often show more analytical, logical, and objective personality traits. However, there is also a shadow side to this function. Many of us now recognize what is known as 'toxic masculinity' – the societal ideals of masculinity that prioritize physical strength, dominance, and heterosexuality at the expense of other qualities (Harrington, 2021). Toxic masculinity discourages emotional expression, suppresses feelings, and promotes aggression. In the context of fatherhood, it can limit emotional openness and hinder empathy and warmth.

For a perspective on constructive paternalistic values rather than toxic ones, we can look at some cultural representations of fatherhood. In Greek mythology, Zeus demonstrates authority, and protection, and imparts wisdom as king of the gods. He assumes the role of a strong figure responsible for maintaining order and providing guidance to his divine children. Similarly, in Disney's *The Lion King*, Mufasa serves as a strong and wise father figure to Simba and shows strong leadership, protective instinct, and the ability to offer wise guidance.

Regardless of your gender, by recognizing and integrating these archetypal aspects within yourself, you can achieve a more balanced empathic energy that is neither too harsh nor too lenient. As a parent, you have to tap into your animus qualities when making decisions, setting boundaries, and providing structure. This requires assertiveness, rational thinking, and the ability to take charge. Simultaneously, you also want to connect with your anima side and be empathetic, understanding, and emotionally present for your child.

By embracing the interplay between the animus and anima, you can have a harmonious equilibrium in your empathic energy. This balance allows you to navigate the challenges of parenthood with effectiveness and sensitivity.

The art of self-parenting

The principles of balance exemplified here have wide-ranging applications beyond the parent–child dynamic alone. They are also relevant in romantic partnerships, caregiver relationships, teacher–student connections, and professional interactions.

Most significantly, we must cultivate equilibrium within our own self-relationship. In adulthood, we in some sense become our own parents. Both self-parenting and parenting others involve harmonizing empathy and discipline, freedom, and structure. We shall treat ourselves with compassion as well as set healthy boundaries and maintain self-discipline. When we feel upset or anxious, we can tap into our inner nurturing side, like a caring mother, to comfort and reassure ourselves that everything will be alright. However, it is equally important to access our inner mentor, like a supportive father, who can guide us in learning from our experiences and finding a way forward.

Unfortunately, many of us find that instead of a loving and caring inner voice, we have a rigid and harsh inner voice. In the realm of psychoanalysis, the concept of the 'introjected harsh inner parent' is used to describe this critical and rejecting voice that stems from our memories of a parental figure who may have been abusive, narcissistic, or lacking in empathy towards us. This voice is often internalized from our interactions with a parent who exudes toxic masculinity.

On the other hand, a harsh inner voice can also emerge in response to an excessively permissive upbringing. Consider the scenario where someone grows up with parents who constantly shower them with praise for every action without providing enough opportunities for personal growth and challenges. As this person steps into the real world, typically during early adulthood, they may suddenly realize that their abilities and skills do not align with society's expectations. This realization can then trigger profound feelings of shame, anxiety, and even identity crises. Consequently, they may develop an inner voice that acts like a strict drill sergeant as a form of compensation. This inner voice relentlessly drives them to keep pace with their peers and compensate for the lack of healthy development and challenges experienced in their earlier years.

Self-parenting involves treating ourselves with the same love and care that we would offer to a young person whom we deeply care about. It requires us to take responsibility for our own lives and become the nurturing and supportive parents we may have wished for. As author Yong Kang Chan (2018) poignantly said: 'It's not enough to just heal the inner child. Our inner parent has to change, too.'

Reflective exercise: Balanced parenting and self-empathy

Take a moment to reflect on the following questions. Write your answers in a journal and consider how these insights can help you balance your parenting approach.

1 As you were growing up, who took on the roles traditionally associated with femininity and masculinity in your home? In modern times, it is not uncommon for fathers to fulfil nurturing and supportive functions while mothers take on the roles of guidance and discipline typically associated with fathers. How did these experiences shape your understanding of masculinity and femininity? Fatherhood/motherhood?
2 Did you have a role model? Someone you admired, looked up to, and aspired to become? Reflecting on your role models, what specific qualities or characteristics do you find most inspiring or aspirational? How can you incorporate these qualities into your own life?
3 Are there any religious, mythical, or archetypal figures that embody the qualities of a divine father or divine mother for you? How can you draw inspiration from their examples to enhance your self-nurturing and self-guidance?

Now, take a moment to reflect on your life as it stands today.

1 Do you need more discipline or motivation? Or do you push yourself too hard, to the point of burning out? Do you find yourself oscillating between these two extremes?
2 Can you learn to be more assertive, disciplined, and actively engage with the world around you? Is there room for growth in these areas?
3 Or would you benefit from practising self-compassion and patience and fostering more empathy towards yourself?
4 Do you find that you have weak energetic boundaries, often being drawn into the intense emotions of others? Can you distinguish between genuine empathy and co-dependency? How can you establish healthier boundaries and cultivate greater emotional autonomy?

Take a moment to reflect on the unmet needs, broken dreams, and expectations that stem from the absence or shortcomings of your own father or mother.

1 How can you release these burdens, find healing, and unburden yourself from past disappointments?
2 How can you provide better self-care and mother yourself more effectively than the mother you never had?
3 Similarly, in what specific ways can you offer yourself the guidance, structure, and protection that you may have missed from a father figure?
4 What steps can you take to balance self-discipline and self-compassion?

Interlude

The day I say 'no more'

A freedom declaration

Dear Father/Mother

I am deeply sorry for the pain you are enduring. Yet today, I must declare my freedom.

It is neither my responsibility to save you nor is it within my power to do so. I never intended to hurt you. I am simply doing what I must to survive in this world, striving to take responsibility for my one and only life.

I regret that my 'no' feels like rejection to you, that my pursuit of dreams seems like abandonment, and that my relationships outside our family appear as a betrayal. But your sadness, anger, and sorrow existed long before I came into this world. Despite my lifelong efforts, I cannot shield you from your misfortunes.

I have tried to calm you during your angry outbursts and breakdowns. When others hurt you, I protected and comforted you, doing everything in my power to please you. Yet, despite my efforts, I could achieve little because I was only a child.

All my life, I have tried again and again to imagine, create, maintain, and preserve the image of our 'happy' family.

But today is the day the lies must end.

Today, I declare:

I can no longer tolerate abuse –

Suddenly, I see it. It shocks me that after all these years, I am only now realizing the cycle of abuse.

Just because you appear calm one day does not mean I can completely relax and trust you. Part of me must remain ever vigilant, always on the lookout for your next outburst, breakdown, blame, or subtle attack.

Hyper-vigilance is the training I received from birth and the only way to protect myself.

From time to time, I am tempted to forget all my traumas and indulge in the fantasy that I have 'good parents'. By that, I do not mean perfect parents, but stable parents who can be a safe haven for me. Maybe I wish for parents more like those I see in my friends' homes, or perhaps like those I have seen on TV. But every time I do that, I open the door of my heart too wide, and my soul is torn out and thrown away.

I have no choice but to kill all hope. Hope is dangerous at this point. For I must stop tearing open my wound again and again so that it can finally heal.

Despair may be what will finally save my life.

Today, I declare:

I am saying no to control and co-dependence –

I am sorry you feel like a victim in this unpredictable, vicarious world.

But I can no longer live under your paranoia and control.

I can no longer allow you to disempower me, remove my independence and autonomy, and rob me of my only chance to grow in this world.

I understand that you do not see a line between you and me, but I am not an extension of you.

I do not live for you, and I cannot share every intimate detail of my life so that you can live through me.

I know my departure will take work.

I am sorry that you may not want me to go.

I am sorry that you feel you have lost the only person you could count on.

I am sorry that you feel like you are going to be lonely.

But that is not my responsibility, and I cannot make it up to you.

You can threaten in all sorts of subtle and explicit ways.

You can destroy your own life and blame it on me.

But I have thought about it repeatedly, and I know my conscience is clear.

I understand that you do not want distance between us, but I know with every fibre of my being how necessary it is. Unlike the confused child I once was, this time I KNOW I am right – a clear, unbroken boundary is necessary between us.

You can have your own life or not, but I must reclaim mine.

So please, let me go.

Today, I declare:

I am saying no to constant criticism and gaslighting –

Sometimes, I wonder if you hate me.

Or, if you regret bringing me into the world. You act as if you mourn every day for the freedom, independence, and big dreams you could have had. I am sorry you lived a life you did not choose for yourself, and I am sorry if it did not turn out the way you wanted. But it was not my choice to be born.

I choose my partner, my career, my sexual identity, and my self-definition. I choose where I live, where I work, and how I live my life.

I decline your opinion on any of the above.

Please let me live with dignity and pride. I will no longer allow your raised eyebrows, derogatory comments, and unsolicited advice to undermine my path.

In case one day you want to threaten me with an 'I told you so', I promise you right now:

I take full responsibility for the consequences of my decisions.

And I am responsible for how my story unfolds.

Please stop disempowering me.

I may never understand why you had felt the need to portray me as weak, strange, sick, and dysfunctional.

Perhaps, you did this to avoid facing your own demons.

But I cannot be the trash can of your psychic junk any more.

Stop disempowering me. I am not 'sick', 'too sensitive', or too fragile. I am robust, intelligent, capable, and independent.

Today, I declare:

I can no longer be your parent in this role reversal –

I came into this world after you. It was never supposed to be my job to save you from your misery. It was enough that you controlled, suffocated, and restricted me. I cannot remain your little helper, saviour or servant for the rest of my life.

Children are not born to be extensions, rescuers or advisors to their parents. They are not meant to become their parents' parents, confidants, or caretakers.

I understand you are the way you are because you have suffered. Sometimes, despite your control and attacks, I feel compassion for you.

With compassion, I see that I have somehow become the parent to the little child inside you who was abandoned. I am sorry that this happened to you. It must have hurt you deeply and made you afraid of what this world offers. When you say the cruellest, most hurtful, and vengeful things, when your own grief and abandonment trauma is triggered, I am learning to see that the little child inside you is protesting.

I am sorry that you are suffering, dear mom/dad. And I am sorry that I cannot put you out of your misery.

But from now on, you do not get to decide the meaning of my life. I am not here to live your unlived life, fulfil your unfulfilled fantasies, or compensate you for the sacrifices you have made.

I understand that you are sad and angry about this boundary I am drawing.

I know you see it as rejection, abandonment, and criticism.

I may not be able to change your mind, but as the adult in this relationship, I have to do what is best for both of us.

If I cannot say 'no' to you, I will never be free.

I can only empathize when your toxic abuse and control do not suffocate me.

So please, let me go.

That will allow me some space for empathy and compassion to grow. That is better for both of us.

To rise,

I remind myself daily that I am an adult, independent, and have my own full life. I no longer have to subject myself to the emotional puppet show. You are no longer a threat to me.

I will take my two-year-old self, who was sitting in the corner trembling and fearing for their life, and I will tell them everything is okay now. I am finally an adult and can stand on my own two feet.

I did not come into this world to heal your childhood wound.

I did not come into this world to live an unlived life, or to fulfil what you wanted for me.

I cannot compensate for what is lacking in your life – I cannot bring glory where you have failed; I cannot make up for your poverty with my abundance.

I will no longer allow guilt to keep me in chains.

All my life, every day, I have done my best to forgive you.

Even when I was little, I only tried to love, to seek love.

From today, I will remember this truth and free myself from a lifetime of guilt.

I owe you nothing.

But I owe myself a whole, living, independent life.

So please, let me go.

I let myself go.

PART 5

Empathy in love

13
Do you have an emotionally unavailable partner?

In an ideal world, we want our intimate relationships to be containers of love that draw us closer to those we care about, a safe space for shared emotions and deep understanding. But for some of us, the reality of a relationship is different. Instead of closeness, you encounter distance; instead of open hearts, you find emotional walls. Navigating a relationship with an emotionally distant partner is a painful and isolating experience, but you're not alone.

Imagine a partner who guards their inner world with an iron shield. When asked about their feelings, they offer superficial or one-word responses. Being with them leaves you perpetually longing for something deeper.

Why do some people get into a relationship but keep their partner at arm's length? Why are they the way they are? Why is there such a gap between what they say and what they do? Are they lying to you or themselves? These are questions that plague many who find themselves with an emotionally unavailable partner.

Identifying an emotionally distant partner can be challenging. Their actions and demeanour can leave you in increasing self-doubt, constantly wondering if you are imagining things or overreacting. This is especially the case if they have little self-awareness and deny their emotional numbness. Dismissing their own feelings may extend to undermining yours, leading to unintentional gaslighting, where their emotional coldness makes you feel like you are the one who's 'mad', too sensitive, or 'too much'.

Recognizing the behaviours of an emotionally unavailable partner can provide insights into your relationship dynamics. Let's start by exploring some common signs of emotional unavailability.

Recognizing an emotionally unavailable partner

One of the key indicators of emotional unavailability is the reluctance of your partner to share their feelings with you. When asked how they are feeling, they often respond with a curt 'fine' or 'okay', even when it is clear that things are not.

When you express your feelings, an emotionally distant partner may respond by offering solutions, intellectualizing the situation, or presenting you with a theory that rationalizes your emotions. They struggle to meet you in the depths of your feelings and resort to withdrawing or deflecting whenever they are faced with any kind of intense emotional expression.

An emotionally unavailable partner tends to withdraw at the slightest hint of conflict. Even with more positive emotions, like excitement, they struggle to meet you at the same level of intensity. Instead of embracing your enthusiasm, they try to tone it down, downplaying or discouraging your excitement. This inability to connect emotionally can leave you feeling as though you were 'emotionally abandoned' – left alone in your feeling world.

Another characteristic of emotional unavailability is the limited range of emotions. They may not even know when they are feeling common emotions such as anger or joy, let alone more nuanced emotions like 'ambivalence' or 'bittersweetness'. They might struggle to articulate feelings beyond saying they are doing 'good' or 'bad' on a given day.

Getting to know an emotionally unavailable partner, including their emotions and history, can be an arduous process. You may feel like you are the one putting in all the effort while they withdraw. For example, they may refrain from discussing their childhood, get defensive when asked, or say they do not remember anything. Even in the context of, say, couple's counselling, they may describe your relationship in factual terms rather than delving into the emotional realm.

To compensate for their emotional distance, they may shower you with physical affection and material gestures. Elaborate dates, expensive gifts, and other displays of outward affection may become their way of trying to bridge the emotional gap. However, when you express your need for emotional closeness instead of physical offerings, they may respond by accusing you of being ungrateful or demanding.

Being with an emotionally unavailable partner can be not only frustrating but also demoralizing. Their fear of intimacy and vulnerability can lead them to push you away, leaving you longing for the emotional closeness you crave. They may also make you feel guilty for desiring a deeper emotional connection than they are able or willing to provide.

There could be various causes for them becoming the way they are. Emotional unavailability is often related to an avoidant attachment style stemming from childhood experiences. They may have a history of feeling unsupported or rejected in past relationships, leading to a tendency to withdraw from emotional connection in order to protect themselves.

In the next chapter, we will dive deeper into why emotionally unavailable partners become the way they are. Through an empathetic lens, we will try to understand things from their perspective, looking into the depths of their fears and insecurities that they try so desperately to hide.

However, this journey is not solely about them, it is also about nurturing your empathic capacity and self-compassion. As you navigate the intricate dynamics of this relationship, you will cultivate patience, resilience, and a commitment to caring for your own needs. The aspiration should be that by fostering a deep understanding of your needs and establishing the necessary boundaries, you can empower yourself to navigate your relationship with grace and wisdom.

Quick scan: Are you with an emotionally unavailable partner?

Here is a list of statements that can help you identify potential signs of emotional unavailability. Reviewing how many or how much they resonate may help you gauge the degree to which and ways in which your partner is emotionally distancing themselves:

- Minimal emotional sharing: They often respond with non-committal answers like 'fine' or 'okay' when asked about their feelings, even if their mood seems to suggest otherwise.
- Limited emotional expression: They have a restricted emotional vocabulary and struggle to find words to express themselves.
- Unease with intense emotions: They seem uneasy or dismissive when you express intense emotions, especially negative ones. They might also try to 'tone down' your excitement and exuberance. This behaviour might extend to how they interact with your children.
- Overly analytical responses: They respond to emotional expressions by offering solutions, theorizing, or intellectualizing feelings, rather than empathizing.
- Feelings are invalidated: They may not explicitly say anything, but their non-verbal language can make you feel irrational, 'crazy', or overly sensitive for having strong reactions to certain situations. When you show strong emotions or have emotional ups and downs,

they joke about or criticize you for being 'crazy' or 'too emotional'.

- Rare intimacy initiation: Intimacy is rarely initiated, and when you're together, they seem eager to return to solitude, which can leave you feeling rejected.
- Evasive about personal history: They are reluctant to discuss their childhood, often defensively asserting it was fine or saying they have a poor memory of it. They are slow to open up about their emotions and past, often speaking about relationships in purely factual terms.
- Theoretical responses: When discussing personal matters, they frequently cite theories, books, or famous quotes instead of engaging on a personal level.
- Intellectualizing: In discussions about your experiences, they tend to analyze rather than empathize, often playing 'devil's advocate' or taking an opposing stance to appear objective.
- Fixation on problem-solving: They might trivialize your feelings, or get irritated and punish you for complaining when they are faced with problems that cannot be solved.
- Conflict avoidance: They shut down, become distant, or react defensively when faced with disagreements.
- Superficial Conversations: They may steer conversations away from deep or vulnerable topics, preferring to keep interactions light and surface-level, or intellectual debates and information-based exchange.
- You feel guilty for seeking more connection: You feel guilty for desiring a deeper emotional connection than what they are willing to provide.
- Reluctance to make future plans: They avoid making long-term plans or commitments, which can be a sign of emotional safeguarding.

14
Why they withdraw
Understanding emotional detachment

For those who fear intimacy, relationships can feel deeply unsettling. Opening up and allowing someone to truly know them requires immense courage, and it is a constant negotiation between the longing for connection and the instinct for self-preservation. This internal struggle often manifests as emotional withdrawal, leaving their partners feeling confused and hurt.

Being in a relationship with someone who is emotionally detached is a continuous learning process, and it can be disheartening at times. To avoid compassion burnout, remember this: their withdrawal is not a rejection of you. It's a defence mechanism, a shield built from past experiences. By delving into the origins of these fears, you can cultivate the emotional skills needed to approach the relationship with empathy for both yourself and them.

In this chapter, we will explore the underlying causes of emotional detachment. Later on, we will discuss practical strategies for navigating these complex dynamics.

Bio-temperament

Your partner's tendency towards emotional detachment could stem from various factors, including inherent personality traits and childhood experiences.

Some people naturally prioritize their 'thinking function' over their 'feeling function', focusing more on the external world than their inner emotions. This predisposition can lead to emotional detachment, although it's usually not the sole cause of significant withdrawal from intimacy.

Innate traits related to self-control might also play a role. A notable psychological study, the Marshmallow Experiment, illustrates this. In the experiment, children had to choose between eating one marshmallow immediately or waiting to receive a second marshmallow. Those who delayed gratification demonstrated greater impulse control. Such individuals often appear less excitable and may need more stimulation to feel engaged. While self-discipline is generally beneficial, excessive self-regulation can become compulsive, affecting emotional openness and connection.

In most cases, extreme rigidity and emotional detachment result from coping strategies or defence mechanisms. Despite a stoic exterior, your partner may not have been born emotionally detached. On the contrary, they might have been highly sensitive and emotionally vulnerable.

Research suggests that some people are naturally more sensitive and acutely attuned to interpersonal and environmental threats (Aron, 2013). To manage daily interpersonal stressors, such as childhood rejection or perceived abandonment, they might resort to withdrawal, detachment, and dissociation as coping mechanisms.

The connection between self-control and emotional detachment is complex and influenced by psychological, environmental, and individual factors. Bio-temperament alone does not inevitably lead to intimacy issues. However, when combined with environmental influences and traumatic experiences, these innate traits can contribute to dysfunctional patterns that hinder warmth and openness in relationships.

Childhood environment

In understanding your emotionally shut down partner, we shall also consider their early attachment experiences with their parents or primary caregivers. These formative relationships likely play a significant role in shaping their emotional responses and patterns of behaviour. While it is impossible to develop an exhaustive list of family situations that could contribute to emotional detachment, here are a few plausible scenarios:

Emotionally neglectful and intrusive parenting

During their early years, your partner may have had caregivers who were emotionally unavailable, cold, or neglectful. When they reached out for connection and support, they were often met with rejection or indifference. This repeated experience of being shut down and denied now significantly influences how they express their needs and seek connection.

Conversely, your partner might have become emotionally withdrawn not due to emotionally unavailable parents, but rather because of overly engulfing parenting. If they had one or both parents who continually invaded their boundaries, withdrawing into their own space may have been their only way to protect themselves. This behaviour was likely a necessary strategy to maintain some semblance of autonomy and individuality.

Some parents, burdened by their own trauma or psychological limitations, place an excessive focus on performance and exert significant pressure on their children. In these scenarios, the child may feel that they are valued only for their achievements and not for who they truly are. This intense emphasis on achievement fosters a deep-seated need to meet others' expectations and avoid disappointment. When combined with the belief that expressing emotions and needs equates to failure, it's understandable that your partner would strive to conceal their emotional vulnerabilities. As their sense of self-worth becomes intricately tied to their success, they might feel compelled to suppress any tender feelings that could interfere with their trajectory of achievement. Sadly, the cumulative impact of these experiences can lead to emotional detachment and a painful disconnection from their authentic self.

Emotionally cold and intrusive parenting are not mutually exclusive, and it is common for children of immature parents to experience both. Your partner, for example, might have been deprived of emotional attunement, responsiveness, and support. At the same time, their parents might have been overly controlling and intrusive, demanding high performance in areas like school, imposing strict boundaries, and restricting their freedom. These contrasting dynamics create a complex and challenging environment for a child. On one hand, they crave emotional connection and support from their parents; on the other, they fear the consequences of being overwhelmed or invaded. This dual experience can lead to confusion and ambivalence, setting the stage for a push-pull dynamic in their adult relationships. This dynamic often reflects their ongoing struggle to balance the need for intimacy with the fear of losing their autonomy, resulting in relationships that are marked by mixed signals and emotional volatility.

Object Relations Theory, developed by British psychoanalysts in the early to mid-twentieth century, emphasizes the crucial role of early relationships with caregivers in shaping one's later interpersonal dynamics. According to this theory, individuals like your partner, who felt emotionally drained or trapped by their parent's behaviour, may have developed certain 'internalized object relations' that caused them to do so. This means they unconsciously expect similar dynamics in all relationships, leading them to intensely protect themselves from potential pain and disappointment reminiscent of their past experiences.

Donald Winnicott, a prominent figure in Object Relations Theory, introduced the concepts of the 'True Self' and 'False Self'. The 'True Self' represents a child's authentic and spontaneous expression of feelings and desires. In contrast, the 'False Self' is a defensive facade, crafted to shield the true self from rejection or neglect by conforming to social expectations. This adaptation often results in adults who suppress their genuine emotions and struggle to form deep, authentic relationships.

Winnicott argues that the 'False Self' develops as a necessary adaptation to early experiences of emotional abandonment, neglect, or hostility from caregivers. If a child's true self is consistently met with disapproval or neglect, they learn to hide their authentic self to avoid further pain. This defence mechanism leads them to maintain emotional distance and self-reliance in adult relationships, even though they deeply desire to be understood and accepted.

These individuals often lose faith in the ability of others to meet their emotional needs, believing that reliance on others will only lead to disappointment. As a result, they may turn inward or seek fulfilment through intellectual, abstract, or spiritual pursuits, which often leave them feeling unfulfilled and perpetually incomplete.

This background explains why a partner might appear emotionally detached. They may harbour fears of dependency, believing that emotional investment will inevitably lead to disappointment. This protective stance, while it may have provided temporary relief during their childhood, results in a deep sense of emptiness and pervasive existential anxiety as they age. Despite their longing for love, their self-perception as unworthy prevents them from fully embracing and accepting love from others, leaving them isolated and disconnected from the benefits of genuine human connections.

Being innately different or neurodivergent

It is also possible that your partner learned to shut down their emotions as a defence mechanism against the painful experience of feeling out of place due to their inherent traits.

Even with responsible parents who did their best, a child who is inherently different from their family can face subtle yet profound challenges. These differences might include unique temperaments or neuro-atypical conditions such as autism or ADHD. Another factor, less frequently discussed, is when a person possesses higher-than-average intelligence.

Intelligence is not just about knowledge and it is not always linked to academic performance, it involves processing information, problem-solving, and critical thinking. If your partner has a higher-than-average IQ or intellectual capability compared to those around them, this might have posed challenges during their childhood.

Never feeling like anyone could share their interests, have engaging conversations, or match them in using more advanced vocabularies, they may have felt isolated and misunderstood for most of their lives. Such experiences during childhood can lead to a sense of themselves being 'too much' for others.

To compensate, they might have made themselves small and silent, doing their best not to inconvenience anyone with their excitability, curiosity, and intensity. They may have withdrawn from social interactions to protect themselves from potential judgement.

Over time, they may have come to rely solely on themselves for intellectual stimulation and emotional support. Accustomed to exploring interests independently, they seek intellectual challenges through books, research, or solitary pursuits, rather than human connections.

Understanding that your partner's high intellectual capacity is accompanied by a deep sense of loneliness and disconnection can offer you deeper insight into their world. Recognizing this can help you appreciate the complexities of their experiences and perhaps approach them with greater empathy and understanding.

Societal and cultural factors

Beyond the personal factors that contribute to emotional detachment, there are systemic and societal influences at play as well, particularly in modern Western society. Here are some critical factors to consider:

HEGEMONIC MASCULINITY IDEALS IN THE MODERN WORKPLACE

Whether consciously acknowledged or not, our lives are inevitably shaped by a cultural paradigm that upholds the ideals of hegemonic masculinity (Connell and Messerschmidt, 2005; Howson, 2006). These ideals, often perpetuated in many Western and Western-influenced societies, have a far-reaching impact on individuals of all genders. Attributes such as strength, independence, and resilience are highly esteemed.

In today's work environment, the dominant standards praise individuals who exhibit unwavering composure regardless of external conditions. Corporate culture lauds those who can maintain an unwavering facade of emotional detachment. Expressing emotions such as sadness, fear, or even exuberant joy may, unfortunately, be construed as signs of vulnerability or a lack of control.

By focusing exclusively on 'masculine' qualities such as strength and assertiveness, attributes like vulnerability, tenderness, and dependence are often stigmatized. These traits, which are inherently human and essential for building trust and fostering genuine relationships, are frequently marginalized.

This cultural emphasis on emotional suppression can lead to profound isolation. As individuals strive to conform to societal expectations, they may inadvertently stifle their innate capacity for empathy and connection with others. The persistent pressure to present oneself as unemotional and impervious can have unintended and detrimental consequences for collective mental health.

The sad reality is that the systemic valorization of emotional detachment not only affects individual well-being but also impacts how we interact as a society. It hinders the development of supportive, empathetic relationships that are crucial for both personal growth and community resilience.

TOXIC DATING CULTURE

Even in the realm of dating, societal pressure often compels individuals to maintain a facade of imperturbability and emotional control. This pressure is deeply rooted in the cultural emphasis on individualism, which highly values personal autonomy and self-reliance. While individualism can foster personal growth and independence, it can also promote a self-centred focus that may deter individuals from fully investing in deep relationships.

The fear of displaying vulnerability can make it challenging to open up emotionally and express true feelings, especially in the early stages of a relationship. Concerns about potential judgement, rejection, or being labelled as needy or dependent often lead to emotional detachment as a protective measure.

A clear indication of this phenomenon is the popularity of books like *The Game* and *Why Men Love Bitches*. These dating guides have become cultural touchstones by promoting strategies that advocate for a cold, hard-to-get demeanour. The underlying premise is that by presenting oneself as aloof or playing hard to get, individuals can create an aura of mystery and intrigue, supposedly boosting their appeal in the dating scene. In this context, emotional detachment is often mistaken for attractiveness, overshadowing the ability to express oneself authentically.

Unfortunately, the societal endorsement of these strategies contributes to a vicious cycle. It encourages people to prioritize maintaining a composed exterior over fostering genuine emotional connections, thereby reinforcing pre-existing patterns of emotional detachment. This cycle perpetuates loneliness and prevents the formation of fulfilling relationships, highlighting a significant disconnect between societal expectations and the human need for authentic emotional intimacy.

From understanding to action

In this chapter, we have explored some of the potential causes for emotional detachment in relationships, shedding light on various factors that contribute to this behaviour. Extending empathy involves acknowledging that your partner's emotional shutdown is likely not a conscious choice but rather a defence mechanism formed from past experiences of disappointment, abandonment, or trauma.

In the forthcoming chapters, we will delve deeper into identifying the specific traits and signs of emotional detachment. We will explore the underlying dynamics that fuel this behaviour and offer practical strategies to foster understanding and empathy within your relationship. By recognizing these signs and learning how to respond effectively, you can begin to create a more open, supportive, and connected relationship. This approach paves the way for both partners to feel seen, heard, and valued.

15
The many faces of emotional detachment

With some insight into the possible origins of emotional detachment, we will now delve further into the specific traits commonly observed in those who struggle with this trait. We will take a closer look at the fears and motivations behind the way they are, ranging from a strong need for control to a fear of dependency, and discuss how these traits affect their relationship with you.

Relating only through the head and not the heart

It can be challenging for someone who is emotionally detached to extend empathy 'on the spot'. This means that when you need comfort, they might not be able to provide it unless you explicitly state your request. For instance, when you are going through a conflict at work or with a friend, you might want your partner to side with you or empathize with your situation. However, they might miss your need for emotional support and instead offer a balanced analysis or even 'play devil's advocate', appearing to support the opposing side.

For many analytical thinkers, their critical thinking abilities can become an obsession with examining all nuances and complexities of any given subject. They feel compelled to consider multiple perspectives and gather sufficient information before committing to a stance. From their viewpoint, being completely logical is either the right or the only thing they can do. Despite their good intentions, their communication style can be hurtful and confusing. You likely want your partner to be more of an ally and a champion, rather than an objective judge.

Over time, your partner may realize that their well-intentioned attempts to empathize often lead to frustration. Consequently, they might lose confidence in their ability to relate, further worsening their tendency to withdraw and avoid emotional situations.

A detached presence

When it comes to life priorities, someone leaning towards emotional detachment may tend to put their intellectual interests above relational pursuits. The tension between desiring intimacy and preferring solitude is likely a lifelong ambivalence for your partner, and it will manifest itself most visibly in their intimate relationship with you. When they spend time with you, they may be physically present, but you can palpably feel their lack of enthusiasm. Even if they deny it, you sense that they cannot wait to return to their personal space, leaving you feeling disconnected and unimportant.

While they may maintain cordial interactions with acquaintances and fulfil their basic need for social interaction through group activities like being part of a sports team or a club, their approach to others often remains that of a distant observer or problem solver rather than an engaged friend or passionate partner.

Emotional detachment can also affect family dynamics, particularly when it comes to interacting with children. Your partner may struggle to fully engage in playful activities with your child because these interactions typically do not provide the same intellectual stimulation as their hobbies or projects. This inability to remain present can be palpably felt by your child, who, even if they cannot articulate it, may sense that they are somehow an inconvenience or hindrance. Unfortunately, such experiences can lead to your child feeling rejected or developing a sense of unworthiness.

Your partner's limitations also result in you having to shoulder most of the emotional nurturing responsibilities that come with being a parent. You may have to pay special attention to and be sensitive to your children's emotions, actively listening to what they have to say and being extra present for them. The combination of not having your own emotional needs met and the burden of extra parental responsibilities is exhausting and can lead to burnout for you.

Sticking to the known

Emotional detachment is often closely linked to a need for control, particularly over oneself and one's environment. Rather than exerting authority over others, emotionally detached people typically seek to master their surroundings, maintain a sense of security, and make things as predictable as possible. This often manifests as a strong inclination towards sticking to familiar territories and routines.

One way they increase predictability and a sense of control is by becoming an expert in a specific area. This might mean dedicating a lot of time and energy to mastering a particular subject, such as politics, science, fitness, or a niche hobby. On the outside, this intense focus might appear as mere shyness, nerdiness, workaholism or hyper-focus. However, at its core, their need to hyper-focus on a few niche subjects is often a defence mechanism designed to shield them from the unpredictable nature of human relationships.

When it comes to socializing, they may prefer familiar people over new encounters. Even if they are more extroverted than introverted, they may only want to be in familiar circles and maintain strict boundaries about whom they let in and out. They likely prefer to keep different areas of their life separate, such as not becoming close friends with work colleagues.

To maintain a sense of control, they might organize their life to minimize unexpected events or surprises. They may be content to stay within their comfort zone and daily routines, not eager to go on new adventures with you. This can be especially disheartening if you have a more exploratory spirit and are eager to embrace new experiences and opportunities. The differences in how you and your partner approach life can sometimes make it challenging to share the joy of novel experiences as a couple.

Fear of dependency

Emotional detachment is sometimes linked to an irrational fear of dependence. For example, your partner may be a workaholic with an unhealthy preoccupation with saving money and achieving financial security. They might feel excessive pressure to forge their path in life, separate themselves from their family, and refuse to accept assistance, no matter how much they need it.

They may mistakenly believe they can become entirely self-sufficient. While this belief gives them a false sense of power and control, it is not based in reality. Interdependence is a fact of life. From the farmers who grow our food to the truck drivers who deliver it, even the simplest activities in our daily lives require the assistance of many other people. The truth is that being overly counter-dependent is a defensive way of coping with deeply repressed anxiety.

Despite how painful it can be for you to be on the receiving end of their coldness, your partner's need to keep you at arm's length and manage their level of dependency does not stem from a lack of interest, love, or empathy. The truth is, they probably won't close relationships like everyone else but can only fully commit once they know they are safe.

Fear of mental intrusion

You might notice that your partner fears their thoughts and beliefs being overly influenced by others. This fear often extends beyond physical boundaries to include their mental and emotional space. It could be rooted in past experiences with overbearing parents who did not respect their autonomy.

Despite desiring mutual understanding and connection, they may fear losing their individuality in a relationship or conforming to 'groupthink'. To protect their inner world, they might be hesitant to openly share their thoughts and feelings, especially in the early stages of intimacy with you.

Healthy relationships involve a give-and-take dynamic where both partners occasionally shift their viewpoints or make compromises. However, for someone who fears external influence on their mind, any change in their stance can feel like a loss of control or autonomy. Consequently, they may be reluctant to reach agreements for the sake of preserving the relationship.

Your partner's strong critical thinking skills lead them to naturally question authority and resist anyone imposing their values on them. While this healthy scepticism can be a strength, it can also make them argumentative, cynical, and overly critical, as they rarely take things at face value.

Being defensive and quick to react to perceived threats to their autonomy can hinder their growth rather than help it. For instance, they might be overly argumentative and combative with their boss at work because they feel a need to resist any 'control' from authority figures.

Conflict avoidance

Your partner's emotional avoidance can hinder their ability to handle relationship conflicts healthily and productively. While they may feel comfortable engaging in intellectual debates, they might become overwhelmed when faced with emotional conflicts.

In an emotionally mature relationship, both parties ideally remain engaged in dialogue and work together to resolve issues, even during conflicts. However, a part of your partner – perhaps a younger, once-traumatized part – may panic and feel threatened when they witness you getting upset or angry. As a defence mechanism, they may withdraw when problems surface. This could manifest as refusing to communicate, ignoring messages, avoiding eye contact, or physically leaving the room.

If you pressure them for communication and engagement during these times, they might reach a breaking point and lash out in anger. Rather than resorting to physical violence, they are more likely to respond with intellectual, nihilistic aggression. For instance, they may become sarcastic, intellectually 'one-up' you, give back-handed criticisms, or humiliate you in a roundabout way.

Consider the role of alexithymia

Understanding your emotionally evasive partner may also involve considering the possibility of 'alexithymia'. This psychological condition is marked by difficulties in identifying and expressing emotions. People with alexithymia often experience a vague sense of emotional confusion and may find it challenging to comprehend or articulate their feelings effectively (Bagby and Taylor, 1997; Bagby et al., 1986).

Recognizing whether your partner might have alexithymia involves identifying specific traits related to their emotional processing, including:

- **Difficulty identifying feelings**: Individuals with alexithymia often struggle to distinguish between physical sensations and emotional states. This confusion can make it challenging for them to recognize and name their feelings.
- **Difficulty describing feelings**: Those with alexithymia typically lack the vocabulary necessary to describe their emotions. This can result in a communication gap where they cannot express what they are feeling in a way that others can understand.
- **Lack of fantasy life**: alexithymia is also associated with a reduced capacity for imaginative and creative thought. People with this condition struggle with forming vivid mental images or engaging in daydreams.
- **A tendency to focus on external events**: Rather than introspecting about their emotional states, individuals with alexithymia are more likely to direct their attention outward. They focus on concrete, external details of situations rather than on their internal feelings and emotional reactions.

Alexithymia has been substantiated through empirical research and is measurable using psychometric tools. One of the most widely recognized instruments for assessing alexithymia is the Toronto Alexithymia Scale (TAS-20) (Kooiman et al., 2002). This scale provides a reliable means to evaluate the extent of an individual's alexithymic traits through self-reported items that assess the core characteristics of the condition.

Research has explored various facets of alexithymia, including its etiology and its relationship with other psychological patterns. Various psychological theories and studies suggest that trauma may play a significant role in the development of alexithymia (McDougall, 1982; Pirlot and Corcos, 2012; Schimmenti and Caretti, 2018).

Alexithymia can significantly impact your partner's ability to connect with you on an emotional level. When they attempt to 'feel' and search within themselves, they hit a brick wall. This ongoing struggle creates a constant source of frustration for them. It may even evoke deep shame and despair as they recognize their inability to fulfil your needs.

Recognizing that your partner might be experiencing alexithymia can help you separate the person from the syndrome itself. As a couple, educating yourselves about this condition can be immensely helpful. Engaging in open, compassionate discussions about alexithymia, possibly with the support of a knowledgeable counsellor, can foster understanding and empathy among you. By developing a shared language and perspective, you can remove blame and shame from the equation and approach the issue as a joint challenge. This collaborative effort can strengthen your relationship despite the difficulties posed by alexithymia.

The 'overcontrol' trait

Thus far, we have extensively discussed your partner's need for autonomy and control. Researchers in psychology have identified a personality trait that may account for much of their psychological needs and behaviours: overcontrol.

Overcontrol is a temperament that represents a distinct way of engaging with the world, similar to other dispositions like introversion or extraversion. People inclined towards overcontrol come across as rule-following, organized, perfectionistic, practical, and meticulous.

Overcontrol should not be confused with being 'controlling' in the sense of wanting to exert power over others. Instead, it primarily relates to self-control. At the core of overcontrolling tendencies lies a deep-seated fear of losing control, which can be linked to unresolved issues surrounding power, trust, and vulnerability.

According to Dr Thomas Lynch (2018), people with over-control often struggle with the following:

1. **Receptivity and openness**: People with overcontrolling tendencies tend to avoid risks and are overly cautious. They are hyper-vigilant and are always scanning for potential threats. They may dismiss or ignore input and feedback from others.
2. **Flexible responding**: They have a strong need for structure and order, which leads them to create strict rules for themselves and others. While they are dutiful and responsible, they may become compulsively rigid and judge those who deviate from the rules.
3. **Emotional expression and awareness**: They struggle to express their emotions freely and may show emotions that do not align with the situation; for instance, they may smile when they are stressed or look flat even when they are joyful. They tend to downplay their distress and adopt a stoic or unemotional demeanour.
4. **Social connectedness and intimacy**: They tend to keep others at a distance, and may come across as distant and cold. However, on the inside, they may compare themselves to others and sometimes feel bitter without showing it.

Unfortunately, overcontrol tendencies are often overlooked because people who have them tend to be private and keep their emotions to themselves. They are also good at handling pain and distress, so they may not seek help even when lonely and depressed. Many people with overcontrolled tendencies have suffered for years without knowing that there is a name for what they have or that there are treatments or solutions for it.

Overcontrol and sexual intimacy

When someone has strong overcontrol tendencies, it can significantly impact their ability to experience pleasure and intimacy in various aspects of their life, including sex. This section explores how overcontrol manifests in sexual intimacy and offers insights into the challenges faced by both partners.

Individuals with overcontrol tendencies often fear being exposed emotionally. They believe that any sign of vulnerability can lead to pain or disappointment. Consequently, even if they are sexually aroused or desire their partner, they struggle to express it openly or spontaneously. This fear of being perceived as creepy, desperate, or needy inhibits their ability to engage fully in intimate moments.

People with overcontrol tendencies tend to view new situations and experiences as potential threats rather than opportunities for positive outcomes. Their fear of losing control when faced with the unknown makes them reluctant to try new techniques, and positions, or explore wild fantasies beyond the conventional. This cautious approach can limit the spontaneity and excitement that often enhance sexual intimacy.

Tom Murray (2022), an expert in the field, highlights that excessive mind-chatter is a significant obstacle for those with overcontrolling tendencies during sex. Their minds are constantly engaged and busy with competing thoughts, which prevents them from fully immersing themselves in the present moment. This mental distraction can be felt by their partner, as they may seem physically present but mentally and emotionally distant during intimate moments.

In short, if your partner has overcontrol tendencies, you may find them tight and rigid even regarding sex and intimacy.

Their fear of emotional exposure, fear of judgement, viewing new experiences as threats, and excessive thinking all act as barriers that prevent them from being vulnerable, spontaneous, and present. Understanding these challenges can hopefully help you navigate intimacy with them with greater empathy and patience.

Closing thoughts: The love–hate paradox in the emotionally anorexic

It may not make sense to you at first – what could be the reason for a partner to form a relationship while remaining so distant from you? Why would they approach you and then withdraw as soon as love blooms?

If you can gain some insights into their lifelong, perennial dilemma of wanting love but fearing it, as well as their tendency to deprive themselves of the nourishment of love, you may have a deeper understanding of such perplexing behaviours.

Imagine a person whose heart has been shattered by pain and trauma, leaving them feeling like a mere shadow of their full self. The wounds may have come from a loved one's betrayal or the pain of witnessing a broken relationship as a child.

They had no choice back then, as a young and vulnerable person, but to shrink their emotional needs and withdraw from the warmth of close relationships, essentially building a fortress around their heart.

This is what we can call 'emotional anorexia', a desolate state of being where someone starves themselves of emotional intimacy and closeness. It is a heartbreaking pattern of behaviour akin to medical anorexia nervosa, where people limit their food intake to an extreme degree. Except in emotional anorexia, someone is depriving themselves of emotional nourishment. Even when they deeply want connection, their fears hold them back. They cannot help but become trapped in a cycle of isolation, unable to reach out to others for fear of being hurt and to connect with their own emotions for fear of losing control.

For all of us, the paradox of love lies in its inherent risk and vulnerability, but this struggle is particularly salient for those who struggle with such fear of attachment. For them, closeness triggers feelings of discomfort, anxiety, and even unconscious anger. As they begin to fall for someone, trust someone, or feel vulnerable in a relationship, some of them become so fearful that they start to resent having fallen in love. This push-pull dynamic may be mild initially but gradually intensify as closeness escalates. As a result, they may engage in behaviours that confuse themselves and others, such as reaching out for connection in small ways but then quickly retreating into their shell, leaving you feeling increasingly confused and even rejected.

Your partner is caught in a profound existential conflict: they deeply desire intimacy, yet they are simultaneously terrified of it. At their core, they yearn for the companionship, love, and understanding that a relationship offers. They want to be seen and heard, to feel connected and valued. However, they also fear the vulnerability that comes with such openness. They are wary of exposing the carefully guarded corners of their inner life, anxious about the potential pain and disappointment that might follow. This duality defines a significant aspect of their existence – they spend their lives longing for closeness while instinctively recoiling from it.

Emotional detachment in your partner can often be traced back to a profound fear of their vulnerability. Despite their outward appearance of stoicism and coldness, the prospect of emotional pain or betrayal from intimate relationships terrifies them. They fear that such emotional injuries might be something they cannot recover from.

This might come as a surprise, considering their usual demeanour. In many areas of life, such as their professional environment, they might handle adversity with apparent serenity. Criticism from superiors, financial setbacks, or other professional challenges often seem to leave them unfazed. Similarly, in their personal lives, they might move from one relationship to another, or engage in multiple one-night stands, showing no outward signs of distress or emotional disturbance even in the face of interpersonal conflicts.

Yet, things are different when they truly find and commit to someone they fall in love with. However much they deny it to themselves, deep down they fear that they will not be able to recover if that person abandons, betrays, or disappoints them. So even if they adore you and enjoy being with you, they keep their distance. Moreover, when you get too close, they have a variety of subtle and not-so-subtle manoeuvres designed to push you away.

Their tactics for pushing you away can be conscious or unconscious, subtle or obvious. They may create physical distance when intimacy grows by avoiding physical contact, such as holding hands or hugging. Alternatively, they abruptly become unresponsive, either by failing to respond to messages or calls or reacting slowly. They may also send contradictory signals, such as saying they want to spend time together but then cancelling plans. They may even leave without warning or explanation when they are particularly triggered. Another way to push you away is to pick fights, find reasons to dismiss you, criticize you for being clingy or 'wanting too much', use work or other 'projects' to justify their emotional distance, or keep conversations superficial and avoid deep emotional topics.

At first glance, their hesitancy to commit might seem like a protective measure to guard their privacy and emotional space. However, the underlying issue is once again their profound sense of helplessness towards life. This aversion to commitment is pervasive, affecting not just relationships but also other areas of their life, such as career opportunities or personal goals, which they might avoid pursuing due to a belief that success is unattainable.

By choosing not to commit, they shield themselves against a deep-seated sense of inadequacy – if they never fully engage, they can never disappoint. If they never pursue their desires, they cannot face rejection.

The desire to be seen, heard, and loved is fundamentally human. Sadly, for your partner, even their longing to receive love may be suppressed by a deep-rooted belief in their unworthiness.

Despite these challenges, your relationship holds significant potential for growth. The fact that they have chosen to be with you shows that a part of them is eager to change, to embrace love and life more fully. Keeping this in mind can provide the strength needed to navigate through relationship difficulties and remain resilient.

In the next chapter, we will explore how you, as the person closest to them, can harness the power of deep empathy to assist them in making positive changes.

16
Bridging the gap with an emotionally distant partner

Having an emotionally avoidant partner can be confusing and painful. When your emotional needs are unmet, it's easy to see their coldness as a personal rejection or a lack of love and commitment. While your hurt feelings are understandable, they may hinder your empathy and push you further apart.

In the last chapter, we explored the experiences or traits that might contribute to your partner's emotional shutdown. For example, they may have had invasive or boundary-disrespecting parents, leading to a fear of being controlled. Alternatively, neglectful or absent parents might have left them without a model for giving comfort and love. If they are neurodivergent or have above-average intelligence, they may have felt out of place in their family or community, retreating into their intellect for safety and comfort.

In other words, your partner's emotional detachment could stem from a fear of vulnerability, hurt, and rejection. To overcome this fear, they need to develop self-trust, trust in others, and the ability to experience deep emotions. This process takes time and must unfold at their own pace. However, it does not mean you cannot play a part in supporting the process. In this chapter, we will explore how, as their most intimate partner, you can leverage the power of empathy to connect with them.

How to support an emotionally distant partner

Meeting them halfway

Since intellectualism is their primary language, 'meeting them where they are' can help create a safe space for them to open up. Demonstrating that you can hold your own intellectually is a valued quality, but it doesn't mean you have to outsmart your partner. Instead, show curiosity about various subjects and engage in healthy intellectual debates without taking things personally.

They may not feel comfortable discussing emotionally delicate subjects, especially those touching on past hurts and family dynamics. To navigate this, start with more surface-level, intellectual discussions on topics like childhood wounds and complex trauma. Even if your partner initially talks about these issues in a detached, unemotional manner, it can still serve as a valuable starting point.

Perhaps you can facilitate these conversations by sharing articles, books, or research. Engaging in philosophical discussions about emotions and relationships might also be appealing to them. These intellectual explorations can help enhance their inner understanding and spark curiosity about their own emotional processes. Gradually, this increased awareness and curiosity can pave the way for deeper emotional engagement and future healing opportunities.

Ultimately, however, there is a difference between rationalizing and feeling feelings. At some point, you can let them know when their intellectualization is getting out of hand and blocking them from their own life. You can express the dissonance and unease you feel when you witness them talk about seemingly traumatic issues in a cold, unemotional way. Aim to sound as non-judgemental as possible, and focus on expressing your desire to connect heart-to-heart and the frustration of not being able to emotionally 'reach' the person you love, rather than blaming them for not being in touch with their emotions.

Noting their emotional window of tolerance

The 'window of tolerance' is a psychological concept that describes the optimal zone of arousal where a person can function effectively without feeling overwhelmed or emotionally shut down. It represents the amount of stress or emotional stimulation that an individual can handle comfortably. When someone steps outside of this window, they become emotionally dysregulated, which might manifest as panic, rage or dissociation.

You can think of it as a thermostat for emotional heat. Just as a thermostat regulates the temperature to keep it within a comfortable range, the window of tolerance helps to manage emotional responses to keep them within a manageable range.

For your partner, their window of tolerance for extreme emotions may be narrow. Due to their history, they may interpret your attempts to seek emotional contact or increase intimacy as an intrusion. When this happens, they can respond in one of two ways: either by entering a state of hyper-arousal, becoming highly anxious and entering fight-or-flight mode, or by dissociating from their own body and mind, entering a state of internal shut-down.

When dealing with situations or topics that have the potential to trigger them, be attuned to signs that indicate they are approaching the limit of their window of tolerance. Observing their facial expressions, body language and eye movements can provide valuable insights. For example, you might notice rapid speech, a wide-eyed and frozen expression, shallow breathing, or physical trembling. If dissociation is their default response, you may see signs such as a vacant look, dimmed eyes, slurred speech, or a general sense of collapse in their posture and energy levels. These signs suggest a retreat inward and a disconnection from the present moment.

Recognizing these signals allows you to understand when to pause or change the course of the conversation. This consideration can prevent you from going too far and help maintain a safe relational space.

Although it can be tempting to push, gentleness and patience are key to helping someone open up. Even during their most withdrawn or disconnected moments, try to refrain from adding demands or questioning them. Instead, provide a quiet, reassuring presence, reminding them that you are there as an ally.

Not colluding with denial

For someone who has tended to intellectualize and suppress feelings, emotional inhibition and dismissing feelings may function almost like an automatic reflex – a lifelong habit triggered without conscious thought. If you are not mindful, it is easy to slip into reinforcing this inhibition and minimizing tendencies without realizing it. For instance, when they discuss challenging or painful experiences, they might downplay their feelings with phrases like, 'There are people who have it worse', 'That's just how life is', or 'Everyone goes through similar things.' While it might feel natural to agree with these seemingly benign statements, doing so can inadvertently encourage them to continue avoiding and minimizing their emotions.

Instead of endorsing these self-dismissive statements, you can encourage them to explore their emotions further. For example, when they reveal vulnerabilities, responses like 'Your feelings make a lot of sense' or 'I can understand why you'd feel that way' can be affirming.

At times, demonstrating spontaneous and natural emotional reactions yourself can be a powerful tool in helping your partner feel more comfortable with their own expressions. For instance, when they share something upsetting, you might express genuine empathy by saying, 'I feel frustrated when I hear that' or 'I am furious on your behalf'. By openly displaying your authentic feelings, you communicate that any emotion is valid and acceptable, modelling how to express them directly.

Being an empathic person, it can be difficult to see someone you care about in distress without jumping in to offer solutions. If you tend to be a natural 'problem-solver', remember that this might not be what the other person needs at the moment. Unless your partner specifically requests help, they likely are not asking for practical suggestions. Often, explicitly showing them empathy can be just as crucial, if not more so, than immediate solutions. During these times, techniques such as paraphrasing what your partner has said to ensure understanding, or validating their feelings, can be incredibly supportive. In contrast, telling them how they should feel or offering unsolicited practical advice might come across as invalidating or condescending. By focusing on listening and validating, you create a supportive environment where your partner can feel truly heard and understood.

Showing appreciation

Love is a multifaceted concept that is understood and expressed differently by each person. While some people show their love through physical touch, gift-giving, or compliments, others may do so in more subtle and nuanced ways. If you and your partner have very different 'love languages', it is understandable that you might feel unloved and let down.

Sometimes, you may need to make an extra effort to recognize the subtle signs that reveal your partner's true feelings for you. It could be how they listen when you speak, the small gestures of kindness they show, or their unwavering support during challenging times. These are all meaningful indications of their affection, even if they struggle to articulate it.

Likewise, you can learn to show your love in a way they can receive it. Your partner may not enjoy small talk, but they may engage more enthusiastically if you invite them to share their critical views on a social issue or their unique perspective on a complex problem. Demonstrating genuine curiosity about their thoughts can make them feel valued and appreciated.

Occasionally, it may be beneficial to explicitly tell your partner that you value their insights and enjoy hearing their thoughts. Saying things like, 'I appreciate your wisdom and the way you see things', or 'Your thoughts always make me think in new ways', can affirm their intellectual contributions. Over time, this positive reinforcement and the resultant emotional safety can encourage them to share more freely, helping them gradually reveal more of their inner world.

Respecting their pace and rhythm

Repeatedly, we have stressed how much respecting your partner's unique pace and innate rhythm is crucial. Feeling vulnerable may lead them to regress at times, becoming defensive and resorting to greater emotional detachment than before. While the temptation is to seek more attachment and confirmation of your connection when they push you away, counterintuitively, giving them space can bring you closer.

For example, if your partner is feeling down, they might not be ready for a direct conversation or to receive overt expressions of sympathy. Instead of insisting on immediate dialogue, subtle gestures can serve as powerful forms of support. Leaving a thoughtful note, selecting a book you believe they would appreciate, or simply placing a cup of coffee at their door can show your respect for their need for personal space. If they are comfortable with physical contact, gentle gestures such as holding hands or a reassuring touch on the shoulder can also be significant yet unobtrusive ways to show you care.

Even during the times when they must withdraw, try not to become disheartened. Keep in mind that, despite their apprehension about intimacy, a part of them does long for it, they just need time to slowly take it in.

Your needs matter, too

When you are trying to encourage an emotionally distant partner to open up, know that the progress is likely not linear. Even when you believe you are making good progress in deepening your connection, you might experience moments where they suddenly withdraw into their idealizations, fantasy world or individual pursuits. When they defensively retreat, reopening their emotional world may seem impossible. During these moments, it is natural for you to feel sadness, frustration, grief, and resentment. *In the midst of all this, it is most critical to extend empathy not only to your partner but also to yourself.*

Many individuals who grew up with emotionally detached or absent parents may, whether consciously or subconsciously, find themselves drawn to partners who show similar traits. In psychology, this tendency is known as 'repetition compulsion'. This is how our inner child tries to get our needs met – we repeat our stories by picking people who behave in familiar ways, but unconsciously we try to change the narrative and hope for a different outcome. Repetition compulsion is very common, but often it leads to more hurt and even re-traumatization.

When your partner responds in a way that feels dismissive or rejecting, it can trigger the same feelings of abandonment that you experienced in your childhood. Their lack of empathy expression can reinforce the belief that you are undeserving of love or attention or that your feelings are not important.

Helping your emotionally evasive partner open up is a meaningful task, but it can be draining. Thus, it's crucial to set and prioritize healthy boundaries for your emotional well-being. Here are some steps and reminders for taking care of your own needs while in a relationship with an avoidant partner:

Grieving what is not there

When we think of grief, most of us immediately associate it with explicit losses, such as the death of a loved one or a pet. However, what we rarely talk about is 'unacknowledged grief' or disenfranchized grief – grieving an invisible loss that society does not recognize or validate.

Grief can stretch far beyond the physical. It can be about mourning a dream that never came to be, the loss of what you hoped the future might hold, or the painful realization that someone close to you isn't emotionally there, even though they are right beside you. One poignant example is being in a relationship where your emotional needs are not met.

When your intimate partner fails to meet your emotional needs and the person you had envisioned them to be doesn't align with who they are, you can find yourself on a grieving journey of disappointment, sadness, and anger. It is indeed disheartening to come to terms with the fact that the person you chose to be with does not quite match what you had thought. Perhaps they have changed, or you did not see their detachment, avoidance, or shadow sides at the start.

Grappling with the loss of what could have been – this kind of grief is subtle and often goes unspoken, but it is real. Be kind to yourself and allow yourself to feel disappointed. It is okay to experience your feelings fully without fighting them.

Regardless of what has happened, even if you discover that you've fallen into a pattern of 'trauma bonding' with an emotionally detached partner, try not to blame yourself for how things unfolded. Life is a series of experiments, and you can be sure that in each moment, you made the best decision possible with the information and resources you had at the time.

Being honest with yourself about the limitations of what your partner can provide and then grieving what is not there allows you to adjust your expectations realistically. This does not necessarily mean lowering your standards but aligning your expectations with reality.

By confronting and embracing grief, you open yourself up to courage and clarity, as well as the possibility of finding a path forward, be it within this relationship or outside it.

Consider branching out

Trying to get all your emotional needs met in your intimate relationship, particularly when you value deep connections and are highly sensitive, can feel impossible. In such cases, it is entirely reasonable to explore external sources to meet your needs.

Taking a clear-eyed look at the reality of your relationship – what it is and what it isn't – can be both challenging and transformative. This honest assessment is not about placing blame but reconciling with reality and taking assertive actions to better your lives.

First, identify specific areas where your emotional needs are not being met in this relationship. For example, you might long for the feeling of having someone consistently on your side, or you might desire a deeper spiritual connection. Decide if these issues stem from changeable circumstances or fundamental differences in personality or values. Consider whether these gaps can be bridged through mutual growth, improved communication or couples counselling.

Then, you might want to reflect on whether some of your needs can be met outside the relationship. If you and your partner are stuck in the pattern of spending too much time together, it can be helpful to expand your social circle without your partner and connect with people who share your passions and values. Sometimes, what we expect from a partner can be found through other channels such as spiritual pursuits, solitude, books, and hobbies.

At first, you may worry that 'branching out' means giving up on your partner or betraying your relationship. That is not the case. On the contrary, by focusing on meeting your own emotional needs, your relationship will likely improve and become more sustainable and fulfilling.

But ultimately, branching out is more than finding people to hang out with or share interests. It is about actively looking for spaces and connections where you can find what is missing in your relationship so you can have a fuller life and not feel compromised and oppressed.

Reclaiming your right to feel and express

If you often find yourself being overly-accommodating of others and tend to be self-sacrificing, especially if this pattern has been ingrained in you from childhood or due to your family dynamics, you may want to check if you have been sidelining your own needs in this relationship. For example, you might have noticed your partner's discomfort with high emotions and conflicts and, to avoid triggering them, held back on expressing your exuberance, frustrations, or needs. However, a healthy relationship requires balance, it should not be about catering to one partner's preferences and comfort. Your emotional needs for connection and bonding are equally important.

Even if expressing yourself feels challenging, and you may question whether it is worth the effort, ignoring the problem can lead to resentment building up and jeopardize your relationship. Thus, if you are committed to making the relationship work, you might have to learn to persist in open communication and work towards getting your needs met.

You can initiate this process by explicitly telling them about your desire for greater emotional intimacy and connection. Try to do so in a non-confrontational and non-judgemental way, using 'I' statements to focus on your needs rather than what they are not doing.

Considering that they may have had limited exposure to empathic responses throughout their life, it is entirely acceptable, and even beneficial, to explicitly describe what empathy means to you in real-life scenarios. For instance, you can say, 'For me, when I am going through tough times, I do not want you to analyze the situation. I only want you to be there and listen to me.' Or, you may say something like, 'It means a lot to me when you simply hold my hand when I am stressed.'

Your partner may need time and space to process and respond to your requests. They might also need to work through their aversion to having demands placed on them and even their shame and guilt of being unable to meet your needs. But these are themes on their growth journey rather than something you can directly help with. So after you have expressed your needs, be as patient as you can and do not push any further. Giving them the space to process what they would like to do would probably be the most loving thing you can do.

Becoming your own best friend

While it is reasonable to expect a certain level of emotional validation from your partner, when you are with someone emotionally detached, you must also reckon with the reality that they may not be able to consistently fulfil this need. Ultimately, and as a part of your own growth, you have to take matters into your own hands and nurture and tend to your inner child's needs. In essence, you can take this as a personal-development opportunity for you to become your own best ally.

To break free from the cycle of disappointment and blame, whether it is directed at your partner or yourself for feeling 'needy', you can learn to recognize and validate your own emotions. Your feelings are intrinsically valid, regardless of whether they seem 'logical', recognized, or are approved by others. A feeling is a feeling and does not require justification.

For instance, you are allowed to feel angry even if others think you might be 'overreacting' or even when you cannot explain the reason behind it. Feeling angry also does not mean you are getting aggressive or blaming someone; you can simply allow this raw emotion to exist and eventually leave your system. Similarly, feeling sadness is valid. Just because there are always 'worse things happening out there in the world', your sorrow is not any less valid than any other one. As much as possible, learn to self-validate, and treat yourself as you would with a good friend. This is a practice of embracing your emotions without subjecting them to any external or internal scrutiny, and knowing that you do not always need to know 'why' you are feeling a feeling for it to be felt fully.

Many of us may not be fully aware, but we often have an internal dialogue that runs through our minds. When this inner dialogue becomes especially harsh or critical, we call it our 'inner critic'. In learning to become your own best friend, becoming conscious of and directing your self-talk can be beneficial. Try to intentionally practise speaking to yourself with kindness, compassion, and empathy. Here are some examples of things you can say to yourself when you are feeling frustrated by your relationship:

- 'It is not my fault that my partner is emotionally avoidant. It is something they need to work on, and I cannot control their actions or feelings.'
- 'My yearning to be with someone who can communicate openly and honestly with me is legitimate. It is okay to admit that my needs are not met in this relationship.'
- 'I am allowed to have my feelings and reactions to my partner's behaviour. It is okay to feel hurt, disappointed, or frustrated.'

- 'With or without their company, I can focus on self-care and engage in activities that bring me joy and fulfilment.'
- 'I cannot change my partner, but I can work on how I respond to their behaviours.'
- 'It's okay to seek support, even when few have supported me in the past.'
- 'I can choose to take care of myself. I will always have my own back.'
- 'I am worthy of love and respect. No one but me can define my worth as a person.'
- 'I am learning and growing from this experience, regardless of the outcome.'

Finding closeness

Navigating a relationship with an emotionally distant partner often feels like riding an emotional roller coaster, where you swing between hope and disappointment. This exhausting dynamic, even when it involves their push-pull behaviours and the tendency to withdraw, does not necessarily reflect a lack of love. To the contrary, it might mean that they are becoming attached and are thus feeling frightened and needing to push you away. Despite their cold and distant demeanour, your partner may be deeply sensitive on the inside. By seeing through their tough exterior into their tenderness, you are in a unique position to build a deep connection with them that would flourish and nourish you both deeply.

However, ultimately you do not want to sacrifice your well-being just to salvage the relationship. If you have tried to express your needs, and they continue to be overlooked, or if your mental health is deteriorating, you must take care of yourself first. After all, you cannot single-handedly change someone unwilling to grow alongside you.

For your partner to break the pattern of inhibition and distancing, they must eventually understand that vulnerability and emotional intimacy are not signs of weakness but manifestations of strength. Although it is not healthy to try to change another person, if through empathy you can embark on this journey of healing and practising empathy together, it can become a profoundly intimate and meaningful quest.

PART 6

Empathy at Work

17
Working for a critical and demanding manager

There are many kinds of bullies in the workplace. Some bullies fit a more typical profile. From a distance, you can tell they are bullies because of how harsh, arrogant, and power-hungry they come across.

However, there are also subtler forms of bullying. Often, these bullies are in positions of authority and rationalize their abusive behaviour by claiming to uphold fairness, high standards, and the common good. They are not typically 'sociopathic' in that they do not deliberately seek to cause harm, and they may not be aware of the negative effects their actions have on others. Nonetheless, simply by acting in accordance with what they believe to be right, they inadvertently compromise the self-esteem and mental well-being of those around them.

In this chapter, we will look at the dynamics of bullying that arise from highly critical and demanding managers. Although their intentions may be good, these managers often project their inner anxieties, such as a fear of failure, onto their employees. As a consequence, their behaviour can manifest as bullying, whether intentional or not.

The covert workplace bully

Bullying can take many forms. Some of the most recognizable include direct threats to physical safety, verbal abuse, and sexual harassment. However, more covert forms of bullying, though less obvious at first, can be equally if not more damaging over time. These subtler tactics include constant undermining, unreasonable demands, spreading rumours, denying opportunities, excessive micromanagement, and persistent nitpicking (Einarsen, 1999). This chapter specifically addresses these latter forms of bullying as they relate to the behaviour of highly critical and demanding bosses in the workplace.

Signs that you are working for a highly critical, demanding boss

If you suspect that you might be working for a highly demanding and critical manager, the following checklist can help you assess the situation. Look for these signs to determine if your boss fits this description:

- Does your manager frequently criticize your work, often without sufficiently acknowledging your efforts?
- Does your manager rarely, if ever, give praise or recognize your achievements, regardless of the effort and quality of your work?
- Does your manager often speak in a critical or condescending tone without understanding the impact on others?
- Is your manager excessively controlling or involved in minute details of your work, making it difficult for you to make decisions independently?
- Does your manager find it difficult to delegate tasks, instead maintaining control by giving overly detailed instructions, requiring frequent updates, and intervening constantly?
- Does your manager often redo tasks completed by others, complain about being overburdened, and blame others for inefficiencies, when in reality, it is them who struggle to relinquish control?

- Are the expectations set by your manager almost impossible to meet, often leaving you perpetually feeling inadequate or like a failure?
- Does your manager exhibit a 'my way or the highway' approach, often justified by a purported aim to achieve the 'greater good'?
- Does your manager set exceptionally high standards and remain inflexible, even when others point out these standards are unreasonable?
- Does your manager show a strong sense of right and wrong, have a black-and-white thinking style, and favour rigid, hierarchical structures?
- While not overtly hostile, do their body language, tone, and demeanour create a subtly threatening atmosphere and unease?
- Do they gossip about your colleague in front of you and behind their back?
- Does your manager frequently appear stressed, frustrated, and dissatisfied?
- Does their leadership style tend to discourage and demoralize team members, leading to high turnover rates?
- Do they seldom exhibit humour and generally contribute to a tense atmosphere?
- Does your manager demand exhaustive research and planning before any decision, even to the point of endlessly delaying the decision point beyond reason?
- Does your manager prioritize quantitative data like statistics and evaluation forms over qualitative inputs such as employee feedback and emotional investment?
- Does your manager focus excessively on minor issues, spending significant time on unimportant details and fretting over potential small errors?

- Does your manager emphasize rules and regulations that have little impact on overall goals?
- Does working under your manager leave you stressed and paranoid, and you find yourself overthinking and obsessively double-checking your work even outside of office hours?

Spotting the hidden aggression

Bullying from highly critical and demanding managers can be difficult to identify as it often masquerades under the guise of pursuing 'high standards' or upholding ethics. These managers are typically seen as dedicated high performers, lauded by company executives for their relentless work ethic and pursuit of perfection. Consequently, their demanding nature is perceived as being in service of 'the greater good', even though it is often driven by their own pathological anxiety.

It is also difficult to pinpoint their bullying behaviours because they rarely express open aggression or anger. They tend to see themselves as a moral, 'good' person, and being angry or lashing out may contradict their idealized image of themselves. For example, they hardly raise their voice because they do not like to appear out of control. However, this does not mean they do not get angry. Quite the opposite – constantly frustrated with the state of the world, corruption, and the feeling that no one pulls as much weight as they do, they are more than irate on the inside. Often, their physical tension, health issues, and inability to relax or connect with others are telltale signs of this suppressed anger they are not even aware of.

However, they may not be fully aware of the impact of their repressed anger. Due to a lack of self-awareness and a defensive posture, they might not see the intensity of their own repressed angst and tension. When they struggle to express their feelings appropriately, this can manifest as passive-aggressive behaviour, which may include frequent nitpicking, increasing demands, harsh reviews, overly critical feedback, and criticisms framed as 'evaluations'. They might also undermine you through gossip, disapproving body language, sarcastic comments, and backhanded compliments. Effectively managing this situation under such a manager demands significant resilience and tact, often more than anyone might typically anticipate in a normal workday.

Flawlessness, but at what price?

Highly critical and demanding bosses are, at their core, perfectionists. They feel the compulsion to constantly correct things, however irrelevant or excessive their corrections might be. However, they do not usually see themselves as 'perfectionists' because nothing in their eyes can be perfect. To them, their pursuit of excellence is deemed necessary and 'normal' – they view others' standards as too low, not their own as too high.

Their ability to deliver flawless outcomes may mean they can quickly climb the career ladder, even when they are relatively young, inexperienced in managing people, and before they have fully matured psychologically to handle complex interpersonal dynamics. They may shine in front of higher management, but working under or with them is a different story. As they laser-focus on achieving 'task perfection', they tend to disregard the feelings and needs of those around them. They nitpick, undermine, micromanage, and never seem satisfied. Even though they believe they are simply doing what needs to be done, others inevitably experience them as critical, punitive, and undermining. Working under them can be humiliating, demoralizing, and even traumatizing.

The psychodynamics of a perfectionist manager

From a psychodynamic perspective, your manager may unconsciously be using defence mechanisms like splitting and projection to manage feelings of inadequacy and the fear of being 'found out' for things they do not like about themselves.

Psychoanalysts such as Freud and Jung have noted that we often use projection as a defence mechanism when we recognize unwanted traits in ourselves that we see in others. This mechanism manifests in various ways. For example, if we repress our anger, we might perceive others as being angry with us, or we might be overly sensitive to the anger of others. Similarly, if we fear abandonment, we might interpret others as being distant and uncaring. Projection allows us to cope with our flaws by denying them and attributing them to others, thereby sidestepping the need to acknowledge and take responsibility for our behaviour.

Perhaps your manager is pushing away what they dislike the most about themselves – such as the possibility of being 'wrong', making mistakes, and acting immorally or dishonestly – onto others. To ease their anxiety, they target their subordinates who make minor errors or possess the very flaws they cannot come to terms with within themselves, and they lay blame on them. For instance, if they are most uneasy about admitting their occasional typos, they might hyper-focus on those who make such errors and treat them harshly.

When people feel anxious, they often regress and adopt a black-and-white way of thinking. In the case of your highly critical manager, this polarized worldview is not just an occasional lapse, it becomes a consistent pattern. Ironically, by categorizing everything strictly as 'good' or 'bad', they tend to label the targets of their criticism as 'the bad ones' while viewing themselves as victims of their circumstances. This mindset serves to shift responsibility away from themselves and exacerbate the cycle of blame and criticism.

To further understand the dynamics at play with them, we should learn about not only the concept of projection but also projective identification. This psychological process goes beyond simple projection. In projective identification, the person projecting their feelings causes the recipient to actually experience these rejected feelings as their own. This can lead to a distortion or damage to the recipient's self-concept.

As outlined in discussions about parents with empathy deficiencies, projective identification involves the projector (in this case, your manager) forcing you to accept and internalize their disowned feelings. Being on the receiving end of projective identification, you are coerced into feeling 'infused' with these projected qualities, which can disrupt and erode your sense of self.

Possibly stemming from adverse childhood experiences or trauma, your manager may have an unconscious feeling that they never quite measure up and grapple with a fear of making mistakes or behaving in a morally corrupted way. As they use projective identification to offload their self-doubt and shame onto you, the target, you might start to feel as if there are flaws to be paranoid about within yourself. You start to live with lingering anxiety that you have something 'bad', clumsy, or incompetent about you that you must constantly watch out for.

Projective identification can lead to feelings of stress, paranoia, and a pervasive fear of making mistakes. If you notice changes in your behaviour and emotions that are uncharacteristic of you in other contexts, it may indicate deeper psychodynamic processes at play. For instance, if you are typically calm and able to maintain a healthy work-life balance, but find yourself obsessing over minor details, excessively scrutinizing your work, unable to detach from work thoughts after hours, and increasingly worried about potential errors or setbacks in this particular job, then projective identification from your highly critical manager is likely influencing your behaviour. This shift suggests that your boss's psychological mechanisms are impacting you, causing you to internalize and manifest your anxieties and fears.

To protect yourself from being overwhelmed by this kind of anxiety, start by recognizing that the root of your feelings of paranoia stems from your manager's fears, not your own. Essentially, you are being used as an emotional receptacle, carrying the burden of their dysfunction. They may not intentionally mean to project their fears onto you, but their psychologically unhealthy state makes it almost inevitable. Unfortunately, the impact of such dynamics extends beyond just hindering your work performance. It can profoundly affect your sense of self-identity and your worldview.

The long shadows of an abusive workplace

Working for or with highly critical or demanding managers can make you feel demoralized and paranoid. Long-term, it undermines your self-esteem, morale, and sense of agency. As soon as you open your eyes in the morning of a workday, you can feel the impact. Your ability to relax and enjoy life diminishes, and you lose interest in activities that formerly pleased you (which are signs of depression). Also possible are panic attacks and other physical symptoms, such as headaches and gastrointestinal problems. These suffocating emotions may continue after you leave work and enter your personal life and relationships. Research has found that victims of bullying often experience a wide range of physical health problems, mental distress, and symptoms of post-traumatic stress (Mikkelsen et al., 2020; Nielsen and Einarsen, 2012). This persistent psychological distress can linger long after the direct exposure to the toxic environment has ended.

Workplace bullying can have profound psychological effects that go beyond immediate emotional distress. It taps into our deepest vulnerabilities and unmet needs for validation and affection, which though not explicitly admitted, we all inevitably carry into our professional lives. When these needs are not only unmet but actively belittled, it can trigger the resurfacing of past emotional wounds, causing us to regress to a more vulnerable and fearful state.

The impact of a bullying manager can be particularly severe if their behaviour mirrors that of one or both of your parents. This kind of dynamic can reactivate old fears and insecurities from childhood, reinforcing feelings of vulnerability, powerlessness, and a lack of worth. These emotional triggers can make us feel as if we are still that helpless child under the authority of an adult, intensifying feelings of being undesirable, irrelevant, and perpetually outside the circle of acceptance and belonging.

Recognizing that your manager's behaviour mirrors that of your parents involves introspection and often requires you to draw parallels between how you feel in the workplace and how you felt in interactions during your childhood or within your family dynamics. To examine if this has been the case, you may start by noticing if your reactions to your manager's actions are unusually intense or emotional compared to other professional relationships. If you find yourself feeling like a child, scared, or unusually submissive around your boss, these could be signs of a parental dynamic.

Consider whether your manager's use of criticism or withholding of approval reminds you of your parents, such as if your manager is never satisfied with your work, just like a parent whose expectations you could never meet. Reflect on how your manager communicates with you. Are there similarities in tone, phrases, or attitudes that echo how your parents communicated?

Most importantly, assess whether you find yourself reverting to roles or behaviours that mimic how you interacted with your parents. This could manifest as trying excessively to please, avoiding conflict, or not speaking up. Observe how conflicts are resolved in your workplace. If the resolution pattern mirrors parental dynamics, such as one-sided resolutions or feeling unheard, it might indicate a deeper parallel dynamic at play.

On an even deeper level, persistent bullying challenges our fundamental understanding of the world, shaking our sense of ontological security – the feeling that the universe is a predictable, reliable place. When faced with relentless and perhaps shocking bullying behaviours, this basic assumption is undermined, leading to existential questions about our place in the world and the reliability of institutions and fellow humans to protect and support us. This loss of ontological security can be extremely disorienting and destabilizing. The feeling that one's very existence is under threat is not only terrifying but can also lead to a profound disconnection from one's sense of self and reality. Recovering from such deep psychological impact takes significant time and often requires therapeutic intervention to rebuild a sense of safety and normalcy.

Seeing beyond the brutal realities with a punitive manager

This chapter explores the often-overlooked form of workplace bullying: working under a highly critical and demanding manager. Unlike the overtly aggressive bullies typically imagined, these bosses can be more difficult to identify as perpetrators because they often maintain a veneer of righteousness. They tend to enjoy a positive reputation and receive recognition from their superiors, making their bullying tendencies even more insidious.

It is not uncommon for individuals in positions of authority to have such personalities. Despite their unhealthy traits, their inclination towards perfectionism, self-sacrifice, and unwavering discipline often earn them praise and favour from higher-ups in large corporations. These traits can become stepping stones to their ascent in the organizational hierarchy.

Although these managers may have a more compassionate side, their rigid and inflexible exterior makes it challenging to empathize with them. In the next chapter, we will explore what drives their behaviours and ways to foster empathy towards them, all while safeguarding your own boundaries and psychological well-being within a potentially toxic workplace.

18

Handling harsh management with empathy

> 'Often times we call a man cold, when he is only sad.'
>
> *Henry Wadsworth Longfellow*

In this chapter, we will explore the underlying reasons behind the behaviours of highly critical managers and offer strategies to manage interactions with them. Our objective is to understand the motivations that drive their actions and expand the capacity to empathize with them. Meanwhile, we must not lose sight of how critical it is to maintain your well-being.

A caveat: the descriptions provided are based on assumptions. Since every individual's history and psychology are unique, they are simply generalizations that would hopefully still give some insights into your specific situation.

Understanding the roots of their harshness

People who are extremely harsh towards others are often just as hard on themselves. They may have pursued unattainable ideals throughout their lives and are constantly chasing perfection. They likely have a harsh 'inner critic' – an unrelenting internal voice that constantly condemns them for falling short. When mistakes happen, this inner critic becomes relentless in chastising and punishing them. This ongoing battle to meet their own lofty expectations leads to chronic stress and anxiety. Then, this stress spills over into their interactions with others, causing them to be more and more intolerant, inflexible, and self-righteous as a person.

When your manager behaves in a highly demanding manner, it may not be because they do not trust you. Instead, they believe that no one will handle tasks and projects with the same caution or meticulous planning they consider as necessary. At the same time, they worry that any mistakes in projects they oversee will reflect poorly on them, which taps right into their deep fear of being seen as incompetent and inadequate. This fear then drives them to resort to bullying or micromanagement.

It is easy to take their constant criticisms personally, but their attacks and nitpicking are not personal. In fact, they are likely harsh not only to you but also to themselves and everyone close to them (although, in some circumstances, they may have singled you out as the 'black sheep' or a specific target of their attacks). For instance, they likely employ a drill sergeant attitude not only at work but also with their loved ones and children. Their relationships across the board, not just in a work setting, tend to lack warmth and playfulness. Therefore, as much as possible, detach yourself and remember that the way they are reflects a lot more about their own psychology than your performance.

The fear of their own vulnerabilities

While expressing and processing their feelings may be the psychological 'medicine' they need most, it is also the skill they lack the most.

Since they are used to being emotionally inhibited all their lives, getting in touch with the true feelings beneath their authoritative facade can become an impossible task for them. They might worry: what if they can no longer manage their impulses and do something 'wrong'? What if they 'relax too much' and become complacent? What if they are too honest with their anger and lash out at someone? Authentic emotions are daunting for them because past attempts to connect with their feelings have often left them feeling overwhelmed and out of control. Perhaps, when they tried to express any feelings in the past in childhood, they were punished. This history makes the task of being direct and authentic exceptionally difficult for them.

The irony is that they may be incredibly sensitive on the inside. But they hide their softer, gentler selves behind a tough exterior because they do not believe it is safe to be otherwise. For example, they may deeply appreciate you and your work, but they would not express it for fear of seeming 'weak' or overly emotional.

The myth of complete control

Highly critical managers often find it impossible to relinquish control, as they associate it with a loss of power and being helpless. This persistent need to control every aspect of their lives is not just a preference, it comes from an unconscious belief that they can manage life's outcomes through sheer effort. They are constantly plagued with stress because the way they function is based on an erroneous belief, which is that they can control things as long as they try hard enough. They feel that they can reach fool-proof perfection with adequate preparation, caution, and backup plans. In essence, they are in denial of a fundamental aspect of what it means to be human: that we do not have complete control over everything and that no matter how hard we try, bad things can happen. Wanting to feel in control is natural for all of us, but at some point, we must know our limits and let go. The denial of this precarious reality means they do not know when to stop micro-managing things, and this can significantly impact their behaviour and relationships.

The silent rage

Passive anger or resentment might be the most significant yet hidden forces driving a critical manager's behaviours. Despite feeling anger towards the world, they often struggle to process or express this emotion in a constructive manner. Their anger most likely comes from constantly falling short of their own high standards, feeling like others are not pulling their weight, and being frustrated by the many injustices and corruption in the world.

Compared to more overt bullies, the anger of these managers is more subdued, often appearing as self-righteousness, irritation, judgement, sarcasm, and uncompromising standards. They're mostly unaware of their own hostility. While they seldom lose control of their behaviours, signs of their constant angst are still visible: a clenched jaw, abrupt or curt speech, and a strained tone of voice. They are constantly on the lookout for the next thing that has gone wrong, the next issue to critique or fix. Despite their efforts to restrain themselves, the tension they hold is palpable to everyone around them.

Occasionally, their suppressed rage would erupt. When these outbursts occur, they not only catch everyone off guard but also lead to self-reproach, as they are likely to regret their loss of control and harshly blame themselves afterward.

Since they don't allow themselves to be honest with their own anger, they may also act passive-aggressively. Passive aggressiveness, unlike overt acts of violence or verbal abuse, can be subtler and harder to recognize, yet it is potentially just as toxic, if not more so. Seemingly minor behaviours, such as gossip, sarcastic comments, and disrespectful body language, might appear insignificant on their own but can accumulate over time and create a toxic atmosphere in the workplace.

Being subjected to this kind of passive or indirectly hostile aggression can be detrimental to your self-esteem and mental health. For example, when you work for them, you may feel hyper-vigilant, like you must tread carefully around them, as you have no idea what will set them off or what they will say or do behind your back. This constant anticipation of negative interactions means you and your colleagues have to divert mental energy towards self-preservation rather than focusing on the tasks at hand. Eventually, work performance is also derailed.

Your manager may also channel their anger towards a seemingly just and moral cause, positioning themselves as an activist or thought leader. This allows them to convince themselves that they are championing the greater good. Instead of facing their personal issues in a constructive way, they distract themselves with a sense of moral superiority. By advocating for what they see as correct and punishing what they think of as wrong, they can also justify their righteous and critical behaviours and attitudes.

Understanding their personal history

Understanding the possible nature and nurture factors that contribute to the behaviour of a highly critical manager can also provide some insights into navigating the relationship with them.

Their behaviours likely stem from a combination of inherent temperament and personal history. While traits like conscientiousness and perfectionism may be innate, these alone are typically insufficient to turn someone into a bully. More often, it would take a series of humiliating, shaming, or abusive experiences during their formative years to mould them into the person they are today.

One possibility is that they have experienced severe neglect or grew up in a chaotic environment with minimal parental support. It might have been a household with absent, mentally ill or alcoholic parents. In such circumstances, they had no choice but to become their own parent. It became their responsibility to ensure they grew up to be a decent and responsible person. In an attempt to make up for the absence of clear parental guidance and boundaries, they have to find their own set of moral codes, rules, and ethics. They have to become their own teacher, critic, and judge. However, without a role model to demonstrate how to temper discipline with softer qualities like forgiveness and gentleness, they have developed a tendency towards severity while neglecting softer attributes such as empathy and compassion. This imbalance continues to be the way they treat themselves and shows up in their interactions with others, often making them overly critical and lacking in sensitivity.

On the other hand, their never-ending quest for perfection may be motivated by the desire to prove that they were not just unlike but better than their parents, who had let them down badly.

Another possibility is that they were raised by abusive, overbearing adults who provided them with no role models of what it means to be sensitive and adaptable. Being insensitive towards others' feelings, being intolerant of vulnerabilities, and neglectful of basic human needs – these were all that they have grown up to learn as 'normal'. As they continue to impose strict rules and high standards on themselves, they begin to project these expectations onto others. This projection often is not conscious, it is the only reality they know. They might not even realize how their behaviour affects others; to them, they are just upholding normal standards.

In addition, if they were criticized and punished throughout their childhood, they may have internalized the deep belief that they are somehow 'bad', inadequate, and incapable of doing the right things. The voice of their inner critic is most likely the result of internalizing their parents' cruel words and name-calling.

Sometimes, being overly critical of themselves can also be a form of self-defence – the unconscious logic is that if they are critical enough of themselves first, they can preempt and ward off external criticism. This is assuming that by identifying and admitting to their own flaws before anyone else does, they can avoid further critique. This defensive mechanism, while protective in their minds, does not work as intended and simply derails their esteem.

Another scenario could be that they were raised in a stringent and fundamentalist religious setting, where achieving perfection and maintaining a moral appearance was crucial for survival. Any perceived 'wrong' actions or violations of the moral code mean the whole family would face rejection from the community; given the repercussions, the pressure for them to appear perfect at all times is tremendous.

In all the scenarios described, their intense self-directed harshness is pushing them towards a highly rigid personality structure. This often occurs at the expense of their basic human needs such as emotional warmth, relaxation, and social interaction. What initially started as a defence mechanism to protect themselves from a chaotic or abusive environment has evolved into a dysfunctional pattern. Ironically, even when they have tried their best to be a 'good person' and did not intend to hurt others, this psychological pattern has turned them into a workplace bully.

The challenges in empathizing with a critical manager

Being around a manager who is rigid and excessively self-critical can severely impact your ability to be the best you can be at work. As mentioned earlier, your manager may unknowingly project their insecurities onto you. If you happen to be someone emotionally sensitive, empathic, and naturally hyper-attuned to your surroundings, you may find yourself more affected by their behaviour than your colleagues might be.

Their behaviours may have taken a toll on your self-esteem, leading you to believe no matter what you do, it will never be enough. Constant worry about being exposed for mistakes can drain all your energy to the point of compassion burnout. When you feel small and vulnerable, on the verge of crumbling, your ability to think, mentalize, stay grounded, and extend empathy or kindness to others is understandably diminished.

Furthermore, they are so rigid in their behaviour that it is challenging to form genuine connections with them or see their softer sides. After all, it is not easy to empathize with someone who hardly seems to empathize with you.

These factors can make it difficult to see beyond their tough exterior and feel safe in their presence, let alone extend compassion or empathy towards them. However, if you are stuck in the same workplace with them, and it is not feasible to leave, it would be beneficial for you to find a different vantage point, to see their softer side, or even to find a way to build some rapport with them.

Building a relationship with a highly critical manager – with dignity

Navigating a relationship with a demanding manager while protecting your own boundaries and mental health requires a strategic and thoughtful approach. Here are some pointers that might help:

Start slow

If you have tried connecting with them on a personal level, you would likely notice that sharing personal matters or feelings does not come naturally to them. Since they are not used to checking in with themselves or reflecting on their feelings, even if you ask about how they feel, they might just hit an empty wall on the inside. Additionally, due to their inherent mistrust, they might be hesitant to disclose personal details, particularly to someone they view as having a lower position in the corporate hierarchy.

To build rapport, you may want to with topics they are more comfortable with, such as work-related issues. Discussing ongoing projects, the general state of affairs at work, or even a challenge you have identified can spark a more engaged response.

This approach can not only initiate interaction but also demonstrate your investment in the workplace's well-being. It could make your manager feel supported, knowing that others share their concerns and are actively thinking about solutions.

Earn trust

A highly critical manager likely struggles to place trust in anyone but themselves. To establish a meaningful connection, gaining and retaining their respect is essential.

Demonstrating through your behaviour that you appreciate the same values, such as predictability and accountability, lays a solid foundation for your relationship. You can do this through simple actions like being punctual, organized, diligent, and fulfilling commitments. If you can build a reputation as a reliable person, you are more likely to advance in your career when you work under them.

One thing to be mindful of is how weary they might be of anything that appears 'too good to be true'. While having a charming personality can be a valuable asset in various aspects of your life, it may not work to your advantage with a manager who is inherently mistrusting. Their rigidity and lack of humour might make them uneasy around people who exude interpersonal charm. If qualities such as playfulness, lightheartedness, humour, and charisma are your usual strengths, you may want to be cautious about how you present yourself when they are around. These are usually great qualities that make you a well-liked colleague, but due to their specific preferences for a studious and serious demeanour, they may not serve you well in this particular workplace.

When working with such managers, never hide away any mistake, as shifting the blame is particularly unacceptable to them. They typically expect you to admit fault and take full responsibility for any errors. However, you should not have to go out of your way to make amends if doing so would violate your dignity. You also would not want to make so much compromise to your boundaries that you lose respect for yourself. Instead of being profusely apologetic, keep your apology straightforward and transparent; simply communicate your understanding of their standards and express regret for not meeting them this time.

Let them know you agree when you genuinely do

Your manager likely holds very strong convictions about what is right and wrong. While you may not share all of their values, expressing agreement with certain moral principles they uphold, such as ethics, fairness, honesty, and order, can strengthen your relationship. If it feels right, consider aligning with them and even contributing to promoting these ethical values within the company. Of course, do not fabricate your beliefs if you disagree. Lying your way into the relationship would be incongruent and likely backfire.

Additionally, your manager is likely always looking for ways to enhance accuracy, and safety, and boost up quantifiable metrics in their projects, and they are desperate to find people who care about these things as much as they do. If you are good at something they value, such as having an eye for details, you can let them know and offer to lend a hand. By doing so, you could position yourself as an ally.

Seeing behind their criticisms

Given how easy it is to lose their trust and how challenging it can be to regain it, as much as you can, you want to avoid actions that are absolute red flags in their eyes. These may include not taking your work seriously, taking shortcuts, being dishonest, or breaking rules.

However, their hyper-critical nature means they can react strongly to minor mishaps that are entirely human, such as being slightly late or unprepared. When faced with their overly critical comments, it is natural to feel humiliated, stifled, and even traumatized.

At these oppressive moments, you might lose the capacity to know how to respond to them in a professional way.

Practising self-awareness can help you catch moments when their critical attitude has triggered you and has regressed into a vulnerable, child-like mind state. Some signs of this happening are a shrinking sensation, feeling younger than your age, feeling like you are about to faint, collapse, or dissociate, feeling the urge to exact vengeance, acting aggressively, crying uncontrollably, shaking, physical pain, intense headache, etc.

When you find yourself triggered, be sure to step away, take care of yourself, and re-ground before responding. Remind yourself that their disproportionate reactions are about them, not you. If you feel traumatized, that is because they had been, and they are projecting.

Often overlooked in dealing with such managers is the fact that, beneath their intimidating exterior, there is an incredibly scared person. Their intolerance to errors means that when mistakes occur, they are also triggered and become psychologically regressed. Even if they are not responsible for the mistakes, their inner critic always finds a way to blame them, perhaps saying they didn't supervise well enough or trusted others too much. Remember, when they blame others, deep down they are blaming themselves.

When they find errors, a part of them panics, and their vision narrows; they will likely act defensively and struggle to listen or empathize. This is also why it would seem that no matter what you say, you cannot make it right, and even when you are justifiably explaining your position, there is no way of getting through to them.

Remember that behind their seemingly unyielding exterior is most likely a person who desperately wants to be understood and supported. They have spent their entire lives trying to avoid mistakes, and they have hardened to become who they are today, but that does not mean it has not been tiring, painful, and lonely.

Having been subject to their harshness, it is tempting to want to retaliate. But see if you can adopt a different perspective and see them as a desperate, scared child. In your dealing with them, instead of revenge, it is best to soften them with kindness, influence them with your wise perspective, and set an example yourself of what it means to be a more balanced human and work partner.

Seeing the potential

Some critical bosses go so far as a bully that they are impossible to be around or work for. When working for such a person, the best you can do is learn to protect yourself and maintain your dignity, to not shrink in the face of their hyper-criticalness, to stand your ground, and to manage any potential triggers and regression.

However, if your manager, despite their highly critical tendencies, has a softer side and provides an opening for connection, there might be an opportunity to establish an alliance. If you feel inclined or motivated, you can not only work for and with them but also contribute to their growth as a leader.

While these leaders may have various dysfunctional traits, they are not typically sociopathic and do not intend to harm others. Typically, they prioritize achieving task excellence over their own ego being stroked or people pleasing, and they are not just chasing praise for the sake of it. They probably care more and work harder than most. In fact, they can be so self-sacrificing that they reach a point of burnout. Sadly, they may have the best intentions for the projects or the company but are often misunderstood because they cannot modify their rather unhumanistic approach.

If you have a good, close relationship with them, the best thing you can do is to support them to accept imperfections of any kind, mostly in themselves, and that growth will trickle down to them being more tolerant of others.

Once your harsh manager recognizes they do not need to control everything and that perfection is not mandatory, they may be able to harness their potential for generosity, altruism, and wisdom. By turning their blind spots into insights and utilizing their meticulous and conscientious nature, you can even play a role in helping transform them into a powerful and moral leader.

Turning challenges into opportunities

In summary, your highly critical and demanding manager has likely developed their harsh demeanour from early life trauma, such as experiences of humiliation, narcissistic control, or a lack of love and care. They lack the emotional intelligence to empathize with others effectively, so they rely on rules and regulations and the pursuit of perfection to make themselves feel safe.

While they might be a noble person on the inside, in their pursuit of excellence and perfection, they have neglected to develop their emotional skills. When their emotional immaturity is combined with power in the workplace, they can, unfortunately, become a toxic workplace bully.

Considering their harsh and unyielding nature, it is challenging to empathize with them. To expand your capacity for empathy, avoiding taking their actions personally becomes easier when you remember their vulnerabilities and understand what they are trying to protect themselves from. If you can see through their facade the loneliness behind them, you have the potential to become an ally. This not only makes your experience in the company smoother but also has the possibility of advancing your career.

As they become more self-aware, there is a likelihood that they can become fairer in their judgements, more open to delegation, and achieve a healthier balance between their analytical mind and creative spirit. Ultimately, guiding them away from excessive self-criticism can contribute to creating a more positive work environment overall. Thus, if you can approach them with compassion and find ways to support them, you actively participate in a meaningful and valuable endeavour.

19
Thriving in a complex workspace

In any organization, the variety of human behaviours, thoughts, and emotions adds a layer of complexity. In workplaces where people interact, much of what shapes dynamics is hidden, driven by unconscious processes. Building empathy at work means looking deeper to understand these underlying psychological mechanisms in ourselves and others.

Time-tested psychoanalytic concepts like regression, projection, and transference are valuable tools for understanding workplace dynamics. This chapter will introduce you to these psychological phenomena, helping you empathize with both your colleagues and yourself. With this knowledge, you'll be better equipped to navigate your workplace with greater strength and wisdom.

Why do we behave like children?

Regression is a defence mechanism that, during stress and anxiety, makes us revert to an earlier stage of development. We might start thinking, feeling, and acting in childlike, simplistic, and vulnerable ways. This can range from subtle behaviours, like thinking in black-and-white terms (good/bad, right/wrong), to more obvious and extreme actions, such as throwing temper tantrums or having emotional meltdowns. When we regress, we also tend to use coping mechanisms from childhood, like shutting out the world and pretending everything doesn't exist or dissociating from our feelings and bodies.

Regression occurs in most relationships, not just professional ones. However, it is particularly noticeable might be amplified in work settings. This is due to the intricate power imbalance and unique psychodynamics embedded within hierarchical organizational structures. (Pines, 1985; White, 2018). As you might have experienced, groups can provide support, fulfilment, and enrichment, but they can also trigger deep insecurities, resurface old traumas, and cause daily frustrations. Essentially, group dynamics can bring out both the best and worst in everyone involved.

Upon entering a workplace, it's not uncommon that you are once again confronted with dilemmas that you thought were in the past. These dilemmas can trigger regressive behaviours as you deal with the complex dynamics of the workplace. Once again, you are confronted with the dilemma of having to choose between authenticity and fitting in. Do you stay true to yourself, or do you conform? How much of what you say and do would you edit to avoid judgement and rejection? How much of your true self must you sacrifice or edit to avoid the scrutiny and envy of others?

Or perhaps, your ambivalence towards authority figures resurfaces – craving good guidance but doubting their trustworthiness. You wonder: does your boss recognize your skills, or do they see you as a threat? Could you be their 'favourite child'?

Moreover, the family dynamics we experienced in our childhood home often reappear in work groups. There's usually a designated scapegoat, a dominant 'queen' or 'king', a 'golden child' or 'teacher's pet', a 'class clown', a mediator, and other roles mirroring familial patterns. Just as in life, thriving in this dynamic and uncertain environment requires finding your footing and keenly discerning who your allies and adversaries are.

Regression happens not because you are psychologically immature, but because of a healing instinct. Although regressive behaviours can be disruptive, they serve a deeper psychological purpose. You unconsciously repeat history while secretly hoping for a different outcome. This behaviour stems from the innate human desire to be acknowledged, seen, and ultimately find a 'family' that loves and accepts us unconditionally. In psychology, this is known as 'repetition compulsion'.

Repetition compulsion reflects the human tendency to recreate familiar patterns, even when they were originally distressing or painful. We unconsciously reenact unresolved issues from our past in an attempt to master or overcome them. This concept explains why individuals may repeatedly engage in regressive behaviours in the workplace, despite the potential for negative consequences.

Despite its irrational and unconscious nature, there is a strong allure in believing that a workplace can fulfil our deep-seated need for belonging. When you catch a glimpse of the possibility of forming a 'tribe' within your professional environment, your attachment system is activated. The mere potential of these individuals becoming 'your people' – who finally see, hear, and love you for who you are – can evoke attachment anxiety, triggering regressive behaviours as you deal with workplace dynamics. Consequently, instead of being the resilient adult you are, your longing sometimes leads you to act out your inner child or inner teenager in a professional setting.

Regression in the workplace is common and entirely natural, and you are not alone in experiencing it. Even those in high positions, including your manager, inevitably go through periods of regression at work. Unfortunately, when a group of people experiencing regression comes together in a room, things can get messy. Traumas collide, expectations falter, and fantasies are shattered. Without self-awareness and insight, workplace drama can become unmanageable and even re-traumatizing. In the following sections, we will explore how cultivating self-awareness and understanding these psychological phenomena can help you handle the challenges of regression in the workplace more effectively.

Transference – are you even in the here and now?

In the workplace, transference often occurs when someone is triggered and regresses.

Freud coined transference as a common, spontaneous phenomenon where one falsely links past experiences with present ones. In transference, emotions, thoughts, and behaviours from your childhood involving significant figures are transferred onto current individuals in your life. Consequently, authority figures or colleagues at work can elicit emotional experiences as if they were people from your past.

No one enters the workplace as a blank slate. Whether the influence is positive or negative, we all carry a plethora of personal experiences, assumptions, expectations, worldviews, and relationship patterns with us. If you notice yourself reacting in irrational ways, it is likely that your emotions are rooted in unresolved issues from your younger years. These unprocessed memories or experiences can evoke strong reactions even in seemingly inconsequential situations.

Not all transference is negative. Positive transference can benefit your workplace well-being and even your career progression. For instance, if you had a positive mentor or loving figure in your upbringing (such as a teacher or grandparent), and your manager evokes memories of them, it can enhance your ability to connect with authority figures at work. Your positive transference allows you to feel secure and confident when expressing yourself to them. However, overly positive transference, particularly in the form of idealization or idolization, can have negative consequences. For example, if you view your boss as a god-like figure, assuming they always know best, you risk compromising your capacity for independent, critical thinking, and your career growth might be stifled.

Unfortunately, in many cases, transference is negative. A classic example is that if you grew up with strict or critical parents, you might then feel a strong sense of anxiety or panic when your performance at work is evaluated or become hyper-sensitive to criticism. If your parents have chronically neglected you in your early years, you may be sensitive to being overlooked or having your opinions overruled. If you were traumatized by tyrannical or bullying parents when you were young, even though you are now a grown-up, you can still be hyper-vigilant when it comes to people who seem to have power over you, such as managers, supervisors, or even a loud and domineering colleague. Negative transference can adversely impact your judgement, trigger irrational emotions, even provoke angry outbursts and nervous breakdowns, and hinder your ability to maintain perspective or assert yourself. If you feel compelled to reenact relational patterns from the past, such as tolerating abuse or being drawn to abusive people, it can even result in re-traumatization.

Furthermore, whatever mechanism you used to cope with your childhood - from defensive humour to emotional repression to trying to please everyone - all of that can be replayed. For instance, in dealing with a demanding and unyielding parent/boss, you might try extra hard to please, suppress your own needs, and do everything you can to make them happy until you eventually exhaust yourself and burn out. Or, you may reach a point where you assume that nothing will change no matter what they do, so you choose the passive route of 'quiet quitting' or passively deflecting responsibility.

Transference isn't limited to authority figures, it can easily colour your perception of colleagues as well. It's not unusual to unconsciously treat coworkers as siblings, mirroring past family dynamics. While this can foster positive collaboration and support, it can also trigger unhealthy patterns of envy, rivalry, or feelings of oppression and unfair treatment. For example, if you were bullied or marginalized by a sibling, you might find yourself feeling apprehensive and inferior when a colleague speaks assertively, interrupts you, or exhibits strong leadership qualities. These past experiences can resurface, creating unnecessary tension and conflict in your professional relationships.

This transference of sibling dynamics can manifest in various counterproductive behaviours within the workplace. Just like rivalrous siblings, you and your colleagues might fall into patterns of unhealthy competition, sabotage, or undermining each other, hindering collaboration and creating a toxic work environment.

Transference is not a one-way street: managers and bosses can also project onto their employees. For instance, consider a manager who has assumed a 'parentified' role within their family throughout their life. This means they were always seen as the 'responsible one', even when they were just a child. Their parents may have been immature, vulnerable, and chaotic, leaving the manager to handle all the chores, take care of everyone, and prevent things from falling apart. Consequently, as a manager, they continue to act as parental figures to everyone and everything. They perceive those around them as either incompetent or vulnerable, always stepping in to fix things, staying late at work, and struggling to delegate tasks until they eventually burn out. Another scenario could involve a subordinate who reminds the manager of their highly irresponsible parents, leading the manager to feel constantly aggravated by them and to discriminate against them.

Ultimately, your success in the workplace extends beyond 'hard facts' like numbers and performance, it requires emotional resilience and quality relationships with others. Gaining insight into why and how regression may occur at work, and acknowledging the existence of a younger, more vulnerable inner child within your adult self seeking love and attention, give you emotional intelligence at work. Essentially, identifying your triggers fosters self-compassion, and recognizing similar dynamics in others enables you to extend empathy to others.

Spotting signs of transference

Reflect on the following points to self-assess whether transference is currently at play when you are at work:

TRANSFERENCE OF FEELINGS

- You often feel that your boss sounds exactly like one of your parents – for example, in a critical, demanding, or unyielding way.
- You feel towards your colleague how you would with your brother or sister.
- You are frustrated that your boss or the organization did not protect you the way they should.
- You are frustrated that your manager or supervisor did not provide you with the guidance you need.
- You feel a compulsion to please your manager and become their 'favourite'.
- You are not able to let it go when you feel you have disappointed your manager.
- You often feel guilty for not having done a good enough job by the team or your manager.

WHEN YOU ARE ACTING OUT OF TRANSFERENCE

- You stay at work longer than you should, either to avoid punishment or to please your manager.
- You struggle to challenge your colleagues even if you know they are plainly wrong.
- You drown in shame and feel desolate when you feel left out by your colleagues (which might have echoed your experience at home or in school as a child).

- You tremble in fear and become muted when someone is expressing anger (just like your violent sibling/parent once did).
- You feel that no matter what you do, you will never be good enough, so you hide and avoid responsibilities.

Empathizing with yourself

When your emotional reactions seem disproportionate to the current situation, they often signal the influence of other forces, including unresolved issues from the past. However, with the right mindset, these seemingly inconvenient triggers can become powerful opportunities for personal growth.

Self-reflection is key to uncovering the deeper patterns and beliefs driving your behaviour. By paying close attention to your own feelings and those of others, you gather valuable data. Instead of simply accepting situations at face value, pause and ask yourself insightful questions like: 'Who might this person represent for me?' or 'Who might I be for this person?' By identifying the underlying transference at play, you gain a deeper understanding of your reactions.

Creating space for reflection can be challenging, especially in a fast-paced work environment. That's why it's crucial to intentionally incorporate regular reflection time into your day. This creates a buffer against emotional reactivity when triggers arise. Establishing a daily ritual, such as taking a walk outside for fresh air or utilizing your commute for emotional reflection, can be incredibly beneficial.

Openly discussing your experiences, whether through conversations with trusted individuals or journalling, can be incredibly valuable in untangling complex interpersonal dynamics and mental barriers. Conversations about transference, in particular, can be especially beneficial when held with those well-versed in the subject, such as therapists or trauma-informed coaches.

These safe spaces allow you to delve into how past relationships might be impacting your present interactions, empowering you to work towards positive change.

The following reflective exercise is designed to help you gain a deeper understanding of your workplace dynamics and the role you play within them. Honest self-reflection can illuminate patterns, triggers, and underlying issues that may be influencing both your professional relationships and personal growth. Take your time to consider each question carefully, and try to approach this process with an open mind and a willingness to explore your thoughts and emotions.

EXPLORING YOUR WORKPLACE EXPERIENCE:

- **Identifying triggers**: In what specific work situations do you find yourself reacting differently than usual? What factors might be contributing to these altered reactions?
- **The role of transference**: Would your response be the same if a similar situation arose with someone who doesn't typically trigger strong emotions in you?
- **Echoes of the past**: Are there aspects of this situation that feel strangely familiar or evoke a sense of déjà vu? What past experiences might be influencing your current perception?
- **Seeking validation**: Whose opinions and approval do you value most in the workplace, and why?
- **Unveiling fears and insecurities**: What are your deepest fears and insecurities within the professional context?
- **Navigating power dynamics**: Who do you feel intimidated by in the workplace, and what specifically about them makes you feel this way? When interacting with your manager or a specific colleague, approximately how old do you feel emotionally? Are you embodying a

fully functioning adult, or does it feel like you're a child in an adult body?

- **Recognizing behavioural patterns**: Have you observed recurring patterns in how you interact with others at work? For instance, do you often become defensive, experience dissociation, or passively withdraw? How do these behaviours impact you, your professional opportunities, and those in your professional circle?
- **Understanding your relationship with power**: What is your relationship with power, and how does it manifest in your interactions with others?
- **Unpacking childhood conditioning**: When facing conflicts at work, what patterns have you developed based on childhood conditioning that are now surfacing?
- **Identifying projections**: What is the one trait you cannot stand in others, and who in your past exhibited this trait? Does the person who triggers you remind you of the worst version of yourself or who you most want to avoid becoming?
- **Expressing unspoken truths**: Imagine this person is sitting in front of you, and you can say anything without negative consequences. What would you tell them?
- **Aligning actions with values**: What are your core values, goals, and aspirations in the workplace? How do your current behaviours and relationships align with or diverge from these ideals?

By thoughtfully reflecting on these questions and exploring your emotional responses, behavioural patterns, and the influence of past experiences, you can gain invaluable insights into your workplace dynamics and unlock opportunities for personal growth. Use this newfound self-awareness to develop an action plan for enhancing your emotional intelligence, communication skills, and professional relationships.

When you are the manager

As a manager, dealing with transference from an employee can be a complex and emotionally taxing experience (Bernstein, 2013). You may find yourself in situations where an employee's behaviour seems illogical or their emotional responses appear exaggerated and out of proportion to the circumstances at hand. In many cases, the true nature of the problem may only become apparent when you begin to feel emotionally drained and your effectiveness as a leader starts to suffer.

Managing transference requires a nuanced approach. While it's crucial to address the situation directly, it's equally important to remember that you are not equipped to be their therapist. Your role is to maintain professionalism and strive for a resolution where both parties feel heard and respected. A key to successfully navigating transference lies in recognizing its root cause: the projection of past feelings and experiences onto the present situation. This understanding allows you to approach the situation with empathy, recognizing that the employee's behaviour, while potentially challenging, stems from a place outside of the immediate work context.

To better understand the dynamics at play, consider that the last time your employee experienced a relationship with such a profound impact on their survival, autonomy, and welfare was likely during their childhood, with their parents or primary caregivers. The inherent power imbalance between a parent and child bears striking similarities to the hierarchical nature of the boss-subordinate relationship in the workplace. As a result, your interactions with the employee can easily trigger deeply ingrained memories and unresolved conflicts from their early parent-child relationships, leading to emotional reactions and behaviours that may seem irrational or disproportionate to the current situation. Recognizing this parallel between parental authority and managerial authority is key to empathizing with your employee's struggles and developing effective strategies to navigate these complex dynamics.

Addressing an employee's transference

As a manager, it can be challenging to determine if an employee's behaviour stems from genuine workplace concerns or if they are projecting past experiences onto you. Here are some signs that transference might be at play:

- Their emotional responses to workplace situations seem exaggerated, misaligned with the context, or overly intense.
- You notice a consistent theme or pattern in their reactions, suggesting underlying issues or past experiences might be influencing their behaviour.
- Information from their personal life, such as growing up in a highly competitive environment, sheds light on their intense reactions to similar situations at work, even when unwarranted.
- You find yourself reacting to this employee in ways that are atypical for you, perhaps feeling unusually punitive or vindictive compared to your interactions with other team members.
- You experience a palpable sense of discomfort or tension in their presence, sensing unresolved issues or emotional baggage impacting your interactions.
- Interactions lack the natural flow, humour, or playfulness you typically share with other employees. You might feel like you're walking on eggshells or unable to be yourself around them.
- You feel unfairly portrayed as a villain or monster, even when your actions haven't been harsh or punitive. Their perception of you seems skewed, not aligning with your actual behaviour or intentions.

- Untrue rumors about you, likely stemming from the employee, circulate at the workplace based on distorted or biased interpretations of things that happened.
- The employee seems to forget you are a person with a life outside of work, treating you more like a character in their narrative than a real human with their own complexity.

Recognizing these signs is the first step in addressing potential transference. By understanding the dynamics at play, you can approach the situation with greater empathy and implement strategies to foster healthier, more productive working relationships.

Unfortunately, transference issues are highly resistant to change. Changing a person's behaviours, let alone their worldview, is rarely feasible in the workplace. After all, you are not their therapist.

Transference is often deeply ingrained, making it highly resistant to change. Individuals prone to transference with authority figures may interpret interactions through a filter confirming their existing worldview, such as 'no one can be trusted' or 'everyone is trying to undermine me'. This can make it challenging to address the issue directly without triggering further defensiveness.

If you choose to address the issue, proceed with caution and sensitivity. While you may have some insights into their history due to workplace interactions, avoid making assumptions about the specific nature of their transference. Instead of direct confrontation, approach the conversation with genuine curiosity. Use open-ended questions that empower the employee to share what they feel comfortable disclosing (Ablon and Bernstein, 2011). Pressuring them to be vulnerable or authentic before they are ready can have unintended negative consequences.

While you cannot change an employee's deeply ingrained patterns, you can focus on creating a healthier work environment.

Clearly communicate your expectations for professional behaviour and interaction. Address specific behaviours and their impact on the workplace, rather than attempting to analyze their underlying motivations. Maintain professional boundaries by treating all employees fairly and consistently, avoiding any actions that could be perceived as preferential treatment or crossing professional boundaries.

As a manager, your role often parallels that of a parent in the workplace, and striving to be a 'good parent' comes with its own set of challenges. When an employee is experiencing transference, they may unintentionally trigger emotional responses from you (counter-transference). To effectively navigate these situations, you have to have a strong sense of self-awareness regarding your own emotions and triggers, distinguishing between what belongs to you ('your stuff') and what stems from the employee's projections ('their stuff').

When an employee's behaviour provokes an emotional response in you, take a step back and assess the situation objectively. Ask yourself, 'Is this reaction based on my own past experiences, biases, or insecurities, or is it a direct result of the employee's behaviour?' By separating your own emotional baggage from the employee's projections, you can respond more effectively and avoid getting caught up in a cycle of defensive or aggressive reactions. Investing in training that focuses on cognitive empathy and mentalizing can be incredibly valuable for managers dealing with transference in the workplace.

Empathizing with an employee's story and emotional pain does not mean condoning their destructive behaviours or avoiding assertive actions within your responsibilities. Often, simply acknowledging the phenomenon and devising workarounds is all that you as a manager can do. If an employee's personal trauma and frequent regression significantly impede their performance, addressing these issues professionally or, if necessary, letting them go is within your rights. After all, the office is not a therapy room.

However, if you manage to navigate through the projection and dismantle the transference, it could be a life-changing experience for them. This is known as a 'corrective experience', which works by therapeutically contradicting long-held beliefs. Practically, it involves challenging and reshaping preconceived notions about authority figures and relationships. For instance, consider an employee who perceives all authority figures as critical and demanding, as they project past experiences with a strict parent onto current workplace dynamics. Through effective communication, empathy and patience, you can gradually disprove these projections. By acknowledging their concerns, providing constructive feedback without harsh criticism, and having open dialogue, they may come to realize that not all authority figures are inherently punitive. If you can be the agent of change for them in that way, you are not just allowing them to function at work but also to grow as a whole person.

Ultimately, being a manager who can effectively deal with transference issues requires a delicate balance of professionalism, empathy, and self-awareness. By understanding the complexities of these dynamics and developing the necessary skills to navigate them, you can create a work environment that promotes productivity and supports the personal growth and well-being of your employees, which may elevate your role as a manager to one that is profoundly meaningful.

Empathy and leadership: Keys to a successful career

The workplace is a stage where professional lives and personal histories intertwine. To thrive, we need more than just skills and knowledge, we need to understand the psychological realities at play. The echoes of past relationships, particularly those with authority figures, resonate within the power dynamics of boss-subordinate interactions.

However, this intersection also presents an opportunity. By cultivating self-awareness – understanding your own triggers and biases – you can transform workplace challenges into catalysts for growth. Recognizing the influence of past experiences allows you to engage with empathy, turning potential conflicts into opportunities. This empathetic approach is not just about navigating difficult situations, it's about unlocking the potential for genuine human connection within the professional sphere.

By embracing the complexities of human dynamics and committing to continuous self-reflection, you pave the way for impactful leadership and a more fulfilling career journey.

Closing thoughts
From walls to bridges

In our journey thus far, we have learned that empathy is not just a concept from a book but a practical wisdom woven into our daily lives. There is no one-size-fits-all solution to the barriers blocking our empathy, and we must adapt how we use empathy to life's unique challenges.

Rumi once astutely said, 'Your task is not to seek for love, but merely to seek and find all the barriers within yourself that you have built against it.' When we enter relationships with our emotional scars and unconscious defence mechanisms, we often find ourselves ensnared by blame, shame, and a need to protect our vulnerabilities; these tendencies hinder our capacity for empathy and compassion.

Throughout this book, we've delved into various tools for cultivating genuine and effective empathy, where we learned about defence mechanisms, attachment patterns, and the dynamics of group interactions. We have also discovered that acknowledging our underdeveloped and wounded aspects and viewing reality without denial can liberate us from projections that hinder our empathy.

It has become clear that early experiences, such as growing up with parents who struggle with empathy, shape our present selves. We have also come to experience the strength of self-empathy, which empowers us to become our own best ally regardless of what happened in the past. In matters of love, we learned to recognize emotionally distant partners and gained insight into the roots of emotional detachment. In the workplace, we learned about concepts such as regression and transference and what drives a critical and demanding manager.

If there is one thing to remember from this book, let it be that self-empathy and empathy for others must go hand in hand. No amount of pretending that your anger, resentment, and disappointment do not exist will allow you to connect with your empathic capacity. The only way to truly forgive and extend empathy, even in the most challenging circumstances, is to face your truth, the rawness of your own emotions, and process them. When you can extend your most profound understanding and compassion to yourself, your capacity for empathy will expand and ripple out to everyone around you.

But the gift of empathy does not stop with our immediate connections. In a world marked by political tension, division, and conflicts, a significant shift is under way as people awaken to the transformative potential of collective empathy.

As you close this book, I hope the insights you have encountered resonate beyond these pages. In a world often quick to build walls, may we all find the courage and compassion to build bridges.

'I want to tell you to live in the messy world, throw yourself into the convulsion of the world.

'I'm not telling you to make the world better, because
I don't think that progress is necessarily part of the package.
I'm just telling you to live in it. Not just to endure it,
not just to suffer it, not just to pass through it, but to live in it.
To look at it. To try to get the picture.'

Joan Didon, Commencement address at the University of California, Riverside, 1975

References

Introduction

Aurelius, M. (2016). *Meditations.* Value Classic Reprints.

Chapter 1

Aron, E. N. (2013). *The Highly Sensitive Person: How to Thrive When the World Overwhelms You.* Kensington Publishing Corp.

Greenberg, D. M., Baron-Cohen, S., Rosenberg, N., Fonagy, P. & Rentfrow, P. J. (2018). Elevated empathy in adults following childhood trauma. *PLoS One*, 13(10), e0203886.

Martin, R. A., Berry, G. E., Dobranski, T., Horne, M. & Dodgson, P. G. (1996). Emotion perception threshold: Individual differences in emotional sensitivity. *Journal of Research in Personality*, 30(2), 290–305.

Mehrabian, A., Young, A. L. & Sato, S. (1988). Emotional empathy and associated individual differences. *Current Psychology*, 7, 221–240.

Chapter 2

Allen, J. G., Fonagy, P. & Bateman, A. W. (2008). *Mentalizing in Clinical Practice.* American Psychiatric Pub.

Corradini, A. & Antonietti, A. (2013). Mirror neurons and their function in cognitively understood empathy. *Consciousness and Cognition*, 22(3), 1152–1161.

Hein, G. & Singer, T. (2008). Understanding others: Empathy and cognitive perspective taking in the human brain. In *Inaugural Herzliya Symposium on Personality and Social Psychology: Prosocial Motives, Emotions, and Behavior*, Herzliya, Israel, 24 March 2008 – 27 March 2008.

Kahneman, D. (2011). *Thinking, Fast and Slow*. New York: Farrar, Straus and Giroux

Keysers, C. & Gazzola, V. (2007). Integrating simulation and theory of mind: From self to social cognition. *Trends in Cognitive Sciences*, 11(5), 194–196.

Martingano, A. J. & Konrath, S. (2022). How cognitive and emotional empathy relate to rational thinking: Empirical evidence and meta-analysis. *The Journal of Social Psychology*, 162(1), 143–160.

Shamay-Tsoory, S. G. (2011). The neural bases for empathy. *The Neuroscientist*, 17(1), 18–24.

Shamay-Tsoory, S. G., Aharon-Peretz, J. & Perry, D. (2009). Two systems for empathy: A double dissociation between emotional and cognitive empathy in inferior frontal gyrus versus ventromedial prefrontal lesions. *Brain*, 132(3), 617–627.

Sharp, C. & Bevington, D. (2022). *Mentalizing in Psychotherapy: A Guide for Practitioners*. Guilford Publications.

Waytz, A. & Mitchell, J. P. (2011). Two mechanisms for simulating other minds: Dissociations between mirroring and self-projection. *Current Directions in Psychological Science*, 20(3), 197–200.

Wicker, B., Keysers, C., Plailly, J., Royet, J. P., Gallese, V. & Rizzolatti, G. (2003). Both of us disgusted in My Insula: The common neural basis of seeing and feeling disgust. *Neuron*, 40(3), 655–664.

Zaki, J. & Ochsner, K. N. (2012). The neuroscience of empathy: Progress, pitfalls, and promise. *Nature Neuroscience*, 15(5), 675–680.

Chapter 3

Bower, G. H. & Sivers, H. (1998). Cognitive impact of traumatic events. *Development and Psychopathology*, 10(4), 625–653.

Brunsteins, P. C. (2018). Empathy and vicarious experience. Congruence or identical emotion? *Philosophies*, 3(2), 6.

Hawk, S. T., Fischer, A. H. & Van Kleef, G. A. (2011). Taking your place or matching your face: Two paths to empathic embarrassment. *Emotion*, 11(3), 502.

Krach, S., Cohrs, J. C., de Echeverría Loebell, N. C., Kircher, T., Sommer, J., Jansen, A. & Paulus, F. M. (2011). Your flaws are my pain: Linking empathy to vicarious embarrassment. *PloS One*, 6(4), e18675.

Müller-Pinzler, L. K. (2016). The Social Emotion of Embarrassment: Modulations of Neural Circuits in Response to Own and Others'

Social Predicaments (Doctoral dissertation, Universiteit van Amsterdam [Host]).
Orloff, J. (2017). Empathy to a fault. *Alternative Medicine*, (35), 28.
Pally, R. (1997). Memory: Brain systems that link past, present, and future. *The International Journal of Psycho-Analysis*, 78(6), 1223.
Paulus, F. M., Müller-Pinzler, L., Westermann, S. & Krach, S. (2013). On the distinction of empathic and vicarious emotions. *Frontiers in Human Neuroscience*, 7, 196.
Wondra, J. D. & Ellsworth, P. C. (2015). An appraisal theory of empathy and other vicarious emotional experiences. *Psychological Review*, 122(3), 411.
Zaki, J. & Cikara, M. (2015). Addressing empathic failures. *Current Directions in Psychological Science*, 24(6), 471–476.

Chapter 4

Abdullah, S. H. & Salim, R. M. A. (2020). Parenting style and empathy in children: The mediating role of family communication patterns. *Humanitas Indonesian Psychological Journal*, 17(1), 34–45.
Bi, S. & Keller, P. S. (2021). Parental empathy, aggressive parenting, and child adjustment in a noncustodial high-risk sample. *Journal of Interpersonal Violence*, 36(19–20), NP10371–NP10392.
Brik, R. (2023). *My Father's Eyes, My Mother's Rage*. Library and archives Canada.
Engels, R. C., Finkenauer, C., Meeus W. & Deković, M. (2001). Parental attachment and adolescents' emotional adjustment: The associations with social skills and relational competence. *Journal of Counseling Psychology*, 48(4), 428.
Feshbach, N. D. (1987). Parental empathy and child adjustment/maladjustment. In N. Eisenberg & J. Strayer (Eds.), *Empathy and Its Development* (pp. 271–291). Cambridge University Press.
Glickauf-Hughes, C. & Mehlman, E. (1998). Non-borderline patients with mothers who manifest borderline pathology. *British Journal of Psychotherapy*, 14(3), 294–302.
Harari, H., Shamay-Tsoory, S. G., Ravid, M. & Levkovitz, Y. (2010). Double dissociation between cognitive and affective empathy in borderline personality disorder. *Psychiatry Research*, 175(3), 277–279.
Li, X., Bian, C., Chen, Y., Huang, J., Ma, Y., Tang, L., . . . & Yu, Y. (2015). Indirect aggression and parental attachment in early adolescence:

Examining the role of perspective taking and empathetic concern. *Personality and Individual Differences*, 86, 499–503.

Mannarini, S., Balottin, L., Palmieri, A. & Carotenuto, F. (2018). Emotion regulation and parental bonding in families of adolescents with internalizing and externalizing symptoms. *Frontiers in Psychology*, 9, 1493.

Meng, K., Yuan, Y., Wang, Y., Liang, J., Wang, L., Shen, J. & Wang, Y. (2020). Effects of parental empathy and emotion regulation on social competence and emotional/behavioural problems of school-age children. *Pediatric Investigation*, 4(02), 91–98.

Mier, D., Lis, S., Esslinger, C., Sauer, C., Hagenhoff, M., Ulferts, J. . . . & Kirsch, P. (2013). Neuronal correlates of social cognition in borderline personality disorder. *Social Cognitive and Affective Neuroscience*, 8(5), 531–537.

Morelli, S. A., Rameson, L. T. & Lieberman, M. D. (2014). The neural components of empathy: Predicting daily prosocial behaviour. *Soc. Cogn. Affect. Neurosci.*, 9, 39–47. doi: 10.1093/scan/nss088

Sosic-Vasic, Z., Eberhardt, J., Bosch, J. E., Dommes, L., Labek, K., Buchheim, A. & Viviani, R. (2019). Mirror neuron activations in the encoding of psychic pain in borderline personality disorder. *NeuroImage: Clinical*, 22, 101737.

Stern, J. A., Borelli, J. L. & Smiley, P. A. (2015). Assessing parental empathy: A role for empathy in child attachment. *Attachment & Human Development*, 17(1), 1–22.

Chapter 5

Anderson, I. M. & Williams-Markey, K. (2024). Clinical features of depressive disorders. In *Seminars in General Adult Psychiatry* (p. 64). Cambridge University Press.

Busch, F. N. (2009). Anger and depression. *Advances in Psychiatric Treatment*, 15(4), 271–278.

Celani, D. (2010). *Fairbairn's Object Relations Theory in the Clinical Setting*. Columbia University Press.

Clarke, G. S. (2018). *Fairbairn and the Object Relations Tradition*. Routledge.

Corradi, R. B. (2009). The repetition compulsion in psychodynamic psychotherapy. *Journal of the American Academy of Psychoanalysis and Dynamic Psychiatry*, 37(3), 477–500.

Fairbairn, W. R. (1952). *Psychoanalytic Studies of the Personality*. Routledge & Kegan Paul.

Fisher, J. (2014). *The Treatment of Structural Dissociation in Chronically Traumatized Patients.* Oslo: Universitetsforlaget.

Fisher, J. (2017). *Healing the Fragmented Selves of Trauma Survivors: Overcoming internal self-alienation.* Routledge.

Frankel, J. (2002). Exploring Ferenczi's concept of identification with the aggressor: Its role in trauma, everyday life, and the therapeutic relationship. *Psychoanalytic Dialogues*, 12(1), 101–139.

Frankel, J. (2019). Identification (with the aggressor). In *Routledge Handbook of Psychoanalytic Political Theory* (pp. 199–207). Routledge.

Geiser, F., Imbierowicz, K., Conrad, R., Wegener, I. & Liedtke, R. (2005). Turning against self and its relation to symptom distress, interpersonal problems, and therapy outcome: A replicated and enhanced study. *Psychotherapy Research*, 15(4), 357–365.

Levy, M. S. (2000). A conceptualization of the repetition compulsion. *Psychiatry*, 63(1), 45–53.

Ogden, T. (1983). The concept of internal object relations. *The International Journal of Psycho-Analysis*, 64, 227.

Prysak, M. A. (2018). Suicide vulnerability and risk: Fragmented sense of self and psyche (Doctoral dissertation).

Richo, D. (2002). *How to Be an Adult in Relationships: The five keys to mindful loving*. Shambhala Publications.

Stimmel, D.T., Rayburg, J., Waring, W. & Raffeld, P. M. (2005). The relation of internalized and trait anger to psychopathology. *Counseling & Clinical Psychology Journal*, 2(3), 112.

van der Hart, O., Nijenhuis, E. R. S. & Steele, K. (2006). *The haunted self: Structural dissociation and the treatment of chronic traumatization.* W W Norton & Co.

Chapter 6

Bateman, A., Campbell, C., Debbané, M., Fonagy, P. & Luyten, P. (2023). *Cambridge Guide to Mentalization-Based Treatment (MBT).* Cambridge University Press.

Bowlby, J. (1979). The Bowlby-Ainsworth attachment theory. *Behavioural and Brain Sciences*, 2(4), 637–638.

DeFife, J. A. & Hilsenroth, M. J. (2005). Clinical utility of the Defensive Functioning Scale in the assessment of depression. *The Journal of Nervous and Mental Disease*, 193(3), 176–182.

Di Giuseppe, M. & Perry, J. C. (2021). The hierarchy of defence mechanisms: Assessing defensive functioning with the Defence Mechanisms Rating Scales Q-Sort. *Frontiers in Psychology*, 12, 718440.

Drapeau, M., De Roten, Y., Perry, J. C. & Despland, J. N. (2003). A study of stability and change in defence mechanisms during a brief psychodynamic investigation. *The Journal of Nervous and Mental Disease*, 191(8), 496–502.

Frederickson, J. (2021). *Co-creating Safety: Healing the fragile patient.* Seven Leaves Press.

Kernberg, O. F. (1992). *Aggression in Personality Disorders and Perversions.* Yale University Press.

Reid, J. & Kealy, D. (2022). Understanding and working with the effects of parental pathological projective identification. *Smith College Studies in Social Work*, 92(2), 150–167.

Seligman, S. (1999). Integrating Kleinian theory and intersubjective infant research observing projective identification. *Psychoanalytic Dialogues*, 9(2), 129–159.

Tanzilli, A., Di Giuseppe, M., Giovanardi, G., Boldrini, T., Caviglia, G., Conversano, C. & Lingiardi, V. (2021). Mentalization, attachment, and defence mechanisms: A Psychodynamic Diagnostic Manual-2-oriented empirical investigation. *Research in Psychotherapy: Psychopathology, Process, and Outcome*, 24(1).

Vaillant, G. E. (2000). Adaptive mental mechanisms: Their role in positive psychology. *American Psychologist*, 55(1), 89.

Chapter 7

Bacon, I. & Conway, J. (2023). Co-dependency and enmeshment – a fusion of concepts. *International Journal of Mental Health and Addiction*, 21(6), 3594–3603.

Bennett, R. & Oliver, J. (2019). *Acceptance and Commitment Therapy: 100 key points and techniques.* Routledge.

Brooks, B. (2024). *You Deserve to Be Happy.* Independently published.

Dahl, J., Stewart, I., Martell, C. R. & Kaplan, J. S. (2014). *ACT and RFT in Relationships: Helping clients deepen intimacy and maintain healthy commitments using acceptance and commitment therapy and relational frame theory.* New Harbinger Publications.

Green, R. J. & Werner, P. D. (1996). Intrusiveness and closeness-caregiving: Rethinking the concept of family 'enmeshment'. *Family Process*, 35(2), 115–136.

H Raven Rose (2012). *Double Happiness: Shadow Selves*. eXu Publishing.

Luoma, J. B., Hayes, S. C. & Walser, R. D. (2007). *Learning ACT: An acceptance & commitment therapy skills-training manual for therapists*. New Harbinger Publications.

McLaren, K. (2023). *The Language of Emotions: What your feelings are trying to tell you: Revised and Updated*. Sounds True.

Minuchin, S., Baker, L., Rosman, B. L., Liebman, R., Milman, L. & Todd, T. C. (1975). A conceptual model of psychosomatic illness in children: Family organization and family therapy. *Archives of General Psychiatry*, 32(8), 1031–1038.

Chapter 8

Begley, T. M. (1994). Expressed and suppressed anger as predictors of health complaints. *Journal of Organizational Behaviour*, 15(6), 503–516.

Burch, B. (1989). Mourning and failure to mourn: An object-relations view. *Contemporary Psychoanalysis*, 25(4), 608–623.

Freud, S. (1924). Mourning and melancholia. *The Psychoanalytic Review (1913–1957)*, 11, 77.

Hollis, J. (1993). *The Middle Passage: From misery to meaning in midlife* (Vol. 59). Inner City Books.

Hosseini, S. H., Mokhberi, V., Mohammadpour, R. A., Mehrabianfard, M. & Lashak, N. B. (2011). Anger expression and suppression among patients with essential hypertension. *International Journal of Psychiatry in Clinical Practice*, 15(3), 214–218.

Tolle, E. (2004). *The Power of Now: A guide to spiritual enlightenment*. New World Library.

Chapter 9

Affrunti, N. W. & Ginsburg, G. S. (2012). Maternal overcontrol and child anxiety: The mediating role of perceived competence. *Child Psychiatry & Human Development*, 43, 102–112.

Albano, A. M., Chorpita, B. F. & Barlow, D. H. (2003). Childhood anxiety disorders. In E. J. Mash & R. A. Barkley (Eds.), *Child Psychopathology* (2nd ed., pp. 279–329). The Guilford Press.

Ashley, P. P. (2002). Explicating the whole mother: Integrating shadow aspects of the 'too good mother archetype'. Union Institute and University.

Bar-Haim, Y., Lamy, D., Pergamin, L., Bakermans-Kranenburg, M. J. & Van Ijzendoorn, M. H. (2007). Threat-related attentional bias in anxious and nonanxious individuals: A meta-analytic study. *Psychological Bulletin*, 133(1), 1.

Bird, G. & Viding, E. (2014). The self to other models of empathy: Providing a new framework for understanding empathy impairments in psychopathy, autism, and alexithymia. *Neuroscience & Biobehavioral Reviews*, 47, 520–532.

Bloom, P. (2017). *Against Empathy: The case for rational compassion*. Random House.

Bögels, S. M. & van Melick, M. (2004). The relationship between child report, parent self-report, and partner report of perceived parental rearing behaviours and anxiety in children and parents. *Personality and Individual Differences*, 37(8), 1583–1596.

Bohm, L. C. (2017). Mother-daughter love: A passionate attachment gone awry. In *Psychoanalytic Perspectives on Passion* (pp. 101–107). Routledge.

Brenning, K. M., Soenens, B., Van Petegem, S. & Kins, E. (2017). Searching for the roots of overprotective parenting in emerging adulthood: Investigating the link with parental attachment representations using an Actor Partner Interdependence Model (APIM). *Journal of Child and Family Studies*, 26(8), 2299–2310.

Byrne, A. & Eysenck, M. W. (1995). Trait anxiety, anxious mood, and threat detection. *Cognition & Emotion*, 9(6), 549–562.

Buschgens, C. J., Van Aken, M. A., Swinkels, S. H., Ormel, J., Verhulst, F. C. & Buitelaar, J. K. (2010). Externalizing behaviors in preadolescents: Familial risk to externalizing behaviors and perceived parenting styles. *European Child & Adolescent Psychiatry*, 19, 567–575.

Chorpita, B. F. & Barlow, D. H. (2002). Childhood anxiety disorders. *Child Psychopathology*.

Clarke, K., Cooper, P. & Creswell, C. (2013). The Parental Overprotection Scale: Associations with child and parental anxiety. *Journal of Affective Disorders*, 151(2), 618–624.

Creveling, C. C., Varela, R. E., Weems, C. F. & Corey, D. M. (2010). Maternal control, cognitive style, and childhood anxiety: A test of a theoretical model in a multi-ethnic sample. *Journal of Family Psychology*, 24(4), 439.

Decety, J. & Hodges, S. D. (2006). The social neuroscience of empathy. In *Bridging Social Psychology* (pp. 121–128). Psychology Press.

de Vignemont, F. & Singer, T. (2006). The empathic brain: How, when, and why? *Trends in Cognitive Sciences*, 10(10), 435–441.

Engelbrektsson, H. (2020). EMPATHIC DISTRESS: The Dark Side of Caring? (Dissertation). Retrieved from https://urn.kb.se/resolve?urn=urn:nbn:se:his:diva-18836

Faleschini, S., Matte-Gagné, C., Luu, T. M., Côté, S., Tremblay, R. E. & Boivin, M. (2020). Trajectories of overprotective parenting and hyperactivity-impulsivity and inattention among moderate-late preterm children: A population-based study. *Journal of Abnormal Child Psychology*, 48, 1555–1568.

Hartmann, E. (1991). *Boundaries in the Mind: A new psychology of personality*. Basic Books.

Hodges, S. D. & Biswas-Diener, R. (2007). Balancing the empathy expense account: Strategies for regulating empathic response. In T. Farrow & P. Woodruff (Eds.), *Empathy in Mental Illness* (pp. 389–407). Cambridge University Press.

Ickes, W. (2001). Measuring empathic accuracy. In Hall, J. A. & Bernieri, F. J. (Eds.), *Interpersonal Sensitivity: Theory and Measurement* (pp. 219–241). Erlbaum.

Jackson, P. L., Meltzoff, A. N. & Decety, J. (2005). How do we perceive the pain of others? A window into the neural processes involved in empathy. *Neuroimage*, 24(3), 771–779.

Krol, S. A. & Bartz, J. A. (2022). The self and empathy: Lacking a clear and stable sense of self undermines empathy and helping behaviour. *Emotion*, 22(7), 1554.

Lamm, C., Bukowski, H. & Silani, G. (2016). From shared to distinct self–other representations in empathy: Evidence from neurotypical function and socio-cognitive disorders. *Philosophical Transactions of the Royal Society B: Biological Sciences*, 371(1686), 20150083.

Manley, S. M. (2017). Parental Overprotection and Child Anxiety Symptoms: The Mediating Role of Perceived Control of Anxiety (Master's thesis, University of Toledo).

McLaren, K. (2013). *The Art of Empathy: A complete guide to life's most essential skill*. Sounds True.

Preston, S. D. & De Waal, F. B. (2002). Empathy: Its ultimate and proximate bases. *Behavioural and Brain Sciences*, 25(1), 1–20.

Rapee, R. M. (2009). Early adolescents' perceptions of their mother's anxious parenting as a predictor of anxiety symptoms 12 months later. *Journal of Abnormal Child Psychology*, 37, 1103–1112.

Reinecke, A., Becker, E. S. & Rinck, M. (2010). Three indirect tasks assessing implicit threat associations and behavioural response tendencies. *Zeitschrift für Psychologie/Journal of Psychology/Journal of Psychology*, 218(1), 4–11.

Rogers, C. R. (1995). *A Way of Being*. Houghton Mifflin Harcourt.

Sharp, C. & Fonagy, P. (2008). The parent's capacity to treat the child as a psychological agent: Constructs, measures, and implications for developmental psychopathology. *Social Development*, 17(3), 737–754.

Shields, R. W. (1964). The too-good mother. *International Journal of Psycho-Analysis*, 45, 85–88.

Thomasgard, M., Metz, W. P., Edelbrock, C. & Shonkoff, J. P. (1995). Parent-child relationship disorders. Part I. Parental overprotection and the development of the Parent Protection Scale. *Journal of Developmental & Behavioural Pediatrics*, 16(4), 244–250.

Turner, S. M., Beidel, D. C., Roberson-Nay, R. & Tervo, K. (2003). Parenting behaviours in parents with anxiety disorders. *Behaviour Research and Therapy*, 41(5), 541–554.

Waal, F. B. D. & Ferrari, P. F. (Eds.). (2012). *The Primate Mind: Built to connect with other minds*. Harvard University Press.

Wagner, S. L., Pasca, R. & Regehr, C. (2019). Firefighters and empathy: Does it hurt to care too much? *Journal of Loss and Trauma*, 24(3), 238–250.

Chapter 10

Bowlby, J. (1979). *The Making and Breaking of Affectional Bonds*. London: Routledge.

Fonagy, P. & Target, M. (1997). Attachment and reflective function: Their role in self-organization. *Development and Psychopathology*, 9(4), 679–700.

Taipale, J. (2016). Self-regulation and beyond: Affect regulation and the infant-caregiver dyad. *Frontiers in Psychology*, 7, 889.

Chapter 11

Schore, A. N. (2008). Paradigm shift: The right brain and the relational unconscious. *Psychologist-Psychoanalyst*, 28(3), 20–25.

Chapter 12

Chan, Y. K. (2018). *Parent Yourself Again: Love yourself the way you have always wanted to be loved*. Yong Kang Chan.

Harrington, C. (2021). What is 'toxic masculinity' and why does it matter? *Men and Masculinities*, 24(2), 345–352.

Chapter 14

Argov, S. (2002). *Why Men Love Bitches: From doormat to dreamgirl – A woman's guide to holding her own in a relationship*. Simon & Schuster.
Aron, E. N. (2013). *The Highly Sensitive Person: How to thrive when the world overwhelms you*. Kensington Publishing Corp.
Connell, R. W. & Messerschmidt, J. W. (2005). Hegemonic masculinity: Rethinking the concept. *Gender & Society*, 19(6), 829–859.
Howson, R. (2006). *Challenging Hegemonic Masculinity*. Routledge.
Neil, S. (2005). *The Game: Penetrating the secret society of pickup artists*. HarperCollins.

Chapter 15

Bagby, R. M., Taylor, G. J. & Ryan, D. P. (1986). The measurement of alexithymia: Psychometric properties of the Schalling-Sifneos Personality Scale. *Comprehensive Psychiatry*, 27(4), 287–294.
Kooiman, C. G., Spinhoven, P. & Trijsburg, R. W. (2002). The assessment of alexithymia: A critical review of the literature and a psychometric study of the Toronto Alexithymia Scale-20. *Journal of Psychosomatic Research*, 53(6), 1083–1090.
Lynch, T. R. (2018). Tribe matters: An introduction to radically open dialectical behaviour therapy. *The Behaviour Therapist*, 41(3), 116–125.
McDougall, J. (1982). Alexithymia: A psychoanalytic viewpoint. *Psychotherapy and Psychosomatics*, 38(1–4), 81–90.
Murray, T. (2022). Making Nice with Naughty: An Intimacy Guide for the Rule-Following, Organized, Perfectionist, Practical, and Color-Within-the-Line Types. Clinical Training & Consultation, PLLC.
Pirlot, G. & Corcos, M. (2012). Understanding alexithymia within a psychoanalytical framework. *The International Journal of Psychoanalysis*, 93(6), 1403–1425.
Schimmenti, A. & Caretti, V. (2018). Attachment, trauma, and alexithymia. In O. Luminet, R. M. Bagby & G. J. Taylor (Eds.), *Alexithymia: Advances in research, theory, and clinical practice* (pp. 127–141). Cambridge University Press.

Taylor, G. J., Bagby, R. M. & Parker, J. D. (2016). What's in the name 'alexithymia'? A commentary on "Affective agnosia: Expansion of the alexithymia construct and a new opportunity to integrate and extend Freud's legacy". *Neuroscience & Biobehavioral Reviews*, 68, 1006–1020.

Chapter 17

Einarsen, S. (1999). The nature and causes of bullying at work. *International Journal of Manpower*, 20(1/2), 16–27.

Einarsen, S. & Mikkelsen, E. G. (2002). Individual effects of exposure to bullying at work. In *Bullying and Emotional Abuse in the Workplace* (pp. 145–162). CRC Press.

Leymann, H. & Gustafsson, A. (1996). Mobbing at work and the development of post-traumatic stress disorders. *European Journal of Work and Organizational Psychology*, 5(2), 251–275.

Mikkelsen, E. G., Hansen, Å. M., Persson, R., Byrgesen, M. F. & Hogh, A. (2020). Individual consequences of being exposed to workplace bullying. *Bullying and Harassment in the Workplace*, 163–208.

Nielsen, M. B. & Einarsen, S. (2012). Outcomes of exposure to workplace bullying: A meta-analytic review. *Work & Stress*, 26(4), 309–332.

Soares, A. (2013). When darkness comes: Workplace bullying and suicidal ideation. In *Workplace Bullying* (pp. 67–80). Routledge.

Chapter 19

Ablon, J. & Bernstein, S. (2011). *Collaborative Problem Solving: An effective approach for managing conflict in the workplace*. https://www2.mediate.com/pdf/CPSInTheWorkplace.pdf

Bernstein, S. D. (2013). Detecting and responding constructively to transference in the workplace. *Journal of Management & Organization*, 19(1), 75–85.

Pines, M. (1985). *Bion and Group Psychotherapy*. Jessica Kingsley Publishers.

White, S. (2018). *An Introduction to the Psychodynamics of Workplace Bullying*. Routledge.

Closing thoughts

Warren, J. (2022). Joan Didion's 'lost' commencement address, revealed. https://news.ucr.edu/articles/2022/01/10/joan-didions-lost-commencement-address-revealed